500 Happy Returns

Nottingham High School's Birthday

Edited by

John Knifton

Table of Contents

	Introduction	7
1.	The Night	14
2.	Waking Up	16
3.	Leaving the House	29
4.	Arriving at School	60
5.	Starting the Day	79
6.	The Morning's Lessons	103
7.	Break, and More Lessons	135
8.	Friday Means Fish and Chips	151
9.	Lunchtime and Games	178
10.	Mainly Rugby	200
11.	Ending the Day	232
12.	Free at Last! Free at Last!	237
13.	Home or Homework	251

About the Author

John Knifton is an author and local historian who lives in Nottingham, England. John spent his childhood in South Derbyshire and went on to study Modern and Medieval Languages at Emmanuel College at the University of Cambridge. John then returned to the East Midlands to train as a Modern Foreign Languages teacher. He has taught mainly French, and occasional Russian Studies, some Religious Studies, Film, Politics and, most of all, football, at Nottingham High School since 1975. He is happily married to Gaynor (née Southall), whom he met while she was working at the school as an art teacher.

John Knifton's most widely known publication is *Lauda Finem: The History of Nottingham High School*. The second edition of this history of the High School was published in 2012 and can be purchased from Amazon.co.uk.

For more information on John Knifton's publications and future projects, please visit www.johnknifton.com.

Best wishes to my friend

Malcolm

Acknowledgements

A book such as this clearly requires a great deal of help and cooperation from a large number of people. May I therefore put on record my most sincere thanks to a number of individuals.

Firstly, I would like to thank Mr. Fear who might have put a very abrupt stop indeed to my bright idea had he felt so inclined. Likewise, the Acting Headmaster of the Junior School, Mr. Jones, and the Headteacher at Lovell House, Mrs. Cummings, both extended me the same generous support.

As regards the nitty-gritty details of actually persuading occasionally reluctant boys to produce their contributions, I am very grateful indeed to the Main School's Head of English, William Ruff, and his hardworking band of teachers, and equally, to Rachel Slater, Head of English at the Junior School and, at Lovell House, to Claire Smith and Julie Bignall.

This book would have been equally impossible without the help of the Main School's ICT staff, and in particular Mark Chambers, who, thank goodness, had the happy gift of being able to rediscover literally hundreds of Microsoft Word files when, like naughty little schoolboys, they either hid where they shouldn't have been or, more worrying still, existed in the computers of some would-be viewers, but remained resolutely invisible to others.

Likewise, I would like to express my gratitude to every single person who managed to produce their own particular contribution. This included many members of the teaching staff and support staff, and a very large number of the boys. Greatest praise is due, of course, to the youngest boys of all, in Lovell House. They are to be commended for their enthusiasm for the day and for life in general.

Not to be forgotten, either, is the young man whose beautiful picture forms the cover of the book. He is Rishabh Motiwale of Year 9 and he took his photograph at 12.53 p.m.

All these different people have enabled the production of a book of a viable length, and, even though I say so myself, a source of constant fascination, not least the boys' obsession with fish and chips. Perhaps the greatest recognition of all is due to the catering staff who prepared this wonderful and much anticipated dish.

My most sincere thanks, however, go to Miss Lauren Knifton, without whom this commemorative work would never have reached either Kindle or you, dear reader. (French teachers, know your limits!). Lauren put in many hours of painstaking work to ensure, among other things, uniformity of formatting for almost eight hundred entries, all of which needed to appear in the same font and size, and with the same style, layout and position relative to all the rest.

But that's enough of that! Let's get started on reading it! Where's my bit got to? Which one is the best? What did my friends have to say?

Introduction

In 2011 the BBC, in conjunction with YouTube, asked British people to film a tiny slice of their everyday life. The 11,526 videos which resulted from this request were eventually whittled down to produce an extremely moving 90 minute film entitled "Britain in a Day". It told the story of just one single day, November 12th 2011. It was seen from the perspective of 314 different people.

As soon as I saw the film, I immediately had the idea of attempting to chronicle a day in the life of Nottingham High School, but instead of using video film, I would ask people to supply a hundred written words. Everybody in the school, therefore, was invited to write a short description of what they had done in any given part of their day. This would include all the teachers, all the support staff, all the catering staff, all the caretakers and all the boys from the very youngest in Lovell House to the young men of Year 13. I had hoped that the day in question could be the school's 500th birthday, but unfortunately this date, February 2nd, would fall on a Saturday. Instead I chose Friday, February 1st, as the closest working day to the school's Quincentennial.

People were free to write whatever they wanted that was school related, from waking up in the morning, eating breakfast, coming to school, assembly, tutor set, lessons, lunch, activities outside the classroom, to going home and falling asleep, exhausted with the workload, at night. Inside or outside the classroom, they could write about whatever they thought was worth recording.

Not everybody stuck to the rules, of course, and a number of the contributions are considerably more than a hundred words, a total which is clearly for some individuals just a short note for the milkman. Unfortunately, not everybody could be persuaded to contribute. Many of the school's most colourful characters, especially the caretakers, cleaners, canteen staff and, indeed, some of the teaching staff, are absent. Looking on the positive side, we do have the best part of some eight hundred short compositions which, when put together, form a fascinating and perhaps poignant snap shot of school life at the beginning of the twenty first century.

Hopefully, these words will be read in the future at the school's thousandth birthday celebrations.

If they still have fish and chips that far in the future, I am sure that there will be boys eager to anticipate and appreciate them. If they still play rugby, there will be boys there to play it, and to meditate constantly about what wonderful players they are.

And surely boys will have homes to rush back to at the end of their day of study, mothers and fathers to love, brothers and sisters to play with, homework to do, and certainly, copious quantities of food to consume.

Hello there, people of the future! We were pretty much like you!

But before we start, though, let's look at just five extracts from my recently published history of the High School, "Lauda Finem"……

On Sunday, February 2nd 1513, the school opens on its first day. The very first classes are held in the nave, or perhaps the north transept, of St. Mary's church. The very first Master is called John Smyth. He describes himself as "…Deyne of Notyngham and parson off Bylbrough", and he has already taught a number of pupils at the parsonage there.

The very first school wardens are William English, Dame Agnes Mellers' son-in-law, and the Mayor's Clerk, William Barwell.

The school will teach good manners, grammar and literature, and every day the pupils "…beginn theyre lernynge to saye with an hye voyce whole Credo in Deum patrem etc."

They will study "…good literature bothe Laten and Greeke, and good autors such as have the verrye Romayne eloquence loyned with wisdom, specially Cristen autors, that wrote their wisdome with clean and chaste Laten, other in verse or in prose…to encrease knowledge and worshippinge of God and Our Lord Christ Jesu, and good Christen life and maners in the Children".

Hours, though, will be long. In the summer, the pupils will work from 6 a.m. to 8 a.m., and then from 9 a.m. to 11.30 a.m. In the afternoon, they will study from 1.p.m. to 3.30 p.m., and then from 4 p.m. to 6 p.m. In winter, it will be 7 a.m. to 11.30 a.m., and then from 1 p.m. to 5 p.m.

By Monday, February 1st 1717, the Free School has moved to a more suitable location in Stoney Street. A plaque which can still be seen nowadays in St.Mary's Church is believed to describe the education on offer at this time. Subjects include "Jewish, Roman and English History, the Heathen Mythology and the French tongue, and the Latin".

Over a hundred years later, on Tuesday, February 1st 1860, the school is perhaps a little neglected, according to an account by Mr. J. Braithwaite, of Bournemouth. In December 1929, he was considered to be the School's oldest Old Boy:

"The old Grammar School in Stoney Street, in the Broadmarsh, is very dull and cheerless. The upper school consists of one large room and one small classroom. There are no cloakrooms or conveniences of any kind, and the sanitary arrangements in the small playground at the back are most primitive."

"The whole building needs painting and whitewashing, but no money whatsoever is spent. The Governors are busy saving up to have enough money to build a new school."

"Work begins at 8 o'clock and finishes at 5, or after, with two hours' break at midday, In winter we have to use artificial light consisting of tallow candles... "long eights" they are called. One "dip" is allowed between two boys, and lighting up is the signal for all sorts of play. We amuse ourselves by blowing the candles out and in again, making a nasty smelling smoke; and another favourite amusement is to warm a slate pencil in the flame, bore a hole in the candle at a calculated distance, fill the hole with gunpowder or a cartridge of gunpowder paste, cover the opening with tallow, and await results, which are often startling! Jumping crackers are sometimes let off but that is not a popular game, as the whole class is punished by being kept in an extra half-hour."

"Latin and Greek are the principal subjects taught in the upper school, with a sprinkling of the "three R's" slipped in for variety. When Mr.Cusins becomes headmaster, he makes us work, and puts us through a course of History, Geography, English Composition and Mathematics. We also keep up our Latin and Greek, as well as French and German."

"The French master is a nice old chap, one of the old French aristocrats, and we all like him and get on well under him. The German master is a martinet, a typical Prussian, with a deep gruff voice and bad manner. Out of class, we imitate his guttural pronunciation, and so, in making fun of him, we are unconsciously learning the correct pronunciation of German."

Another of the school's birthdays, namely Tuesday, February 1st 1916, constitutes what is thought at the time to be the most exciting day ever in the school's entire history.

Overnight, a number of Zeppelin airships have attacked Nottingham, and seemingly every boy has a story to tell. According to "The Nottinghamian":

"Many and marvellous were the tales...it seemed as if everyone in the school was giving his experiences to everyone else as loudly as possible. Apparently, the airship had, at some time or another, been straight over the houses of nine out of ten of the boys."

In actual fact, the only bombs fell miles away from the city centre, between Stapleford and Ilkeston. They had been dropped by one of nine airships of the German Airship Naval Division who were carrying out a major bombing raid over the whole of the Midlands, an action which was later to be known as the "Great Midlands Raid".

The Zeppelin involved over Nottingham was the L.20 (LZ 59), based at Tønder in Denmark. It was commanded by Kapitan-Leutnant Stabbert who dropped seven high explosive bombs, one of which exploded just to the north of the railway viaduct at Bennerley Junction to the west of Nottingham. Later that night the L.20 dropped fifteen more bombs on the nearby Stanton Ironworks near Ilkeston, one of which damaged a railway bridge crossing the Nutbrook Canal.

The following morning, around seven o'clock, the boys awake to find more than eight inches of snow blanketing the recently attacked city. What more can a boy ask for?

But enough of history.

Somebody is still working frantically at their previous night's homework………

1. The Night

12.23 a.m.

Work. That's all there is for a young student. That's what my mum says at least. But I always like to think that there is so much more to a youth's life than work. I try to get involved in sports and in local events... 'try', that is.

Anyway, "mums know best", as they say. So here I am, working. 12.20 a.m. on a late Thursday night. I've got to finish that English essay. (In hindsight, I probably shouldn't have spent so much time playing on the Xbox.) As I'm coming to a close, I ponder about the day about the day ahead. What picture should I take for the school's collection? When should I take it? During the Physics lesson spent pumping iron in the gym? Or during the Chemistry lesson on the many fascinating uses of elastic nitinol? Meh, I'll just do it on the bus.

As I drift off to dreamland, I think about what exciting activities that life may have in store for today's anniversary. Please not work.

Tameem Reza, 10S

2.21 a.m.

Restless, I cannot sleep, I check my clock to find that the time is 2.21 I need to get to sleep and I am so tired but my body will not let me. Now wide awake I realise that lying in my bed will do me no good, so I tip-toe downstairs cautious not to awake any member of my family. Opening the cupboard I am disappointed at the lack of cereals and snacks, I grab the Coco Pops and fill the bowl I had laid out with milk and eat in half-conscious discomfort. Outside, oddly enough, it is not pitch black, but the trees silhouette against the auburn sky.

Samuel Thomas, 10T

4.35 a.m.

Awake. The only sound is the brushing of my eye lashes against the pillow. I contemplate getting up then consider the coldness of the room with a tentative foot and stay put. The daylight is beginning to show itself around the edges of the bedroom curtains. The thought of four year seven groups of (as yet) unwritten reports begins to nag at me. I push the thought to the back of my mind along with the rest of the clutter and business of tomorrow, pick up my kindle and begin reading...

Mel Kirbyshire, Art teacher

2. Waking Up

5.00 a.m.

I wake up at 5.00 a.m. feeling incredibly tired. I have a luxurious blazing bath for about 5 minutes then get dressed quickly in less than 2 minutes, I go downstairs to see my beautiful cats, I pick up my cat and stroke him lovingly, then start to make my lunch for school. After I make my lunch I decide to have a nice lovely hot cup of tea, and I drink it in 3 minutes then just stroke my cats until it is time to leave at 5.50 a.m. for the bus.

William Hodgkinson, 8T, age 13

5.30 a.m.

My alarm that I have set on the phone goes off at 5.30am. I get up out of my bed and switch off the alarm. Unfortunately, I cannot keep myself awake so I fall back to sleep only to be woken up by my mum at 7 o'clock! I take a quick shower lasting for about 5 minutes and quickly get dressed in a matter of seconds, then I eat my breakfast while watching some uninteresting programme on the television. I leave to get to the bus stop at around 7.45. I wait for the bus to come, and when it does I'm ready to get to school....

Alok Dangi, 7T, age 11

5.45 a.m.

Time to wake up! Truly, it is the worst time of the day, when the alarm clock strikes full volume at the brink of dawn. But in this winter, the dawn is more than an hour away. Why do I get up so early? I need to catch the 6.45am tram while my Father needs to board the 6.40 train to Derby via Nottingham. Now I need to freshen up, do yoga for 15 minutes, brush my teeth and have a shower. Finally, putting on my school clothes, away I go! I do not have time for breakfast, only supplements.

Sagnik Santra, 9S, age 13

5.45 a.m.

I wake up to the bleeping of the alarm, but it is just too early. The snooze only lasts five minutes but it feels like an hour! Eventually I get up realising that if I don't I will miss the train. Eating my breakfast I realise that I am still hungry. Oh well, I will have to eat at school. In ten minutes it will be time to go and wait in the cold. It will only last another ten minutes and then it will be time to sleep on the way in. However the time till then is quite a while. I must eat and get ready which is difficult so early but the show must go on.

David Steele, 11Y, age 15

6.00 a.m.

My Friday starts off with me waking up 6:00 in the morning. I groan when I realise that it is time for school as I get out of my bed. Of course I sometimes oversleep, making my mum quite annoyed; I blame my alarm clock.

I glumly go to the bathroom to brush my teeth and use mouthwash, and then I change my clothes into my uniform after putting on deodorant. Next, I go to the kitchen to have my breakfast, usually cereal. I do my jobs so quickly, so that I have to wait for my little sister and mum to be prepared. I also have spare time so I just have a little rest. But it isn't long before I must go to my bus stop and prepare myself for another boring day at school.

I wish I had more time to relax and have fun at home or have time to hang out with my friends, but looking on the bright side, tomorrow is the weekend! Yay!

Naim Rahman, 8S, age 12

6.00 a.m.

I wake up to the thunderous sound of my father's alarm, at six o'clock, early in the morning. It is so early that the sun hasn't even decided to wake up yet. I stagger downstairs and my eyes are still closed, but my body is fully awake. I push the door open in the kitchen I put down some toast in the toaster and prayed it didn't burn. Next, I go upstairs in a flash. I am delighted with my breakfast; I shower, and get ready for school. It is time for my next mission, the bus run... I leave the house within minutes, running as fast as my body will allow me; I have to get the bus on time. I make it.... just. I am on the seventeen, and now my next mission, school...

Morgan Fearon, 9T

6.00 a.m.

I wake up. I'm freezing cold and I'm struggling to stay awake. But I have to get up otherwise my mum and dad will have to come and chivvy me along. I walk downstairs. Then I sit down and watch the TV for ten minutes. Normally it is football news. My sister comes downstairs and then I have breakfast. I get my way through my breakfast; I then put my bowls and plates away. I walk upstairs and then brush my teeth and get dressed. I then do my piano practice and pack my bag.

Adam Fear, 7H, age 11

6.01 a.m.

The pitch black sky is signalling the start of a day so tedious, yet a day so many people are looking forward to: Friday. My legs are as heavy as lead as I trudge down the stairs. It's so cold in my living room that I'm shaking more than a rattlesnake's tail. I have to force myself to eat the bowl of cereal in front of me, chewing is just too difficult, I'm too tired. I am witnessing a sunset whose beauty was like nothing I had ever seen before, and the best part is the day had only just begun.

Matthew Moir, 9T

6.02 a.m.

My eyes are open slightly; the light seems to be burning the retina inside my eye. I begin my journey to the bathroom, tripping over the uniform from the night before and feeling as if the carpet is trying to swallow me whole. I make my way past the doorframe where there is a bath full of hot boiling water for me to sink into, simply because the shower is broken. I put one foot in the bath and I say ouch because it is too hot. I man up and lie in the bath and fall asleep. I miss the bus. Mum begins her daily rant about how I'm so lazy, and all I can think is: where is my bed?

George Cowen, 11Y, age 15

6.03 a.m.

Sleeping in my nice cosy bed, then being awoken by the ringing sound of the alarm, arousing me immediately. I slip out of bed half asleep and walk into the bathroom; I came out and got dressed into something warm. Down the stairs I went and into the kitchen and let my dog out. My toast popped out, I snatched it and stumbled outside. The cold wind rush making me regain my senses after the anaesthetic of sleep. I call Marli and he runs to me excitedly because he knows what's happening. Time for a walk.

Edward Bousfield, 8Y

6.04 a.m.

It's that time again. Always the same, the same time, same people, same feeling. Its morning; and as ever I'm not in the mood to be woken up. The door swings open and in swoops mum. She has the impossible task of wakening the beast. I am asked to get up, nothing. I am told to get up, nothing. I am dragged by my feet into the bathroom, nothing. Eventually I begin to stir. Only in period two do my eyes finally open to see the blinding light of the Spanish lesson. My Friday has begun.

Jacob Longstaff, 9S

6.05 a.m.

Here it is, Friday the start of the weekend. It's a day to remember, as it is the 500th anniversary of when the school started teaching pupils and we have a party in the quad tomorrow to celebrate it. So up with the alarm and jump into the shower to get ready for what the day has in store for me. I arrive for my 7.00 a.m. start and get on with answering my emails. After catching up with paperwork and putting away the stock that has been delivered I feel I have earned a cup of tea. 10.00 a.m. and I join Angela from reprographics along with the caretakers for mid-morning break. The talk is all about the party in the quad, who is going, who is avoiding it like the plague, nothing will deter me as I am really looking forward to it. This will be a chance to meet up with the staff members who have left, but want to come along to celebrate this fantastic occasion and of course any excuse buying a new dress. All the ladies are talking about how they will be making a big effort and dress up. Still can't sit here chatting, work to do and all that.

Susan Ford, cleaning manager

6.15 a.m.

It's 6.15 a.m. and my alarm is making that blaring infernal noise, awakening every sense within me, I turn over and press the snooze button with the early morning brain fog. I slowly ponder whether or not I should I should actually get up. It's so snug and warm under the covers. If only I could stay here the whole day. I make the decision, the time has come, I throw back the covers, race to my underwear drawer, pick up the first pair of clean boxers I could see and with my towel in one hand and my boxers in the other I head straight for the shower.

Dominic D'Sa, 8Y

6.20 a.m.

Wake, Friday, rise, shower, tea, scouts, necker, woggle, uniform, drive, arrive, banter, coffee, pigeon-hole, laptop, consent forms, missing, lists, cheques, accounts, income, costs, Ennerdale, fire-station, consent forms, programme, badges, bookings, charity, copy, laser-quest, consent forms, maps, google, route-card, training day, consent forms, fish-and-chips, pudding, theory, shopping, socks, blisters, Compeed, plasters, leaders, flags, salutes, day hike, consent forms, activities, quiz, summer camp, letters, consent forms, parents, pickups, late, pub, crisps, beer, friendship, commitment, loyalty, betrayal, farewells, home bound, family, good night kisses, television, nightcap, bedtime, tick-lists, consent forms, tick-lists, consent forms, sleep, consent...............

Ben Thomas, Design Technology teacher

6.29 a.m.

I wake up from my long 8-hour sleep, tired and cold, but ready to finish the week and jump into the long and restful weekend. I resentfully get out of my bed and walk towards the shower that will keep me awake. For 10 minutes, I wash myself and feel the warm water run down me and wake me up. After I exit my shower, I return to my room and dry off whilst drinking a cup of tea and wait for until it's time to change and then I wait for the day to roll out.

Jonathan Flett, 9Y

6.30 a.m.

I wake up to the sound of the alarm, shower and then knock on each of my two boys doors. "it's 7.00 a.m. and we're leaving at 7.30 a.m. Roads in chaos from the recent snowfall, will we be on time? I fly through the door of Lovell House as the Council House bell strikes 8.00 a.m, made it! A quick shout "hello" as I rush through the corridors to Early Birds, anxious parents awaiting my arrival. The boys are excited and full of life! Now refereeing a football match! Another day is beginning.

Judith Robinson, Teaching Assistant, Lovell House

6.31 a.m.

I wake up. I hate mornings! It's too early to wake up! Why can't I go back to bed! I bring myself to my senses and slowly drag myself out of my cosy bed. I venture out into the wilds of the bathroom. The cascading water feels like my only luxury of the day. I return back to my cave, my bedroom, to find my uniform lay out on the bed – thanks mum! 7, after having my energy supply for the day I'm forced to make the morning trek to the bus stop. Here goes another day of hell. I hate school all the teachers are grumpy!

Harry Ashdown, 8H

6.32 a.m.

Waking up on any day is hard, but when it's Friday, it feels that little bit easier, because it's Saturday tomorrow! I can smell the pancakes that my Mother is making; this day just gets better and better. I go to the bathroom, brush my teeth, and wash my hair and face also. The pancakes are awesome. Why can't I have them every day? Capital FM is essential for the ride to school; it helps me relax for the working day ahead of me. I leave for school at 6.50 a.m., and usually it takes 30 minutes to arrive there.

Ali Hussain, 10L, age 15

6.33 a.m.

The bright beam that is morning wakes me from my most peaceful slumber. The dawn of the new day signals start to, yet another, mind-numbing school day. I stumble out of bed- moved only by the thought of breakfast. As is the norm I arrive at school not long after on the packed transport that is the tram. Still bleary-eyed I shamble to my classroom, enter and I collapse into my chair, throwing off the heavy burden of my bag. I sigh and brace myself for the tedious day ahead of me. The day has only just started and I am already eager to leave.

Kit Hobbs, 8Y

6.34 a.m.

It starts with a slight shudder, then a severe shaking. My beautiful dreams destroyed in a matter of seconds by a marauding force of nature. It stops. I see nothing, hear nothing and feel nothing except the laziness and lethargy slowly settling into their new positions within my bones. I stare upwards, squinting in the dim light, and the dreaded words emanate from the safety of my lips... 'Ten more minutes, please?' My plea is met by a strike of lightning, which encourages me to move away from the safety of my blankets and into the emotionless, dim passageway ahead.

Ashok Shankar, 9T

6.35 a.m.

I awake seeing the time of 06.35 on my clock. Switching off the alarm that was set the night before, I gradually make my way downstairs dreading the Friday that is to come. I also remember the maths prep that I was meant to do last night; the first sigh of the day fills my lungs, but there is still breakfast to look forward to! My sugar free Alpen awaits in its cardboard box in the cupboard under the work surface. After the maths prep (completed hastily and probably poorly done) I watch the rest of the minutes away and have my breakfast; crunch, crunch, crunch. Another day awaits me, "What fun!"

Jack Blowers, 9H, age 13

6.36 a.m.

It's the morning. I roll over. My eyes glued together with sleep. The sound of my alarm deafens me. I slumber out of bed. I slowly turn off my alarm, go to my draw and pull out my uniform. My dog is wagging his tail, ready for a walk. I put on my coat and grab his collar and open the front door presenting the morning darkness. The air is fresh and the streets are silent. I put on my wellingtons and set off. I stroll slowly down my road. I get near to the beginning of the long path and let my dog off.

Oliver Kerr, 9H, age 14

6.39 a.m.

"Owais! Wake up! It's time for school!"

"Waaaaahhhh? Oh ok I'm coming", except of course I'm not! I continue to sleep for a couple of minutes until it hits me! Friday morning......Almost the weekend! I open my eyes only to shut them almost instantly. Opening them slowly, I adjust to the light. I get up, pull on my clothes and spray myself with way too much lynx. Out of my bedroom and straight downstairs I go, using my momentum to carry me through to the kitchen. Chores….. I open the cupboards, pull out the bowls and lay them on the table. Nobody is downstairs yet and it seems I am up slightly earlier than usual. Into the dark, cold and wet garden, I head straight for the rabbit hutch and pull out the rabbit food. "Elvis," I call, "where are you? It's breakfast time." I open the hutch and pick up my beloved gold, white and black guinea-pig. He squeaks happily. After about five minutes he starts to sniff my hand.

"You hungry, Elvis? Here, have some food." I pour some food into his bowl and Blackberry, my sister's rabbit, appears. He begins to eat as well.

Owais Abid, 8S

6.40 a.m.

I wake up at the ridiculous hour of twenty to seven. The daily routine consists of me waking up my mum before walking down to feed my cats and pet tortoise. I brush my teeth while waiting for the shower to warm up. After my shower I have to have a few minutes lying comfortably in my warm bed looking at my phone. After approximately ten minutes I get dressed, normally after having cleaned up my cat's sick due to it eating too fast, and set off to catch the bus at the bus stop.

Alex Chadwick, 11H, age 15

6.41 a.m.

As my eyes open to see the shadowy pupils of my dad staring down at me, I know that another day in prison Is upon me. School. It's Friday, I think to myself; yet I refuse to get out of bed for a shower.
I fall back to sleep.

It's now 7.00 a.m. and I have about twenty five minutes until the train leaves. I still refuse to get out of bed until abruptly; an angry man drags my feet, along with me, out of the bed and onto the floor. The urge to inflict pain on him is counteracted by my sheer exhaustion.

Anger, pain and resentment are just three of the many feelings that I am enduring.

Joe Scaffardi, Senior School pupil

6.42 a.m.

My alarm has just gone off, but I set it half an hour early so it felt as though I had lay in #tacticalalarm. I drift in and out of sleep for the next thirty-eight minutes, and finally at twenty past eight drag myself from bed into the shower. I walk downstairs greet my dog and let her into the garden, I get my Weetabix out the cupboard, and tip my yoghurt into the bowl alongside them. As I put on my blazer, I walk out the door, get into the car and off to school I go.

Campbell Minogue, 11L

6.43 a.m.

I stumble down the steps to my car ready to drive the 52.3 miles up the M1 from Rugby to the High School. Some say I am crazy. "How do you do it every day?"

"Does it not just wear you out?"

In reality it isn't that bad, I actually quite enjoy the hour or so I get to myself. It is the perfect time to think about the day ahead and dare I say it some last minute planning happens too! At about 07.45 I turn in to Science Lane awake and prepared for the day ahead.

Mr S. P. Robinson, Biology teacher

6.44 a.m.

My eyes are squinting, trying to ward off the radiant rays of sunlight that are drifting through the gaps in my curtains. The sunlight is bathing my skin with warmth as I am struggling to fight off the sunbeams in an attempt to wake up but I know that I have to wait for my alarm clock to bleep away, signaling the start of a new day at school. I am rubbing away the sleepiness from my dreary eyes. I wonder how the pupils of Nottingham High School would have felt as they woke up for their first day of school 500 years ago, knowing what I know about the legacy that they began.

Atif Hussain, 9T

6.45 a.m.

I had to wake up at 6.45 like any other day, I normally just lie in bed for 15 minutes until 7 o'clock but today I fell asleep again and didn't wake up till 7.15! Now I have to rush getting ready and get all my books together from homework the night before, and whilst doing this I have my toothbrush in my mouth at the same time. Once I have all my things ready I head downstairs and start shovelling cereal in my mouth, getting as much in my mouth as I can in the time I have left. I don't want to be hungry during the first 3 periods of school. When I have finished, I rush outside to the bus stop, as I am late, but I can see that the bus is not the 'good' one but the 'bad' bus, so then I have to sit in an un-comfy bus with all my bags underneath my feet so there is no leg room. A great start to the day!

Remy Coulthard-Boardman, 7T, age 12

6.46 a.m.

The repetition is killing me. Wake. Sleep. Wake. Sleep. I am awakened at 6.40 by the tiresome voice of a radio presenter, his voice filled with a dull enthusiasm as he plays tracks made for people younger than him. I get up and have a shower, how exciting. In the morning even the shower is tired, spitting and dripping water almost as if its telling me to go back to sleep, I wish. Next is breakfast which is an exciting concoction of half-burnt toast and the stench of early-morning anger. Then, I am forced out of the door and into a world full of angry teenagers stuck on repeat.

Rahul Badiani, 11H

6.47 a.m.

Today is a special day. They always say breakfast is the most important meal of the day – usually porridge for me with a light smidgen of All-Bran. But today I have a real hankering for some toast with a thick coating of marmite. I search for the jar, my tummy rumbling at the thought of all that yeast extract, riboflavin and niacin. After applying the blessed marmite to my overdone toast I begin heartily engulfing my awesome meal. I feel ready for a big day of learning stuff.

David Somers, 11L

6.48 a.m.

My drive into work this morning is the same in many ways, the same 6.45 a.m. depart, the same 16 mile journey and the same route. However, my thoughts are different; I don't spend time thinking about period 1 or Friday afternoon games. Instead, my thoughts are about one thing, in particular one person, my Grandfather 'Raymond Kendall ON' I never knew my Grandfather because he died when I was 2 years old but I do know that he was a pupil at Nottingham High school in the 1930's.

I start thinking about what his journey into school would have been like as a 12 year old boy. His route would have been different, he would certainly have walked to school and he would have probably not had to leave at 6.48 a.m. One thing for sure though is our destinations are the same. I'm proud my grandfather has been a part of the school's 500 years history.

Mr Paul Allison, PE teacher

6.49 a.m.

Suddenly, I wake up from my deep slumber and look at my clock. 6.50, time to get up. I groan and awkwardly climb out of bed. I eat my breakfast, which consists of Weetabix, yoghurt, an apple and a drink, then I tiredly walk up the stairs to brush my teeth. Once I got dressed into my black woven school jumper and black blazer, I sit down to watch some TV. It was time to leave the house. I tie the shoelaces on my shoes and start walking with my brother to our destination; the bus stop.

Philip Davey, 10T

6.50 a.m.

Groggy eyed I burrow deeper into my duvet, fleeing from the cold of the morning. My alarm bleeps louder. I couldn't do it. Why did school have to start so early? Why do we even have to go to school? I willed my eyes to stay open, knowing that if they closed, all would be lost and I would sleep for 2 hours longer. Why was I even tired? Wasn't 9 hours of sleep enough to fully rest my body? I sigh. It had to be done. I rolled to the edge of the one place I loved and threw myself off onto the cold, hard floor. Good morning world.

Josef Stoger, 10H

6.54 a.m.

Waking up to Beatles as your alarm doesn't sound like a bad feeling; but in the morning it is. Overly happy guitar riffs with elephant-like screeching 'ooos'. It won't stop. Well it won't stop, unless I; open my eyes, get tortured by the morning's sun, rub the nesting sleep from the crevices, squint, stretch, yawn, shove away my cat, grab phone, scramble to turn it OFF, realise my phone is upside down.

This should be the easiest task of my day. I think of those well-deserved greasy fried chips, drowning salt and vinegar. So I turn my phone the 'right' way round. With a reassuring smile, I click to stop the distorted, chaotic whirlwind of sound. "Ahh Peace at last."

"DAMN! THAT WAS THE SNOOZE BUTTON."

Harvey Brown, 11S

3. Leaving the House

6.57 a.m.

I wake up and the cold breeze from my open window brushes my face. I fling of the duvet and get out of my bed. Downstairs only my mum is awake, it is 7.00 a.m. I go into the bathroom wash my face with cold water and use some mouthwash. I go back to my room covered in goose pumps. I stand next to the heater and get into my uniform. As usual I have to go into my sister's room and wake her up. Friday is always my best day because it goes fast and you can look forward to a nice weekend. (Most of the time)

Ibraheem Hussain, 8Y

6.58 a.m.

Park the car at the Shepherds mini park and ride, get the bicycle out of the boot and assemble it. Set off for school with a six mile ride ahead of me. Over the A52 and along a track towards the river, ponds either side of me and a bumpy track but there is a little bit of daylight today.

On to the road near Holme Pierrepont and down to the river, the Trent is running high and is a murky brown bubbling mass. Through town, living dangerously on a bike, into the north entrance ready for a busy Friday. Much better than driving all the way and gets you ready for emails, isams, lessons. Get to the desk for ten past eight and I am ready to read the emails from all areas of the school.

Ian Thorpe, Design Technology teacher

6.59 a.m.

I wake up. It is around 7.00. I put my school clothes on. I walk to the bathroom to wash my face. I make my bed. I walk down stairs for breakfast. My mum is downstairs already making the breakfast. I am plated with a cooked cheese sandwich from the electric sandwich toaster which I got last year (I didn't like it) and a cup of apple juice and around fifteen grapes. After my breakfast my dad drives the car out of the garage and we load into it heading to school and work.

Chih-Hsiang Lo, 8T, age 12

7.00 a.m.

The sound of my phone blaring jolts me awake. I instinctively roll over, grab my phone and shut it off. Silence. Peace and quiet. So quiet that I hear a ringing in my ears. I roll over, burying myself deeper into the soft, warm blanket, nuzzling my head against the pillow. Why did I have to get up? The only sounds are of my slow breathing, and my heavy arms and head rubbing against the silky smooth duvet. Complete and utter bliss. What seems like seconds later, my phone goes off again, spoiling the tranquillity of my sleep.

Laurence Oakden, Senior School pupil

7.00 a.m.

My ears rattle to the sound of my alarm clock; it is time to get up. The effort it takes to get out of bed in the morning is unbelievable and it took me at least a minute just to sit up. I finally get out of bed and I open the curtains to find darkness. Despite it only being seven o'clock the birds are already chirping and singing with delight, but I'm certainly not. Outside it's a cold and miserable day and I'm really not looking forward to the long walk, in the rain, to the bus stop.

Joshua Sheehy, 8Y

7.01 a.m.

I arrive at my office and immediately switch on my laptop to check my emails. There is an enquiry from an Old Nottinghamian asking for advice about public speaking; a request from a tutee for a reference for a work experience placement; two emails from publishers' reps asking for my 'valuable time' in order to sell me textbooks; plus several bids for tickets for next Tuesday's Arts Society classical concert. I answer all of them. What my inbox lacks, however, is what I was actually looking for: essays which two sixth formers said they would send me last night, a promise which, once again and predictably, they have failed to keep.

William Ruff, Head of English

7.01 a.m.

I wake up and look out of the steamy window, it looks cold but I can't see any frost. The familiar sound of my dad shouting at me from downstairs, telling me to hurry up and get some breakfast before I have to go to school. I groan, it is Friday, the last and worst day at school. The best thing about it is swimming, but even that is turning out to be quite boring, because we have to do timed swims with year 9. Eventually I get dressed and head downstairs for breakfast. It is going to be a long day.

Joe Kingsley, 8Y

7.02 a.m.

Exhilarated for the day ahead, I am clambering my way out of bed and towards the radiator to clasp my towel. I will need it once the shower has finished ridding me of the sorrows of the previous night of endless homework. As I open the door I am blinded by a scouring light as it is released from the glistening bulb. Edging through the corridor as the walls seem to be enveloping me, I stumble into an out sprung door. Once I reach the shower I black out in the storm of refreshment.

Will Andersen, 11Y, age 16

7.02 a.m.

I'm lying here on this cold Friday morning, awake before my alarm had even gone off, waiting for it. I'm anticipating the to the day slow start so I close my eyes to gain that extra 5 minutes that we all seem to think will help. I listen to the wind whistling past my window and just wait for the dreaded moment that my mother will walk in demanding me to rise from my bed, which usually follows with my ignoring her and the same thing happening ten minutes later with increased anger. Oh the joys.

Sam Rodriguez, Senior School pupil

7.02 a.m.

I get out of bed and go downstairs. I am wearing Ben 10 pyjamas. I start to watch Mr Bean on television. He is a funny man.

George Akins, Reception Class, Lovell House

7.03 a.m.

I hear the familiar yell of get up your going to be late for school. I slowly clamber out of bed, sleep still clinging to my eye lids. Packing my bag is slow work due to the fact that my books are strewn all around the house. As I make my way down the stairs I notice we have five minutes till we need to leave despite this we are still going at the same pace. Finally after a hurried breakfast I jump into the car only to realise my games kit is still in the house.

Thomas Chester, 7Y

7.03 a.m….AAAHHH!

My tight eyes being forced open like breaking into a chest. The long, dark, black out curtains are drawn open. Although I had no idea what is happening, my still eyes fill with dullness. My heart pumps slowly with no enjoyment or thoughts. I feel so vague.

I saunter down the road; the dark grey, overcast morning causing a gloomy mood. Gail forced winds whipped past my blushing cheeks. The tarmac remains damp as the aggravated motorists pass in their hurry. Every inch of my body is wrapped like a parcel to seal out the biting cold.

Rain pounds down whilst I stand like a sitting target waiting for the last bus. Congestion adding to the local smog which I inhale daily. I scrunch my eyebrows together and tip my head to the side. I look from one person to another, back and forth, with a blank look on my face. My eyes are wide as I 'am making several attempts to stay awake.

Vishal Singh, 9T

7.04 a.m.

BEEP! BEEP! Rubbing me eyes tiredly with my left hand, I begrudgingly reachout with my right hand and fumble for the switch on my alarm. I really hate it sometimes-my alarm. Since I cannot at that moment find the strength to rouse myself from my slumber, I shift in my bed and blissfully drift back into the land of dreams. BUZZ! 'BAH!' I yelp, attempting to jump out of my bed but instead only managing to get tangled with my sheets and fall to the ground flat on my back. Hastily, I scramble to my feet with a relieved expression upon my face. I really should have listened to that alarm.

Zico Sandhu, 10Y

7.05 a.m.

I wake up to the sound of my mother's calling. Eventually, I slip out from my warm, cosy duvet into the cold, frozen air. I drag my curtains open to find a mattress of crisp, thick layer of snow on the ground five metres below. I open my bedroom door and drag my feet down a flight of never-ending stairs. I arrive in the kitchen, as my feet frozen from the cold marble floor. On a wooden table, there is a plate with two croissants resting on it. I eat it quite quickly. With my stomach satisfied, I drag my feet back up the stairs to have a shower, brush my teeth, get dressed, and pack my bag for the day ahead.

Oliver Boothright, 8H, age 12

7.06 a.m.

A shrill repetitive ring raises me from my slumber. Dreams of limitless fancy are cut short and reality commences. I pull back the sheets, using the cool air as inspiration to begin movement, and roll lazily off my bed. My head fells dizzy as I begin to stand and sway slowly, waiting for consciousness to fully kick in. Eventually my sense return to me from limitless visions of happiness and realisation arrives. And so begins the tedious and monotonous routine to prepare for the day: shower; get dressed; eat breakfast; brush my teeth and fill my bag for the imminent activities. Déjà vu strikes me as it does most mornings. Time for school.

Abe Chauhan, 10L

7.07 a.m.

I hear her, but I don't respond. I am asleep. I think to myself, it cannot be morning yet. I find a new position in my bed; a futile effort to return to the blissful trance known as sleep. Alas, it eludes me. In one swift movement I push the duvet away. After feeling the sharp sting of the cold, it is soon back where it belongs; keeping me warm. The sweet familiar aroma of cooking bacon enters my nasal passages and urges me to bite the bullet and exchange one love for another; bed for bacon.

Jack Skinner, 8Y

7.08 a.m.

Reluctantly, a heavy shutter lifts, revealing a black hole that takes in the scene that lays before it. The protective cover smoothly slides back, and closes. A slight flicker, and it is open again, this time joined by a twin seven centimetres away. The deep wells twist, focusing to the optimum point. The faintest of gurglings, discernable only by the one who makes it, warn the drowsy body of the coming explosion.

I sneeze, my neck snapping forwards. Through my sharpening vision I survey a pile of cloth, an overflowing bookcase and a mirror returning my sleepy gaze. I have woken up.

Ben Lim, 8Y

7.09 a.m.

At this time my mother is shouting at me to get changed for school. I normally get up 15 minutes after but in the event that im feeling well I do it straight away (not very often). After I do get down, my mother has my breakfast ready and the menu is Croissants and toast ☺ and maybe scones if im lucky. After watching TV for 30 minutes it is 8 AM

It is time to set off for school my sister and my brother as well as me enter the car my sister (15) goes to Fernwood and she gets dropped of first we set off for my school at around 8:15 which and we arrive and I have a brilliant day ahead of me.

Subhaan akhter, 8T

7.10 a.m.

I'm getting ready for the bus, I put my coat on when I realise that I haven't packed my bag.

I run up the stairs and look at my watch, ' I'm thinking 'I'm going to be late again '. I flip open my planner and look at my timetable. I chuck everything out my bag apart from my English and maths things. I put everything I need into my bag and my mum is already waiting in the car. We drive off and when we reach the stop I jump on the bus.

Callum Rittig, 7Y, age 11

7.11 a.m.

Scrape car in the semi-dark
and admit the passenger.
Launch along Leicestershire lanes,
winding, with wicked limits catching out the incautious.
A hill (impassable in snow)
and a ditched car
waiting for gradual recycle or tow.

Left across the border,
unguarded
excepting the speed vigilante.

Pass Ma Murs and her Gourmet Grill
and on to the Tollerton bottleneck;
end of the bridge-creeping HGV.
Boys and bus stops.
Faces recognised, never met.

WBS; pause.

Away along A60
and travel over the Trent.
Cameras, lane changing,
hooters and Hooters.
A lucky break at the light barrier.
Join melée with four-by-fours in the backstreets.
Rest on the car park between the lines.

John G. Allen, teacher of Mathematics

7.12 a.m.

I get up and straight away I put my school uniform on. I then go to eat my breakfast of Kelloggs Cornflakes which I mix with warm milk and put sugar on top.

James Black, Reception Class, Lovell House

7.12 a.m.

I get out of the shower in an instant rush to get dry and fling my clothes on, once I'm dressed I look at my clock "I'm running late" I scream as I realised I've spent over half an hour in the shower and have taken 20minutes to get dressed and make me bed. My mum hears my moans and yet again tells me that I need to start waking up with my alarm instead of waiting till half seven when she wakes my sister up for school.

Lewis Symons, 8T, age 13

7.13 a.m.

My day begins at 7.13 with my alarm ringing loudly followed me turning it off and sleeping another 10 minutes. Finally I decide I need to take drastic action and I drag myself out of bed. When I'm up I head directly into the bathroom to brush my teeth. Before long I get changed, hunt for my tie which I've finally find. I scan my table in my bedroom to be sure I haven't left any books on my table. When I'm absolutely sure there's not books lying around I eat breakfast and leave for school.

Neville Shery, 8T

7.14 a.m.

I swagger out my front door at 7.14 in the morning, anticipating another enlightening day at Nottingham High School. Enjoying my 5 minute walk to the bus stop, everything is going to plan, good light, isn't too cold and excited by what the day ahead has in store for me. Walking down the alley I take to the bus stop, until disaster, I hear my beloved blue Sharpes bus rampaging down the road. I've never missed the bus in my life and with double English today I can't have picked a worse day to be late!

Max Robertson, 11H

7.15 a.m.

I walk out the shower and quickly dry off with my brand new fluffy towel. I walk into my bed room and am suddenly hit by a wave of cold. I get changed in to my shirt and trousers. When I go down stairs a hot piece of toast is on the table begging me to smother it with nutella. When I have eaten the toast my mum tells me to through away my shirt because it's too small. I end up throwing away more than half my shirts. Then I pack my bag.

Harry Warrior, 8T

7.15 a.m.

500 years, eh?

I'm marking the occasion in my own small way with a brand new brilliant white school shirt, and all my thoughts are with the thousands of new shirts that must have been worn on historical events at The School over the centuries.

I unpin, unbutton, unwrap and disassemble the ridiculous packaging on this, 'London Shop' attire that my father has purchased especially to share this moment with me.
Job done.

I look resplendid, with only one more button to go………………..Ouch!

That pin!

I bet that has been pricking boys for 500 years!

Usthman Shiekh, 9T

7.15 a.m.

My eyes slowly open and light floods in, disorientating me for only a moment as the usual shriek and dyslogistic glare of my mother jolts me awake. I groan and clamber out of my bed – heading straight for the shower, sighing with relief as the steaming water cascades down upon me. Now more alert I dry myself and begin to dress; the accepted strangle of my tie pulling tight around my neck and the wearisome, characterless black socks suffocating my feet, were little in comparison to the hurried and bland breakfast which I am forced to endure. After the routine teeth cleaning and slug of Listerine I arduously barge out the door into the sharp, frosty air and go to the bus.

Harry Holdstock, 10T

7.15 a.m.

My hands are cold. Arrive at school at 7.20. I've brought the wrong bag. My hands are cold. Arrive at school at 7.35, sit down. Laptop on, inbox is blinking, cover period 1... Time for a coffee.

Shaun Mitchell, Teacher of Geography, age 28.

7.16 a.m.

So dark. So cold. Gloves. Ignition key. A dashboard full of red and yellow lights. Headlights on. Back out carefully. Wave goodbye. Central locking on. Heated seat on. Music on. Tom Waits. "Who'll come a-waltzing, Matilda, with me?". Out onto Hucknall Road. Red brake lights. Orange street lights. Green traffic lights. Bus lanes. Digital average speed cameras. Brown buses. White vans. Mansfield Road. St.Andrew's church. Traffic queuing for Trent Bridge. Backstreets. The front of the school. I can see my darkened classroom, lit by the corridor behind. Right into Waverley Street. Tram tracks. Science Lane. My very own disabled space. Still Tom Waits. "Never drive a car when you're dead".

Gloves off. Headlights off. Heated seat off. Music off. Ignition off. W3. Go in. Sit down. My own comfy chair. My desk. Look out over the lawns, over the garden. Towards the statue. So calm. So peaceful. So quiet. The best view in the school. The best view in my life.

John Knifton, teacher of French

7.17 a.m.

I walk out the shower and quickly dry off with my brand new fluffy towel. I walk into my bed room and am suddenly hit by a wave of cold. I get changed in to my shirt and trousers. When I go down stairs a hot piece of toast is on the table begging me to smother it with nutella. When I have eaten the toast my mum tells me to through away my shirt because it's too small. I end up throwing away more than half my shirts. Then I pack my bag.

Harry Warrior, 8T, age 12

7.17 a.m.

My Mum walks in, opens the curtains and turns the bright bedroom light on. BBC Radio 1 is shouting at me. I feel so tired and I just can't get out of my bed! My Mum then shouts breakfast ready and somehow that urges me to get out of bed.

"Oatcake filled with cream cheese today" says Mum

I eat my food and then run upstairs as fast as I can. Somehow I have found loads of energy! My sister is ready, I'm ready, and we jump into the car to head for school. Phew!

William Nowicki, 8T

7.18 a.m.

Turning right from Waverley Street into 'Science Lane'. Cross the tram tracks descending to the City from Hucknall and beyond. The lane is in darkness but I can already see that I am the last of the regular 'Early Arrivals' today. However it was better to fill my car with petrol at 131.9p a litre on the way in at Sainsbury's in Arnold rather than face the aggravation of a return visit on the way home to Calverton or an intended hike in price anytime soon. Still plenty of parking space. Remove jacket, tie, laptop and briefcase from the boot, fully armed for the day!

Mark Cleverley, teacher of Chemistry

7.19 a.m.

After leaving the house at 7.03 a.m. and dropping my husband at work, I arrive at 7.19 a.m. to an empty, peaceful school. Logging onto my computer I check my emails as there is usually something that needs doing before Registration. There are announcements that need typing and putting in Form pigeon holes and notices to put up in the Sixth Form Centre. I send emails to staff advising about boys' Exeats. I log onto iSams, the school's database system to authorise Blue Tickets. My colleague arrives and brings me a cup of tea before our official start time of 8.00 a.m. – I feel like I've done a morning's work already!

Dawn Wallis, Administrator

7.20 a.m.

The door opens. The slow wind sweeps across my face like an ice cube slowly melting then freezing again. The only problem is you have to leave so you can catch the school bus. I take m first step. My heart rate starts to increase. The drive way is frozen solid. Every time I make a step the ice breaks into little shards. All the trees are ice sculptures of ice monsters without a face. The two cars covered in ice like a new skin made of ice. I take my last step in the drive and on the path.

Matt Filor, 8Y

7.21 a.m.

I am waiting for the bus with my friends and I walk on and the bus driver asks what I want. I say I want a child return to Nottingham and he says "is that a single?" I look at him in disgust and pay. Two minutes later we are going through an area where the trees are really low and because it is very dark the driver hits a tree and we all have to get off. I am waiting for another bus, on the corner of the street yet again, but it is even colder now and it's started raining. Typical England!

Nathan Gull, 11T, age 16

7.22 a.m.

I'm standing at the bus stop. It's cold, music's playing.

Somewhere down the street a mother's struggling with a child. The noise dies, a door slams and a car engine fades into the distance.

It's really cold. This bus better come soon.

I should have brought my gloves, my hands are freezing. And a scarf. Definitely a scarf.

I'm unbelievable. How did I forget a scarf? I always wear a scarf. At least I've remembered the important stuff. I've got my Maths and Music and…

Oh no.

Where is that blue book?

Oh come on...

French homework.

Ciarán Green, Senior School pupil

7.23 a.m.

Arrive at school/work, go to the gym, have a shower, it's not always warm, today I'm lucky.

Philip Rood, Chemistry Technician, age 55

7.24 a.m.

I am awakening to the sound of my pounding alarm. I drag myself out of bed and stumble down stairs, to the sound of my sister noisily chatting away. I pour my cornflakes into my empty bowl, and then the milk. As I take large mouthfuls I feel the cold milk drip down my chin. As I engulf my orange juice in one big slurp, I am ready to go back upstairs and clean my teeth. I squeeze the Colgate toothpaste onto my toothbrush, sprinkle with a dash of water and plunge it into my mouth. I have little time to lose!

Matthew Croft, 9L

7.25 a.m.

It's raining, again, and the sun is just rising over the horizon, gaggles of wet, tired, miserable commuters are standing on the dark station, the light in the draughty shelter is flickering again, it was fixed not two weeks ago. Where *is* this train? Just then, the station announcement sounds, its tinny voice echoing around the station, "Mngmgnhmgnhgmnhgmnhs mghs" which, after 4 years of catching the train, I know roughly translates as "the 7.33 Northern service to Nottingham is delayed by 10 minutes, we apologise for the delay." Typical.

Fabian Martin, 11T

7.26 a.m.

Out of the house and into the murky morning light, I close the door on the reassuring mayhem of three children and a dog. A short walk to the bus stop, I notice the Number 6 on its way. A bit early for a jog, but I make it. This is my calm time. Daydreaming over Trent Bridge and into the Lace Market, the city's landmarks are a blur. I take a tram for the last leg. It glides through Old Market Square, past the University and up the hill. A load of us get off here, ready for school.

Kieron Heath, Head of Chemistry, age 39

7.27 a.m.

I get inside my car to get to school. The engine starts up with a low growl. And then we set off winding our way to school. After a couple of minutes the traffic starts building up like bricks to make a house. it takes quite a while for the traffic to die down until the streets are deserted. I switch on the radio listening to the news and music. The time strikes forty minutes past seven. Tall buildings loom over me. Five minutes to go. We pass the tram track outside and finally we reach school.

Arjun Srinivas, 7Y

7.28 a.m.

I begin my journey to school by car. At this time the road is clear and there is not much traffic. I set off at this time to avoid sitting in traffic for 30 minutes as I'd rather arrive at school and use that time for doing work or playing pool in the sixth form centre. My drive to school is largely uneventful with nothing but my thoughts and the radio for company. But then a car pulls out in front of me, the car jerks as I slam on the brakes and a swift beep of the horn alerts the other driver to my annoyance. Pheww! That was close!

Jeevan Boyal, age 18

7.28 a.m.

I wake to the sound of my alarm and drag myself from the warm bed to begin the standard everyday preparation for school; I rush to the bathroom so that I can be first in the shower just to find that I am too late, and there is no hot water left. As I slowly trudge down the stairs the smell of bacon wafts up my nostrils and I am revived a little, but still the prospect of French first thing kept my spirits low.

James Chester, 11L

7.29 a.m.

On the way to school I take public transport (the train to be precise). It leaves Newark Castle Station at approximately 7.29 and it makes one stop before getting into Nottingham, so I took my final step to leap onto the train. It is a large train carrying six carriages with red furniture, a first class and vestibule. However my brother and I do not sit in first class. We arrive at our first destination being Lowdham. Lowdham is a minute town with several people from school living there. But only being at Lowdham for a couple minutes, we depart. The next stop is my destination, this stop being Nottingham hence the name of my school Nottingham High School.

Josh Nissim, 9H, age 14

7.29 a.m.

I eat my breakfast. I eat cornflakes with milk on. I have a drink of orange squash.

Alfie Cooper, Reception Class, Lovell House

7.30 a.m.

I wake up and instantly look at my clock. The time is 7.30 and I am ready for the last day of the week. I get up out of bed and begin the walk to the shower. I finish my shower and then I walk back to my bedroom and put my school clothes on, the same clothes I wear every day of the week. Then, I go downstairs and have the same breakfast as usual – 2 Weetabix biscuits - and finally at 7.50, I leave the house with my sister and my dad and I am ready for school.

Kieran Brooks, 11S

7.30 a.m.

For most people, being awake at 7.30 is normal, however unfortunately, this is not the case for me. I rub my eyes and make attempt number one at getting out of bed, attempt failed. But today was a good day, and I succeed in attempt number two after an encouraging shout from my dad. After that challenge, I now have to get downstairs without waking my sister, who for some reason is allowed to stay asleep longer than me. I begin the descent. One step, two step, three step, `creek', oh dear...

Matthew Wiggins, 10S

7.30 a.m.

I wake up in the morning at 7.30 a.m. like I usually do. When I say wake up, I actually mean forcefully drag myself out of bed as my dad knocks at my door and commands me to wake up from my comfy slumber. Eventually when I find the strength to get up and ignore the temptation to jump back in bed I take off my pyjamas (wearing blue with white stripes) and put on my school uniform. I usually get told by my mum to put on a jumper but I never really like them seeing as they always seem to make me itchy. I then drag my feet down the stairs to the kitchen where I hunt for my box of porridge. Today I am in luck. Usually my sister takes the box of porridge and puts it somewhere no one can find and not remember where she put it. As I place my bowl of porridge in the microwave for 2 minutes, my cat pounces into the kitchen towards my feet then looks up at me. This means she is hungry and won't leave me alone till she has her feast of tin foods. 'Bother,' I think as I look for her favourite tin, but there is none left...

Patrick Constantin, 10L, age 15

7.31 a.m.

I am walking to my front door knowing that as soon as I open it my body is going to slowly freeze to death; I'm doing it anyway, but opening the door the wind quite literally blows me away. I start the walk to my bus facing up to the wind using my hot flask to warm up my hands. I am really cold so I drink some of the drink. Ouch! My tongue almost falls off as the tea was boiling. Oh no, my bus is here! I have to ditch my drink and run. The flask is no longer important.

Harry Badcock, 11H, age 15

7.32 a.m.

My dad roars up the stairs, awaking me 30 minutes late. Fear pulsates through my body, as heavy as lead, as I wearily haul myself to the bathroom like a wounded soldier heaving himself to safety. After quickly splashing refreshing water onto my face and putting on my uniform, I am hurled by my dad outside in the bitter, biting wind. I might just make it. I charge like an antelope running from its predator to the car, the humiliating thought of walking into assembly late snapping at my heels. I fling myself into the front seat of the car and begin preparing myself for, I imagine, a tumultuous day at school.

Tayyib Ali, 9T

7.33 a.m.

My dad comes into my room, turning the light on and telling me to get up. I moan and get back under my blanket to shield my eyes from the light. I am finding it difficult to get up because I went to bed late. After about 5 minutes staying in bed I get up to go to the bathroom to brush my teeth and wash my face. Now I go to get ready in my school uniform. After I get changed I go down stairs to have my breakfast which is tea and biscuits. My parents tell me to get up earlier because we always get stuck in traffic. I have finished my breakfast, so I am waiting at the door for my sister who always comes down late. She has finally come now. We go out and set off for another day of school.

Adam Hassan, 10L, age 14

7.34 a.m.

One of the most painful noises wakes me up for school…..my alarm. I turn over to press the snooze button for a vital 15 minutes extra sleep. Eventually I drag myself out of bed and go downstairs to have my Weetabix. Just before I leave for school I remember to eat my two Omega-3 tablets to improve my mental abilities #readyformaths. When I arrive at school everybody seems to buzzing and ready for the weekend as I walk down to assembly. My first lesson is French in the very hi-tech languages lab with Monsieur d'Hiver.

Ali Hart, 11L

7.35 a.m.

Oh great, the bus has just gone straight by me, I have missed it again. To make matters worse, an English essay is due and I have only done half of it. Really? I have missed the bus – again. Now I'm going to be late for assembly and I'll have to sign in and receive a late mark. Not the best morning that I have had.

Tom Burton, 8T

7.36 a.m.

Half-asleep, I am being pushed and shoved in an attempt to board the school bus. I finally get on without any trouble, but I know that the task is far from complete. While walking towards my seat, I am still being pushed, but this time by the awfully arrogant year nines. I try my hardest to stay upright, not to avoid being injured, but to avoid being the laughing stock of the bus. I reach my seat with the satisfying feeling that I have survived another day of the bus-boarding mayhem with no disasters.

Harvey Johal, 10L

7.37 a.m.

I get on the bus with a glum face, but a hint of a smile because it's Friday! I greet the bus driver in mid-yawn. She responds with a tired hello. The first five minutes of the journey I am all alone in the bottom deck of the bus, but when the bus arrives at Halam all my friends on the bus get on. We are all tired so we turn for our iPods and iPhones to play because we are too tired to talk. After a while we get bored of our games and end up talking to each but we always have one earphone in our ear listening to music! We talk to each other about our day ahead, and the good and bad subjects we have today. We also talk about exams and what we are doing over the weekend. We then realise that we aren't even half way through the journey! We end up just looking out the window, bored. There is nothing to talk about and nothing to do. The rest of the journey goes on…

Harry Mills, 8S, age 12

7.38 a.m.

At precisely 7.38am I catch the 79A bus from Rise Park bus stop which takes approximately 10 minutes to travel to the Bulwell tram stop. The bus journey is very bland, however when I arrive at the tram stop things change. Already there are two portly girls in short skirts smoking what can only be described as an illegal substance called weed. The stench was horrendous and the thought of what these people are putting into the bodies is sickening. It is at this moment I despise Bulwell.

Faraaz Ahmed, age 18

7.39 a.m.

I'm tired, but ready. I tie my laces, and then do a double knot. My bag is packed and I lift up on to my shoulders like an Olympic weightlifter. The door creeks open and I take my first steps towards school and the long day ahead. The cars drive past and I gaze at the beaming headlights. Finally I reach the bus stop on a cold and windy day. The cars and Lorries drive past, but no bus? Then finally the bus arrives. I hop on, greet my friends, and a new day is born.

Hamish Mark, 7H

7.39 a.m.

I awake to the sound of my hollering mother and stir under the sheets. Looking across at my carriage clock on the tall dresser at the end of my bed, I see it's twenty to eight. A slump to the bathroom, I jump in the shower. Returning to my room, I see the dazzling poking above my window sill and pull on my clothes. My mother is yelling at me to get some breakfast down me, but I don't have time, the clock ticks ominously and it is already eight. Pulling my bag over my shoulder and shoving some coins into my pocket, I run through the bungalow's red door and close it behind me. I trudge solemnly to the drudgery that is the commute to my school, through the sleepy suburb that has yet to awaken. The station is a small red brick building with two windows. I dash in and speak with haste asking for a ticket to Nottingham. The train is pulling in as I flurry through the closing doors and watch as school pulls up and home pulls away.

George Bond, 8S, age 13

7.40 a.m.

I wait in the hall for my mum to be ready. As she brushes her teeth I put on my shoes. I take out my phone and start playing on a game. Finally my mum is ready and we step outside into the cold morning breeze. I feel refreshed and ready for the day. We walk a short distance to the car and get in. I throw my bags into the back seat and slump myself in the passenger seat. We set off, on the long journey to school. I take out my phone and play on a game as my mum drives me through Watnall into Nottingham. I feel excited as the package I bought off eBay is due to arrive later in the morning.

James Wakefield, 9H, age 13

7.40 a.m.

The sky is a deep cerulean blue, unusual for this time of year, as my feet carry me, dreamlike, towards the school. The gravel crunches beneath my feet and the wind sets leaves quivering in the trees, as if thanking them for some calm before the tumult of voices to come. I breathe deep the crisp morning air, calm, as the first rays of sunshine creep over the aged rocks and caress my face gently. Thousands have walked these very steps, but for now my school and I are together, alone.

Raghav Sudarshan, Year 11

7.41 a.m.

I am getting onto the school bus. There is a lot of pushing and shoving as everyone vies for a spot on the bus. For me, a year 9, it is an opportunity to grab the aisle seats near my mates. I am triumphant as I throw my bags on my seat. Alas, one of my fellow Year 9s has been condemned to a seat next to the Year 10s. I get out my phone and plug in the earphones. The pandemonium of the bus is replaced with my favourite songs. I am now ready for the school day ahead…

Mukul Rathi, 9H

7.41 a.m.

I am outside the bus stop it's freezing as usual. The bus is late again as it always is. Finally five minutes later the bus arrives I climb aboard then go up to the top deck. Everyone is in a glum mood as usual and I say hello and join in with the chatting. The bus journey feels like it goes on forever there are so many stops. When will it end.

Sam Brough, 8H, age 12

7.42 a.m.

It's 7:42 a.m. and I've just sat down on this freezing cold Sharp's bus…there's even a draft here on the top deck. I'm tired. In fact, I'm exhausted; I haven't been sleeping well recently.

Lessons are going well today, especially French, but I can't wait until my cup of tea at break; I'm experiencing withdrawal symptoms, being the true Brit I am.

Lunch has come and it's about time! We are currently trying to plan the route throughout Europe that we're all going to be taking on inter railing this Summer…. The planning isn't going very well (Ben won't shut up).

Lessons have gone slowly this afternoon, but it's time for the weekend now and I'm having everyone round tonight for a few drinks and a chill!

Henry Potts, 6M2

7.42 a.m.

"7:42", the clock says. I have woken up 22 minutes later than planned. As I rush out of my room, I grab at the nearest towel and then I slam the bathroom door. Without any other thoughts but getting myself fresh and clean I make my way through the daily routine of washing. Only 6 minutes have passed since I have woken up. I realise that I am now well on track, so I dry and dress myself calmly. I glumly walk down the stairs, as if I have two young children grasping onto my thighs refusing to let go. "What's for breakfast today?" I sarcastically ask myself as I imagine the usual Sainsbury's own brand corn flakes. But no, in the pantry, I see a fresh new box of Chocolate Weetabix Minis. I open the lid cleanly and carefully with precision and finesse, and a heady whirlwind of wheat and chocolate aromas awaken my senses

James Geeson, 10L, age 14

7.43 a.m.

I wait for the bus. A half melted mound of ice from last week lies next to my feet. It's cold today. Finally the bus arrives. I say hi to the bus driver, no reply... as usual. I take a seat towards the back of the bus next to my friend. I take my water bottle from my pocket and take a sip. My friend takes it from me and throws it to the back of the bus. I get angry. I stand up to retrieve it but the bus driver tells me off. My friend apologises. As the bus breaks, the bottle rolls under my feet. I put it back in my pocket.

Ashhad Noor, 10T

7.43 a.m.

I start to come to school in the car. My Dad drives and I have a black Mini car. I am allowed to sit in the front today on my booster seat.

Millen Rana, Reception Class, Lovell House

7.44 a.m.

After 5 minutes of waiting in the blistering cold, the bus arrives at my stop. I step into the behemoth vehicle and a warm gust of air caresses me as I pay my fare. Drizzle dripping off my shoes with every step I take; I coolly advance towards the back row. I pass the distinctive faces of strangers I see every day, whose names I'll ever know. Tiger-striped bag on the floor, headphones on playing a song I cannot recall, I take out my iPhone to play Temple Run 2 as the bus departs only to inevitably get stuck in traffic and make me late for school.

Jyzu Manzano, 10Y, age 15

7.44 a.m.

I finish my breakfast – toast and orange juice. Next, I triple-check my bag for school. I get ready for the journey. Friday is usually a good day at school, and today it's also my birthday as well.

The bus comes much earlier than expected. I miss it by a matter of seconds as it sails past at the bottom of my road. Annoyed, I trudge back up the hill towards my house. Thankfully, when I get there, my dad agrees to take me on his way to work. We set off towards school, hoping to beat the bus.

Joseph Geldman, 8H

7.45 a.m.

As I wake up at 7.00, I realise I will be at school in 45 minutes, so I begin to become apprehensive of the day ahead. After all I have got English then double French; my most hated subjects. I arrive at school; I am feeling extremely envious of the majority of my classmates who are still relaxing in their comfortable beds. They don't realise how lucky they are! I stumble up the stairs and walk along the corridors, barely able to keep my eyes open, when I realise my French essay isn't completed. Then I realise I have got 1 hour before schools starts...

Luca Costante 10L

7.45 a.m.

I step outside for the first time, the wind sending a chill down my spine. I walk up the road and watch as the familiar cars pass and watch the morning rush-hour fly past the bus stop. As I carefully cross the road, I imagine the day ahead of me.

Oliver Thomas, 7L, age 12

7.45 a.m.

I wake up, knowing a big and long day is a head of me. I walk a few tired and dizzy steps, to the bathroom feeling like it is long walk through the Derbyshire hills. I turn the cold iron tap and out comes the water with a mighty flush. I fling my glass under and fill it as much as I can without it over flowing. I put the glass to my mouth and take a mouthful. My mouth freezes feeling like I have taken a bit out of the Antarctic ice. I am ready for it.

William Hart, 9S

7.46 a.m.

I am getting onto the public bus at 7.46 and am being whisked through the streets of Nottingham; after seeing Trent Bridge CC, now I see the train station, boarded up for renewal, and then I see the canal. We're now moving on quickly down parallel to the broadmarsh centre, turning left and now I'm getting off the bus and catching the tram, through yet more of the sights of Nottingham. I see Old Market Square and looming over it, the council house. Up the hill I spy Royal Centre's large columns towering over the tram stop. Moments later we have passed NTU and are climbing up the hill towards my final sight of the journey, the tower of the school is only just visible above the shrubbery of the arboretum. Finally I have arrived at the school.

Aidan Aungles, 9H, age 13

7.46 a.m.

Out the house, up the drive and away. It's cold, I'm late, another great start to the school day. I hurry up the road. "Why is it so cold?" I wonder to myself, almost slipping on a self-centred, miraculously surviving sheet of ice. I am at the bus stop, late, yet everyone is here. Where is the bus? I am bored, tired (sleep is overrated), did I mention cold? Look here bus, I kept my side of the bargain, where are you? Four minutes later the hulking beast shudders to a halt with a desperate squawk. "Morning" I mumble. A great day begins.

James Gordon 10L

7.47 a.m.

Decisions, decisions …..! Which pile of 'Things to do' should I tackle first? I log on to check e-mails and decide to check that the audio file for my first lesson is still accessible. Then I photocopy some spare copies of today's recipe for my Sixth Form cookery group. I try to guess (intelligently) how many boys will forget them today and promise myself a treat if I guess correctly. But who will know if I cheat …….? I imagine that those who have forgotten their ingredients as well will be in the local Sainsbury's right now. Year 8 pupils start to straggle in and gather in the corridor outside. Same banter, same questions…..

"Wasn't that Maths homework hard last night?"

"What Maths homework ….?"

Time for a coffee.

Tony Holding, Head of Year 8, Head of General Studies, Teacher of French and German

7.47 a.m.

I walk up the stairs ready to go with my coat in one hand and my grey school bag in the other. I put on my blue waterproof coat, my black gloves and my black leather slip-on shoes. I walk out of my front door to meet the cold crisp air. The sun is just becoming visible over the houses in the distance. I start to walk down the street accompanied by my sister. As I come to the traffic lights I watch the cars go past and with them I can see my physics teacher's smart car.

Ben Hartshorn, 9Y

7.48 a.m.

From the ledge below the tower the roofs of Nottingham are huddled together against the cold wind and rain. It's so cold there that my camera's tripod seems to be shivering as much as I am. Below me children scurry on their way to school, and making a panoramic photo of the Nottingham skyline at sunrise on the school's 500th birthday is fast becoming a bit grim. Steadying myself and my camera, I fire the shutter, check the exposure, greet Mr Kilby, who seems amused to see me standing on the roof, finish the job and return to the warmth of the library.

Will Burn, Teacher of English, Head of Year 11

7.49 a.m.

I slowly walk down my road to catch the bus, as I reach the bus stop I see the same people as I do every morning. The bus is usually early; however this morning it is late which means I have to stand in the bitter cold as the icy wind blows in my face making me very uncomfortable. Thankfully, soon after I see the bus approaching in the distance. As I get on I am energetically greeted by my bus driver, Ron, who says the same thing just like every other school day, 'Morning'.

Alex Jones, Senior School pupil

7.49 a.m.

Geography Office, after following the normal routine as ever: walk from Waverley Mount car park, through a growing morning light, down the steps. I see the office light is on – Shaun is in first today. Round the west block corner to hit a chill of air, past the kitchen delivery lorry, through the open door into the corridor – met by a blast of warm air. I walk between familiar photos of our Ecuador trip and OS map of the whole region. I sit at my desk, and discuss last night's football transfer news with Shaun, then down to business.

Mr Colin Sedgewick, teacher of Geography

7.50 a.m.

A subtle chill creeps from under a shallow crack in the door, and it rises in bitter circulation; and I depart my house. Outside it is barely dawn, and a shallow mist is floating in the air. Shivering in the cold, and huddling in vain against the minimal warmth of my coat, I hurry into the car, the tread of my shoes scuffing against the sharp gravel of the driveway. I open the back seat door and throw my bag in hastily, then clamber into the front passenger seat. I plug in my headphones and withdraw from the world outside.

Benjamin Towle, 11Y

7.51 a.m.

The bus is cold and draughty this morning. The top deck of the double-decker normally has a draught that slips through the gaps in the panes. From downstairs comes the high-pitched babble of some small children and forms an awkward and clanking melody to pass the daily commute. The conversation on the top deck is mostly about University offers and grades. It's all we do talk about at the moment. The 40 minute trip is nearly over, with the centre of Nottingham rushing to greet us.

Jack Barratt, age 18

7.52 a.m.

I come to school in the car. I have a small blue i20 Citroen car. I take my brother to school. He is in the Senior School because he is 15 years old.

Rafe Renton, Reception Class, Lovell House

7.53 a.m.

I arrive at the bus stop, and I wait there for the bus. The bus arrives at 7.53, it is late, and I get on along with 6 other people. Once we all sit down the bus continues on its journey, we go around a few sharp corners it is very exciting. We reach my friend's stop at 7.56 and we talk about various thing. Then my other friend get on and sit down at 7.58. We all play on our phones for the rest of the journey.

Will Hustwayte, 7Y, age 11

7.54 a.m.

I'm waiting for the 77 Bus to get to school. It's 7.54 and the bus arrives. I board it. Students from other schools causally talk about what they are going to do today. I hear someone complains about how hard GCSEs are. I inwardly laugh. My bus is packed with students. I pull out my copy of The Economist to read. The person next to me is on her phone. Getting off the bus when I reached Upper Parliament Street I am walking slowly towards the tram. The tram isn't due for another few minutes. I walk inside Starbucks. Being greeted by the barista, I begin to order my drink. I have about 20 minutes to spare as I arrive at the High School tram stop. I walk into Sainsbury and look at the price of milk. 2 for £3. I make a note of it on my phone.

Kevin Lau, 6O2

7.55 a.m.

The day begins with the first coffee. Strong, black with one sugar. The quiet of the classroom belies the chaos ahead. This is the most orderly my desk will be all day. In front of me, my planner lays scribbled on and I look over what we have in store. Games, Music and a visit from a fire engine! I take a final gulp of coffee and welcome the first boy at my door. A bright eyed smile to begin the school day.

Claire Smith Year 1 Teacher, Lovell House

7.56 a.m.

After I hear a shout from my mother instructing me to 'get up' I still decide to go for a sneaky, but short, lie in, as the warmth and comfort of my bed in the mornings persuades me to remain there a little longer. After I get up I then realise that it is an important day in the school's history, so I quickly have as shower, brush my teeth and make my way downstairs, for a quick slice of toast, then I quickly run upstairs, as I did not pack my bag and I again hear the sound of my mother's voice, I rush outside into the car to set out on our 20 minute journey to school, the mornings are always hectic.

Uhan Elliott, 10Y

7.57 a.m.

Get the (much-maligned, 4Mb { there's more memory in a dog biscuit now!}) acorn to reprint year 12 option choice summary. Choose the 21 choices (20%, elucidated yesterday evening) to alter in order to accommodate one recent change. Let the (still much maligned, 4Mb) acorn recalculate the option blocks and totals and then readjust another 15 options choices to balance numbers. That's 36 changes to help one boy (will he ever appreciate the trouble we go to accommodate one boy's potentially fleeting fancy?). Produce a memo to try and encourage the 39 (c.40%) recalcitrants to return option forms.

Dr Andrew Wood, Head of Timetable, teacher of Chemistry

7.58 a.m.

It's all my fault! It always is – whenever there is a Sixth Form misdemeanor, an email pops up in my inbox or an irate colleague reaches for the phone. This morning I am no sooner on the campus, when my iPhone vibrates. Oh, no!... and it is not yet 8.00 a.m.! Tentatively I pull out the phone and check the message….it's a parent thanking the school for supporting her 18 year old son through a very traumatic January filled with external exams. Suddenly the day looks brighter……

Wilma Robinson, Head of Sixth Form

7.59 a.m.

I arrive at school in Balmoral Road car park – plenty of space to park my car at this time.

I say goodbye to my son as he heads off to the gym to deposit his hockey kit. En-route to the North Entrance, I see a member of staff taking a photo with his mobile phone. Inside the entrance, a boy and his friend are looking at a mobile phone.

A Year 7 boy returns a Reading Challenge book and is tested on its content – he easily answers the questions.

Sally Blythe, Library Assistant

7.59 a.m.

As i step out my front door a slight frost catches my wet hair from the morning shower and step by step hands gripped inside my pocket hidden from the cold i vacate to tall walls of Nottingham high school . It's so early i can hardly think as a singing bird rattles its noises inside my clustered mind . Cars full of moaning teenagers wiz past as if they can not wait to drop their children at school . The dull lessons and predictable homework's are my first thought of the day. My second being what lunch is on in the dinning room . I feel like all i do is walk these 300 yards to school and almost the whole way i can see the top of the school.

Harry Bennett, 9T

4. Arriving at School

8.00 a.m.

Chemistry department, my assistant arrives, we go through each teachers requirements, putting together an overall picture of the days experiments.

Always a rush first thing to get the necessary experiments ready and out into the five chemistry labs for the first period start.

During the lunchtime I run a Climbing Club, weather, some sun but cool but the pupils enjoy their session.

Continues like this through the day, preparing, setting out, clearing the days practical's, until the final lessons finishes at 4.00 p.m.

Philip Rood, Chemistry Technician, age 55

8.01 a.m.

I leave my office to check that all of the computers in the two Languages Suites are working correctly. If there are any problems, I try to rectify them and if this is not possible I report any faults to our ICT Department.

I then look through the emails for the matters relevant to today. I prioritise anything important and write a to do list for the day. At around 10.15 I stop work to go and get a nice cup of tea, and if I'm feeling naughty a couple of biscuits.

Rachel Bedrock, Languages Resources Assistant, age 38

8.02 a.m.

Sıradan bir Cuma günü...

Her sabah aynı saat'da kalkmak nekadar zor bişey inanamazsınız. Bu sabah, her sabah gibi 8'de kalkarım, bana gören kolayca zombi sanabilir. Görunmez bir kavahltı dan sonra, tum zorluklara rağmen arabayı binip okula giderim, yolum açıkdır. Okulda resim boyarım, biraz Almanca konuşurum, birazda Ispanyolce yazarım, ama benim için en önemlisi yemekdir. Arkadaşlerimla keyif yaparım ve okulu'da mutfak kulturu çok başarılıdır, onun için büfe'de çok ama çok para harcamam büyuk bir sürpris değil. Bundan sonra eve giderim, bu sıradan bir Cumadir.

Efekan Dundar, 6M2

8.02 a.m.

Hours? Days? Months? Years? In the time on my hands, I take to observing the smooth contours on the wall paper adjacent to me. A sharp glance at my watch. Once again, an appreciation of the crisp decorating surrounding me. Ever the silence. Ever the unwavering glow from beneath the door. The impatience sets in now, tearing at my delicate tolerance threshold, breaking down the walls containing my anger. My voice box booms along the hollow walls, "Hurry up!", but to no response.

My tail between my legs and my pride in a disgruntled heap on the floor, I enter the vacant bathroom.

Daniel Thurgood, 9T

8.03 a.m.

I leave home with my coat and my hat on. The bus stop is just outside my house. When I get on the bus, I sometimes go on my phone or I read a book. Once I get off the bus onto Mansfield Road, there is still a five minute walk to get to school. Once I get into school, I go to my form room where some of my friends are. I pack my bag, then talk to my friends until registration. Mrs Pidgeon reads the notices and then we go to assembly.

Faisal Ahmed, 8T

8.03 a.m.

Friday morning and I arrive at just after 8am and open up the Design Technology studios and workshop. I tidy away a few things that have been left out from the day before and do my morning safety checks.

Next I have some Printed Circuit boards to make. I put on my lab coat to protect my clothes from the etch chemicals. It smells of the workshop – fusty, so I get a body spray out of my bag and give it a quick blast.

Ben Thomas and his 2 year 13 students arrive in the workshop and ask 'what is that smell?' I tell them it's 'Girl' and they all pull faces. Maybe they've been in a boy's school for too long. Year 9s arrive and one announces it smells 'peng in here'. A slang term for good, maybe there is hope after all!

Sally Bales, Design Technology Technician

8.04 a.m.

As I arrive at school I'm excited for the weekend of sport. I'm excited for the day ahead but not the first two lessons. Double German. I get into school and pack my bag, take off my coat and relax in the classroom until someone else arrives. When they do we go downstairs to the dining room and get a drink and a snack. We go back to the classroom and listen to music before making sure we have got everything for the day. We wait for everyone else to arrive and for school to start. Today's going to be a good day.

Tom Walton, 9L

8.04 a.m.

I get to school. I go to the 'Early Birds' club and play chess. I play chess with my friend Adit.

Isa Saleem-Khan, Reception Class, Lovell House

8.05 a.m.

When I get out of the car a blast of cold refreshing air hits me. The sun is out and there is dew on the freshly mown grass. I am then greeted by the familiar sound of the big yellow bus' brakes whining in protest at the immense weight of all the school children on board. I get on and hear the same noise that I had heard a year and a half ago on my first journey, a blend of people shouting, listening to music and all sort of methods of making as much noise as possible. I sit down next to my friends and start chatting.

Johnathan Ross

8.06 a.m.

I have just finished my cold and tiring walk to the bus stop, slightly late as usual, but that's okay because the bus is always late. I get on the double decker green bus only to find that my bus pass has run out, I have to pay the, rather expensive, child fare of £1. I find the usual sort of people on the bus; school children, workers and not much else. Of course, there is the odd irritating person listening to their iPod way too loud. The bus jolts and we set off past the 60's built traditional houses.

James Hoole, 9Y, age 13

8.07 a.m.

As I step on the bus, royal azure all over with the Nottingham High School logo imprinted on the side, all eyes turn towards me and others that are getting on at my stop. I find a seat. Downstairs or upstairs? To me it makes no difference. For I have an aid to get me through the journey. I take them out, the fountain of my living. Earphones. I plug them into my phone and insert them into my ear. The lush flow waves into my head. The cutting beat perforates onto my eardrum. The crafted raw lyrics kiss my brain. The wonder that is music.

Isaac Acharya

8.08 a.m.

It is bitterly cold, the harsh wind is blowing by my face, and I just finish off my orange juice and shove the carton in to the bin. I look up at the timings of the bus and bus number 89 is due but it is late again. I wait for a couple of more minutes and then I can see from the hill a double decker purple bus coming my way, I lift my hand to get drivers attention and the bus parks with a cough of diesel coming out of its huge exhaust. The doors open and I go in, I scan my bus pass across the scanner and turn round to look for an empty seat but all seats are filled with people of all ages and sizes, so there I stand my hand holding the cold steel pole tightly and I am thinking about all the homework's that I have to hand in for Friday morning.

Kaman Bukhari, 9S

8.09 a.m.

I get to school in my white Audi car. I go out into the playground and play football with some other boys who are already there. I love football and support Manchester United and Nottingham Forest.

Arun Sandhu, Reception Class, Lovell House

8.10 a.m.

It's just another ordinary day of my High School life. We've all found our familiar territory on the bus and I'm listening to one of the latest release on UKF Dubstep, trying to share my findings with the less enthusiastic indie hipsters that grace the surrounding areas on the bus. I've just conducted one of my frequent checks of twitter, Ben is in top form as always as he recalls the gruelling memory of Lewis's trip to a certain unnamed fast food chain that will thankfully stay with him for the rest of his school life.

Michael Allen, 11S

8.11 a.m.

I enter through the gates and into the yard at the start of the day preparing myself for the long day ahead. Fridays are increasingly long though as it is touching distance to the glorious weekend. My day instantly gets better though as I see Nathaniel Day. We march in together to the dining hall preparing ourselves for the day ahead.

Mark Needham, 11L

8.12 a.m.

I stand at the bus stop in the bitter cold of a February morning. I am wearing my favourite dark red coat waiting for the bus: late as usual. I am trying to make small talk with the year 8s about the up and coming six nations at the weekend. They have no idea what I am talking about. I see the reflection of the bus in a shop window from around the corner; I am relieved as these awkward conversations about rugby and how hard year eleven is over. We all trudge onto the bus, the weekend is near.

Harry Tindale, 11S

8.13 a.m.

The chilling winds of the morning strike my face as I breathe in the fresh air. The car rolls on the roads on the way to school, often hitting bumps in the ground which shook my body. I stare at the clouds, trying to make shapes from them but I could only see blurry layers of white vapour. The school's outline is now visible; the tower making a faint silhouette against the sky. I look on through the mist as the car wheels past the bus lane and a multitude of students walk through the gates. I step inside my class room, then pack my bag. Finally, I go outside.

Achintya Singh, Senior School pupil

8.14 a.m.

Firing down, a constant burn to my skin and a sting to my eyes; the white lights of W18 capture me. Melancholy has arrived. The last remnants of joy finally dance themselves dead as I fold over my maths book. Quadratic equations grin sinisterly at me. A cold shawl of breeze rushes through the window and cools my still slightly damp hair. Yet then a pit pattering sound echoes down the barren corridor. Could it be? Yes. My friend walks through the door.

"Stuck with those equations?" he asks. To which I desolately nod too. "I'll help." He smiles.

Sasha Burnside, Senior School pupil

8.15 a.m.

It is a bright morning as the sun floods into my room; the light grabs my eye-balls and squeezes them as hard as it can as I strain my neck round to turn off the alarm which has been tearing through my ears for the past 2 minutes. After I get changed I clamber into the car, I look out of the window to see green and brown fields rushing past without saying hello or goodbye. The sun is still squeezing my eyes but not as firm as before, it is giving me a break for it knew, I was nearly at the dark grim hell hole named; school.

Olly Kumra, 9T

8.16 a.m.

As I arrive in school this morning, there is a distinct aura of warmth, not because the heating is finally being put to use, rather because it is time for the school to celebrate five hundred years of its existence. It seems as though there isn't a single corridor that doesn't contain some sort of reminder of this milestone - and for good reason. It is astonishing that the school is still in one piece after such an exorbitant amount of time; but what is even more impressive is how the school has such a positive impact on the students and every day is enjoyable. Today is no different, and the ever-friendly atmosphere sets the tone for a great day to come.

Graham Garside, Senior School pupil

8.17 a.m.

On my way to school I bump into a friend of mine from the girl's school, and end up walking her to school. This works out well as I haven't spoken to her in a while so it is a good catch - up. After leaving her and wishing her a good day I head off to my form room admiring the joyful characters of both our schools. I meet up with my friends and coincidently bump into my tutor along the way to have a quick catch - up before the school day starts.

Jeevan Gosal, 11S

8.18 a.m.

Liam is first in working as usual.

From the reprographics room I pick up the Author Visit letter to parents for the Simon Scarrow event next week by invitation from the Librarian at the Girls' school. The walk along the road has required six ticks of agreement one of which is in green.

There is an email from her about book orders.

I order online a further 19 Tom Palmer books from yesterday's Junior School/Year 7 author event.

At the same time I pick up a box of photocopier paper.

Form period fills the library with 6th form.

Yvette Gunther MA MCLIP, Librarian, Head Librarian/Archivist

8.19 a.m.

I am running late because I am in a traffic jam. We have a big red Volvo (XC90). The cars are moving very slowly and we are just waiting and waiting.

Sasmeet Satyam, Reception Class, Lovell House

8.20 a.m.

As I step out my front door a slight frost catches my wet hair from the morning shower and step by step hands gripped inside my pocket hidden from the cold I vacate to the tall walls of Nottingham high school. It's so early I can hardly think as a singing bird's rattles its noises inside my clustered mind. Cars full of moaning teenagers whizz past as if they cannot wait to drop their children of at school. The dull lessons and predictable homework's are my first thought of the day. My second being what lunch is on in the dining room. I feel like all I do is walk these 300 yards to school and almost the whole way I can see the top of the school.

an unknown Senior School pupil

8.21 a.m.

The bus is late…again, and I know today is going to be an ordinary day. I get on the bus, smile at the familiar faces, and sit down at a seat which really should have my name on it. I'm listening to my music on that same favourites playlist. Life is routine. Suddenly the bus stops at a bus stop. Seems ironic but no one ever catches the bus at the end of Ilkeston Road. A new face. He walks right to the back of the bus and sits next to me. He smiles and says "Oh a High School boy." I smile back and the journey continues.

Mohammed Yazdani, 6I2

8.22 a.m.

The bus has pulled into the bus lane. We stand in unison, as if we are choreographed. A chair next to me is struck. Dust billows into the air, filling my lungs and stinging my eyes. I exit the bus, eyes still streaming and prepare for another school day.

Alex McLachlan 10Y

8.23 a.m.

The day begins, as I have come to expect in my role as School Captain, with the customary lap of the school, this time looking for Dr Sibly – we have arranged a short rehearsal for my morning assembly reading. It is a piece from the bible to mark 500 years since the first lessons were taught at the school, and let's just say the language doesn't roll easily of the tongue! Despite the odd spoonerism, I feel confident, and as I take my seat in the chair stage right, boys from years 7-11 gradually begin to fill the Player Hall. After a brief version of the school hymn from the Brass Quintet, I manage to turn on the microphone without difficulty, and deliver the reading as clearly as I can. Fortunately, the mishaps of the rehearsal do not make a reappearance, and so I settle down to enjoy the remainder of the assembly.

Christian Cummings, Captain of the School

8.24 a.m.

An abortive attempt to sing a few bars of Coney Island Baby briefly fills the stairwell as I approach the music room. Voices not yet fully awake and certainly not warmed up. One sixth-former gingerly picks out the notes on the piano, a year 11 boy attempts to finish a cereal bar AND sing, doing neither well. The group tries to decide which song to rehearse. They all talk at once until one of their number, the pianist, wrestles control of the debate with a strained 'Just shut up everyone! We'll do My Everline'

The door opens and Mr Reid, clutching a stack of folders and photocopies, seizes control of the assembled boys with an authoritative 'Right lads!'

David Allerton, teacher of French and Spanish

8.25 a.m.

I trudge wearily into school, and walk across the yard to the west wing of the school. I walk through the doors, and walk into the year 9 corridor. I walk down to the far end of the corridor and open my locker. I pack my bag for the day and leave it on the side. After this, I go and talk to my friends. I talk about the football matches coming up. I then go downstairs and into the yard where I start playing football for the rest of break.

Harjit Nijran, 9Y, age 13

8.26 a.m.

Don't want to get up this morning but manage to get myself out of bed. Have a shower, brush my teeth and go downstairs to have breakfast. I finally leave the house to walk to school and arrive at school at 9:00, but I have to go straight to assembly because I am late and then it is off to Geography, the lesson doesn't last that long though but the rest of the day awaits me. Can't wait till 4 o'clock.

William Grogan, 10L, age 14

8.27 a.m.

I walk into the school, casually swaggering up to the door, talking to my friend who goes on my bus about the football score from yesterday. Whilst chatting to him I accidently bump into a colossal 6th Former. We exchange our apologies and then my friend and I laugh about what had just happened. Our depleted swaggering walk turns into a trudge up the stairs towards our grey, dull lockers. I then meet the rest of my drowsy friends who can't wait for the day to end. And we all slowly pack our bags.

Sabahath Khan, 9Y, age 13

8.28 a.m.

I glance up from the book I am reading. The bus is currently trundling along the route to school. I check my watch. 8:25- we seem to be on time. I can hear the shouts of excitement at the back of the bus, but pay them no heed. I go back to reading. Fiction is so much more interesting than reality.

Unfortunately, I soon finish my book, and am reduced to flicking through the (sizeable) appendices and gazing blankly through the window. After what seems to be an age, the bus pulls into the bus lane. A new school day has begun.

Dominic Stafford, 11Y

8.29 a.m.

I arrive at school and go straight to my form room ready to be registered for the day ahead, I take a seat among my friends as we wait to be told the notices for the day. On my mind is French vocabulary as I am soon to be taking a French test. Mrs O'Brian arrives, greets us with her signature smile and informs us of the day ahead. She tells us about a meeting we will attend to discuss our future plans and potential careers, then we leave all discussing the lessons we are about to attend.

James Lago, 10S

8.29 a.m.

Having just got into school, I go to the music block to put my trumpet in the store cupboard. On the way out, I meet two members of a brass quintet that I am part of. I am understandably surprised when they tell me that we are playing in assembly this morning, playing a piece that I have never seen. We immediately settle down for a rehearsal, and are soon joined by the other members. Our teacher, Mr Douglas, writes out the parts, for he hadn't known that we were playing either. We had a quick run through, and then went to the Player Hall to perform.

Joseph Silcock, 10T

8.30 a.m.

I open the school shop at 8.30 a.m. until the first bell goes at 8.45 a.m. Some mornings are busier than others – when the exams are on the sale of stationery increases considerably. Today there is a parent and a year 7 pupil here on the dot of 8.30 a.m. The boy needs a pair of rugby shorts. Straight after they have left a pupil comes in for a PE vest and pays cash – which is unusual as most boys charge their purchases to their end of term accounts. Two more year 7 boys come in for Rugby socks – it's year 7 games this morning!

Irene Epworth, School Shop Manager

8.30 a.m.

I climb out of my father's automobile to be ambushed by an aggressive gust of wind, ruining my hair which I have spent at least five minutes perfecting in the downstairs bathroom of my home half an hour earlier. My day has already started appallingly and I have not yet arrived in school. As I walk towards the gates I begin mentally preparing myself for the mindless, football related drivel I must endure before lessons begin. Nevertheless I feel somewhat optimistic as to what the day may have to offer, barely able to contain my excitement for the upcoming school assembly.

Patrick Kassell, 10L

8.31 a.m.

As the bus turns into the bus lane, there is the usual laughter of the people who are awake in the morning and the grunting of the unhappy girls who are acting like they have just woken up. Ben and I are as awake as we are ever going to be today and as usual we are annoying anyone we can. We just have the attitude that it is one more day to the weekend.

Harry Kerr, 11S

8.31 a.m.

I arrive at school listening to music. I put my bags and coat on the rack and walk into the classroom. Nobody else from my form is in the classroom yet. I wait for a bit and keep listening to my music. A couple of minutes later a couple of my friends arrive. We talk until the bell rings. We move to our seats and wait for our form teacher to arrive. He arrives 3 minutes later. Our form teacher begins another of his signature rants and we wait it out then leave to assembly. The deputy headmaster talks about the 500th anniversary of the school which is tomorrow. He finishes speaking and we slowly file out of the hall, and walk to our first lesson.

Oliver Craven, 8H, age thirteen

8.31 a.m.

I'm at my desk having a coffee and waiting for the arrival of unwell, injured or just Friday tired boys. I never know what real or imagined symptoms will come in but I am prepared - it co be straight forward – a headache, a grazed knee or a sore throat or it could be one of the more 'interesting' ones –a tick attached to a scalp from an adventurous trip to the cheviots which needs removing, a glass pipette that has gone straight through a finger or just someone that needs a chat and encouragement– coffee drunk, ready to go!

Sarah Jacob, School Nurse

8.32 a.m.

I've got loads of late homework so I'm in a rush, I run to form period and I'm greeted by the new lights in my form room. They're far too bright. I've got a detention, great. I sat down in my usual spot and secretly go on my phone under the desk; my form teacher sees me and tells me to put it away so I do. The bell rings and I leave for assembly, dreading singing hymns in the hall. I sling my bag in my locker and do up my blazer buttons, tripping as I go down the stairs.

will Sanderson, 11H

8.32 a.m.

I'm walking into school, looking up at the schools towering possibilities. I'm looking up at the school; it is massive yet still does not look like it could ever be big enough to contain the many resources the school has to offer. I'm in school and I'm packing my bag. I check my time table and see it is time for form period. My form teacher has just arrived and is letting me into the form room. He is now telling me and the rest of the class about many of the lunch time and out of school activities. The bell is now ringing and I know it is time for assembly

Toby Allington, 7S

8.32 a.m.

I'm sitting in my classroom. Only one more day left until the weekend. Groups of boys are sitting around me. I continue to talk to my friends. Spontaneous laughter suddenly erupts from one of the groups, for no apparent reason. Looking around I see the groups of people, doing homework, crowding around phones. It's a typically average day. I sit down; concentrating hard on my biology notes, and trying to decide which

I should revise first for the imminent test. I keep going, despite the ruckus around me. My head is whirling with facts and names. Ventricles and veins, atriums and arteries, tricuspid and bicuspid valves. The bell goes, its tinny drone echoing around the hall. It's time for register. There's no hurry to get to my seat. The teacher is usually a bit late.

Ben Gutteridge, 9L

8.33 a.m.

I arrive at school in a flurry after the usual 2 hour morning shift at home, such is the typical start to the day of a working mum. In the Geography Office, Mr Sedgewick is on the phone. 'Oh, wait one minute' he says as I walk in, 'Here she is' and hands me the phone, whispering 'It's the police!' I feel instantly guilty and quickly rack my brain to think what potential crime I may have unwittingly committed and been caught doing on my mad dash into school. 'HA! Got you!!' he and Mr Mitchell cry out and then roll around laughing at their ability to wind me up so easily – yet again. Grrrr.. Another typical day in the Geography department at NHS……

Amy Lemon, teacher of Geography

8.33 a.m.

Quickly off the bus, avoiding the stampede, I run as fast as I can across the school premises, whilst rain pelts my face. As I open the door, majestic waves of heat strike me in the face and only then do I know my day has begun. I stand by the heater for as long as my hands can take and walk over to my years' corridor to be greeted by a mob of teenagers catching up on last night's football matches on TV. I start my own argument and the only thing stopping me is the bell.

Robbie Rizk, 10H

8.33 a.m.

Stepping off the bus and smelling the fresh air of the open world, I think to myself; 'I am so glad to be off the bus full of crazed Year Eights and painfully loud music'. Now, I turn and begin the monotonous walk down to school whilst thinking about the large amount of work I would have to copy up after yesterday's disastrous hockey tournament - with two loses and two draws, we were almost certainly the worst team there. Without realising it, I am already walking past the war memorial. I take a deep breath and prepare myself for another day's gruelling work.

Simon Warrener, Senior School pupil

8.34 a.m.

Every Tuesday morning after I have got off the bus, I race into the music school, drop off my bags and then got to sign in for Brass Quintet. After signing in I proceed over to Mr Douglas' room. I then help to set up for the rehearsal and warm up on my trumpet. After warming up we have a very entertaining rehearsal (which usually goes smoothly) in which we work hard to become a better brass quintet. After the practice, I put my trumpet away, grab my bag and go to my first lesson, trying not to be late.

Max Carty 10L

8.34 a.m.

My day normally starts with me rushing into the car half-dressed rush to school at 8:30. When I walk into my classroom before school starts I normally see people doing last-minute homework. When the first bell rings to start the day with your tutor sets. I really like my tutor set because there is normally a lot of laughter between my year and the year 9's at my drama part of being a prop in the play. When the bell rings to end tutor set it is a sad long walk to geography.

Ritho Evans, 8T

8.35 a.m.

Friday 1st Feb 2013 is an unusual day for me as I am involved in the interviewing the boys who hope to be accepted into year 7 to start in September. Today we are tackling the 'D to G' surnames. These boys will become real people for 15minutes and for some it will be the changing point of their lives; the day they were accepted into Nottingham High School. It might make a difference to the school too. There may be a future School Captain amongst them or the next Chancellor of the Exchequer who knows. The decisions are tough but I cannot let my heart play a part in this, the head rules every time. But before I go to see next year's boys, there is a little matter of a missing rugby kit that has just presented itself to me in my office.

Carol Fletcher, Head of Year 7

8.35 a.m.

I scramble off the bus after a late start, in anticipation of the last concert band rehearsal before the National Concert Band Festival. I walk swiftly along Forest Road, fighting the drizzle with my school bag, a saxophone and a clarinet dangling off my shoulder. After signing in at the hatch, I am relieved to enter the warmth of the music school, and to see that I am just on time for the rehearsal. After a 10 minute walk in the bitter cold, tuning up is painful (exaggerated by the wince on the conductor's face). "One, two three" and we're in.

Matt Glendening, 10Y

8.36 a.m.

I arrive and the Headmaster comes to see me regarding files that I have prepared for his interviewing parents of boy's who have taken the entrance examination.

Sixth formers arrive to collect the latest Yearbook, I tick each one off.

My telephone is ringing - yet another parent asking if their son was successful in passing the entrance examination - they have previously been advised decisions will be posted out on 8th February.

I open emails on my laptop to find more reports sent from feeder schools, I am now endeavouring to get them to the Headmaster before commencing his interview schedule.

Lynda Goodwin, Admissions Co-ordinator, age 52

8.36 a.m.

I get to school and run around in the playground. Mummy leaves so I say goodbye to her. I put my school bookbag in the box. I am in Gruffalo group.

Euan Dodd, Reception Class, Lovell House

8.37 a.m.

I walk down the stairs, down some more stairs and go through the glass double doors of the bus. I arrive at school a few moments later with my mind worrying about the lessons soon to come, but first I must attend assembly. After a quick ten minutes, I push my way through a horde of year sevens and walk on a little more until I arrive at the player hall, awaiting the fiendishly boring twenty minutes that await me. I walk down a row of endless chairs, sit down, grab a hymn book off the floor and prepare myself for a long day ahead.

Jyodh Bilan, 10H, age 14

8.38 a.m.

I stand with the barbershop around the organ in the Player Hall, contemplating that a few years ago singing in assembly, even in a group would fill me with fear. But today, I don't mind. If I have learnt anything from the school, it is to have no inhibitions. Cutting Harmony are going to sing the school hymn in Latin (we had to iron out a few pronunciation errors) and Veni Creator – a song that Dame Agnes Mellers decided should be sung every day by all the boys. However, this will be the first rendition for at least 400 years.

Edwin Peverill, 10S

8.39 a.m.

I play at the top of the playground with my friend George. The bell rings, so I line up with the rest of my class. My teachers (Ms McCluskey and Miss Higgins), collect me and I hang up my coat. My Clarks shoes got mixed up so I swap them back with my friend.

James Freeston, Reception Class, Lovell House

5. Starting the Day

8.40 a.m.

As I hear the bell at 8.40 a.m., I head off to my weekly music lesson in the Music Block. I do the usual things: practice the Grade 6 pieces that I will do for my exam, as well as scales and sight-reading. After 25 minutes, I walk to my first lesson: English. In this we are learning about poems written in the First World War and about Shakespeare's Henry V. Now we are going to write a 500-word essay on how Wilfred Owen conveys emotion in his poem, 'Dulce et decorum est'.

Ben Mills, 10S

8.41 a.m.

I take the cash and cheques received from the safe to process for our G4S collection later today. I log all the income on a spread sheet. I ensure it all has an orange form to record the income.

Catherine Scholes, Finance

8.41 a.m.

Friday 1st February 2013 begins as any normal day at Nottingham High School. We go for our achievement assembly only to find out that our school is celebrating the 500th anniversary of the teaching their very first lessons at the High School. In the achievement assembly we sing happy birthday to the High School. Following this, various trophies and certificates are handed out to the pupils. Then we go to our next lesson which is English.

I am really proud to be part of this fabulous school and consider myself lucky to be part of the celebrations. I really enjoy the day.

Rohan Shah, 4C, Junior School

8.42 a.m.

Another busy day has begun. Firstly I deal with a parent's query at reception, then put the registers and dinner registers out for the teachers to complete. I collate the names of the boys who want to do after school sports next half term and ensure that we have all the parental permission slips for a Year 2 school trip. I start to construct the Friday Bulletin which is sent out each week with parent information and the phone rings 'Good Morning! Oh, Tom is feeling unwell today? I will let his teacher know. I hope he's feeling better soon'.

Mrs Barbara Marson, Junior School Secretary

8.43 a.m.

I wake up and look at the time, it's almost quarter to nine. Clearly my alarm didn't go off so I rush to get to school. I then sit through a vibrant lesson of double geography in which I learn about the development of China. I then go to the gym in my double free and break time to stay fit and active. I arrive back at school from my time at the gym with my friend, and I eagerly await the schools' fine Fish and Chips for lunch. After devouring my lunch I prepare myself for an afternoon of hard work.

Sam Jaffe, 6X2

8.43 a.m.

As the clock ticks down and the High School dawns on a new day, everyone begins to arrive. At 8:45am, the bell rings and all forms prepare for registration and then assembly. As my teacher takes the register, we all prepare are bags and make sure homework is complete. The notices are also read out. We then make are way to the Player Hall for assembly. The whole school gathers and Dr Sibly (Deputy Head) presents it. We usually sing a hymn, before making our way to first period.

Dom Harris, 8T

8.44 a.m.

I now have the all too common frantic dash from bus to registration office; laden with two instruments, three bags and an unrealistic hope to finally be on time to one of Mr Douglas' increasingly early rehearsals. With the upcoming, ever-daunting prospect of many national music competitions crammed into an unutterably short space of time, we start rehearsing '1513' – a newly commissioned composition, which brilliantly captures the quincentennial anniversary; incorporating both 'Greensleeves' and the school hymn into its melody. The second daily dash ensues – playing the school hymn in assembly, which, in itself, presents a challenge to any tubist: wading through the swarming crowds asking what on earth my instrument actually is.

Harry Smith, 10H

8.45 a.m.

As I look across the Player Hall from my seat on the balcony, I feel the familiar fluttering of nerves in my stomach. I look to my left and to my right, to observe my fellow choir-mates. They too look nervous, but composed, as we are well prepared for what will surely be a memorable assembly. We stand as Dr Sibly enters the Player Hall to the sound of the Brass Quintet, and then we prepare to sing. Fifteen minutes and a historical assembly later, the last note of the School Song leaves my lungs, leaving me feeling rather invigorated.

Nathan Cox, 11L

8.46 a.m.

Today is another day at school; letters are being handed out and a notice as well of course. It is now time to go to assembly.

As I am walking to assembly I feel proud as I am a part of this school and that the school has a real togetherness. I then see people talking to each other, companions, and friends improving their skills for later life. They are also gaining friends. I feel proud to be a part of a community in the school and proud of being able to be in this school with real feel of happiness. I feel a real sense of accomplishment being in this school, together with all my friends, and colleagues. In assembly it is all about 500 years since the school had its first lesson. I feel that the school has achieved a real goal and I am proud to be a part of this momentous time.

Will Ash, 7S

8.47 a.m.

I come into the classroom and sit down on the carpet. Miss Higgins does the register. I choose my lunch. Today I am going to have battered haddock with chips and beans. Yummy!

Adit Goyal, Reception Class, Lovell House

8.48 a.m.

I walk straight into the magnificent player hall, excited as the red velvet certain is down which made me feel as if I was in the royal concert hall. As the deputy headmaster walks up onto the stage, the brass band plays a soft tune. He starts to speak about how the first ever pupils to the school did not learn how to read or write, back then it was, considered a past time. It was now getting uninteresting and I just wanted to be at home watching the Heineken Cup rugby match I recorded.

Alex McConachie, 9Y

8.49 a.m.

I am signing certificates which I will give out in Achievement Assembly. I walk into the hall for the assembly and the school start to file in and sit down.

I stand at the front of the School in the Junior Hall and explain that it is the School's 500th birthday and as fitting any birthday we will sing 'Happy Birthday' to the School.

The pupils and staff sing the song and start to sway from side to side in rhythm.

I then hold up a birthday card and ask if it is anyone else's birthday?

> Mr E. Jones, Interim Headmaster, Junior School

8.50 a.m.

The cold brisk winter wind hits me hard in the face as I round the last corner of the music block. As I enter, I am greeted with a warm wall of heat from the nearest radiator. I ask a passer-by if Concert Band is on. Apparently not. Disappointed, I begin to retrace my steps to go to assembly. I am about to enter the Player Hall, when suddenly my phone vibrates. It reads simply: "Concert Band is on". By this point I am already crossing the threshold of the hall. I am stuck in two minds. But there's no going back.... I prepare myself for the inevitable consequences of this mistake...

> Sam Brown, 10T

8.51 a.m.

Year 6 are told that we have a special speaker in the morning, we don't know who it will be but we do know that it will be something unpredictable. We all go to the Founder Hall and look around and see a woman with part of her left arm and left leg. She tells us that she was born with them lost and how when she was a baby she had to use her brother's skateboard that she 'borrowed' but technically stole for a few years. Her brother was fine as she thought until she went swimming one day with her floats and her brother asked her if she would like to swim without her floats and then she asked if she could go in the shallow end and her brother and chucked her in the deep end. She fell down to the bottom of the pool and then pushed herself up again.

She next goes onto her swimming. She tells us that she came 1st in a race against the girls and the boys were swimming to as they were running late on time and she would have came 3rd out of 6th in the race with the boys. She then goes onto her Paralympic swimming and how she had to wake up early in the morning and swim for 3 hours and then go to school and then do more training. She said that she was chosen for the Atlanta 1996 Paralympics. She came 3rd in her first race and slept with the bronze medal under her pillow and gave herself a neck injury which affected her in her other races. She then says about her Sydney 2000 that she came home with one silver medal and two bronzes.

Thom Hughes, 6S, Junior School

8.51 a.m.

Oh better get some more of that photocopy request done for John, ah yes 40 copies of each exam paper, I remember. Suddenly my door opens – a voice says 'gosh this has had a change around' it's Roger Kilby from Maths; every time I see him I suddenly recall all the times I thought he was the Headmaster of the school, some confusion huh? He asks about the A4 books he's ordered & I tell him I'm waiting for them to arrive. He leaves some laminating for me to do. It's not everyone's dream job but I love it.

Angela Manders, Reprographics, age 44

8.51 a.m.

"Friday, Friday - got to get down to the orthodontist on Friday", I remember muttering to myself while descending the stairwell. "I really need to get that exeat signed by Dr. Sibly. Or else, face the wrath of Mrs Elwell."

It's Friday. I've arrived (late!) at school, and for some inexplicable reason I have still not got round to getting one of the Deputy Heads to sign my exeat. After getting my books from my locker, I journey to the 'SMT corridor'. But both deputies are absent. How very peculiar. I take four paces to Elwell's office. Give me strength!

Tom Jayamaha, 10L

8.52 a.m.

I am going to assembly now; it will probably be more entertaining than the last one. The teachers make us sing very old boring hymns every time; I don't really see the point. We have two assemblies a week and all are extremely similar: a big long speech/story, a hymn, and notices. It is very repetitive. Today the assembly is about Rosa Park and the black civil rights movement: finally something interesting to listen to! Now we must all stand and wait for the leader of the assembly to leave. Hurray! We get to leave the assembly and go to the first lesson.

Tayyib Khaliq, 10H , age 15

8.52 a.m.

Mr. Jones sends us to the Founder Hall, because an Australian Paralympic swimmer has come to talk to us! Year six rush up the stairs to see who it is. At the top of the stairs, we see it is Elizabeth Wright who has only a left arm and a left leg.

A little while later, we sit down and wait for the talk to start. We wait for a few minutes, then Elizabeth starts by talking about her birth and childhood and that she was born without half of her right arm and half of her right leg (congenital limb deficiency). When she was a baby she couldn't crawl properly, so she 'stole' her brother's skateboard to help her move around. Three years later, her brother got revenge by: taking her 'floaties' off and throwing her into their pool. Surprisingly, she swam really well!

The talk by Elizabeth inspires me not just to try and win, but to try my best, and if I win, even better.

Nihit Batra, 6S, Junior School

8.53 a.m.

I walk downstairs to the Junior Hall, to the final, most important assembly of the week. Taking my seat, I sit quietly and wait patiently for Mr.Jones. With a cheerful welcome the assembly kicks off. Certificates of achievement and trophies of excellence, are awarded in all categories. Student of the Week, the most prestigious certificate; the ultimate achievement, chosen by all the teachers, it's the most challenging certificate to gain; granted to the most deserving student. I applaud. Today there is nothing for me… I leave orderly with everyone, ready for the first lesson, ready to try again!

Razeen Surtee, 5A, Junior School

8.54 a.m.

On a lovely Friday morning, we run to the Founder Hall to see the special treat that the teachers have organised for us. When we enter the Hall, our eyes shoot immediately to look at the guest who is waiting to greet us.

Calmly sitting on my chair, I notice that she is a disabled person, but she isn't just any disabled person, she is a Paralympian. This amazing guest swam for Australia and her name is Elizabeth Wright. She had won two bronze medals and one silver medal!

She tells us a story about how her brother had once chucked her into the deep end of the pool. She was only five when she experienced this horrible event, but when she rose up from her torture she started floating. The reason she started floating was because she had one leg and one arm, so she had a great balance. Elizabeth treats us to a video of the Olympics held in Sydney in the year 2000.
Finally at the end she is asked so many questions that I can't keep count. Overall she enjoys receiving the questions and answering them. We all thank her for a lovely time and I know that I will never forget this day.

Zayem Shahid, 6L, Junior School

8.54 a.m.

The door creeps open, and behind it lies the dark, imposing figure of Mr Williams.

"Get to assembly, boys."

And in a similarly stealthy manner, he creeps away into the shadows. The door is left invitingly ajar; all to allow six grinning boys – and one rather worried one – to traverse through to a Sibly special. Our jaws slack loose, and we tip-toe out of the Music School and into the West Block, arms outstretched. All except two, who, being precociously more careful, need no more than a shadow and the distinct '*tip*-tap' of stiletto heels, both getting progressively closer, to bolt across front lawn.

Annanay Kapila, 10L

8.55 a.m.

As I enter the magnificent hall, escaping the biting cold, muffled chatter is clouding the room like a thick mist. An ocean of faces, whose origins can be traced all around the globe, floods the hall. But before I can take in any more I am being ushered towards a row of seats; my friends piling in, behind me. I glance up; my gaze is held by the stunning ceiling. The thick tree trunk-like beams arch along the curved ceiling. Directly above me a large chandelier is hanging precariously on a single chain, reaching for me. Suddenly I snap out of my trance as I notice that silence has swooped across the hall and everyone is standing.

Nikhil Sahdev, 8Y

8.55 a.m.

At 8.55 we go to achievement assembly that we have every Friday in the hall.

I know that I am going to get my gold award in Mathletics and I am very excited. I sit next to Abdullah and Akash who are my best friends in the whole school

When I am given my certificate, Joseph and Isaac are given theirs too by Mr Jones and he shakes our hands, then a photo is taken of us. I have 3050 points on my certificate.

When I sit down, Akash looks at my certificate. Other boys receive their times tables and sport awards and I think that they have done very well in getting their awards.

William Appleby, 3, Junior School

8.55 a.m.

On Friday the school celebrates its 500 year anniversary. To start the day off everyone gathers in the Junior Hall to sing happy birthday to the school. We think this is thrilling. I enjoy it so much, as do the rest of the school. Mr Jones announces the celebration is going to be on Saturday and there will be a cake baked but not with 500 candles as this is too much. It is a fantastic achievement to reach 500. This is a fantastic and joyful way of celebrating the 500 year anniversary and it will be one of the highlights of 2013.

Hassan Malik, 4C, Junior School

8.56 a.m.

Today's going to be interesting… I've lost my voice! Not good for a music teacher really!

It's Achievement Assembly today at Lovell House. The laptop is connected to the interactive white board so that the boys can follow the words of the new song they have been learning, on the large screen. As each boy comes up to receive their award we all sing "Well done"

Well everyone except me that is!!!

    Lynn Kawalec, Head of Music (Junior School and Lovell House), age 47

8.56 a.m.

On Friday we hold an Achievement Assembly which is to celebrate the School's five hundredth birthday. Wow, can you believe it, 500 years of Nottingham High School.

When we are sitting down at the assembly, Mr Jones announces it is the School's five hundredth birthday and all the boys begin to cheer in celebration.

Following the School 500 year celebrations, we move on to achievements for pupils. These achievements recognize good behaviour, hard work and improvement in pupils. There are a number of awards handed out to pupils, who are all very happy to receive them.

Fareed Khan, 3M, Junior School

8.56 a.m.

Year 6 get to have talk from a famous paralympian called Elizabeth Wright. She talks to us about how she became a paralympian and what inspired her. Her disability is that she only has a left arm and leg! To walk she has a special leg. She was born in Australia and she was part of the Australian team. There is a video she shows us a clip of one of her races she swam. At the end of our session everyone gets In a big picture with her, three people get to hold her medals Overall it very enjoyable!

Reuben Passi, 6G, Junior School

8.57 a.m.

I walk into the Player Hall and take my seat with hymn book in hand. Dr Sibly, in the absence of the headmaster, walks into the hall and the school rises as he walks by while the organ is playing. He then reaches the front of the hall and announces the hymn for the assembly. The hymn having come to an end, the school is seated and Dr Sibly begins his assembly; an insight into the first lessons taught at the school. Being a rather commemorative day, the Barbershop group assist the school in singing the original Latin version of the school song before the bell rings and lessons begin.

Monty Kirk, 10S

8.57 a.m.

All of the boys in Year 6 at Nottingham High Junior School are quietly seated in the luxurious accommodation of the Founder Hall. We are all eager to find out about the mystery guest coming to visit us, as we have been informed about it previously. Little do any of us know that the guest will be a retired Paralympic swimmer! Her name is Elizabeth Wright and she has won three medals over two Paralympic games: two bronze medals and one silver.

Elizabeth was born with a congenital limb deficiency. Her right arm is missing at the elbow and her right leg is severely shortened. She also has a half leg in that her right leg is half the width that it should be therefore she requires a prosthetic leg.

Ever since she discovered the Paralympics, Elizabeth Wright was desperate to participate when she was old enough. Her main aim was to swim in front of a home crowd at the 2000 Sydney Paralympics but she got the chance to shine four years before that in Atlanta where she won her first medal, which was bronze in the 50m butterfly (S6 category). Then she won two more medals in the year 2000; silver in the 400m freestyle and bronze in the 4 x 50m relay.

After a wonderful career, Elizabeth retired at the tender age of 21. This is a great day for me and the highlights have to be meeting Elizabeth Wright and also, holding one of her bronze medals!

Sebby Gould, 6S, Junior School

8.57 a.m.

Year 6 walk into the Founder Hall, where we meet an Australian Paralympian named Elizabeth Wright. She has won silver and 2 bronzes in swimming at the 2000 Sydney Paralympic Games. She has a disease which means she has missing limbs. She has no right arm and no right leg, so obviously it is difficult for her to move around.

She is inspiring because she tells us about her life and how she grew up and overcame her difficulties. It is a great experience meeting her and learning about how she won her medals.

Skye Hamilton, 6L, Junior School

8.57 a.m.

The whole Junior school gathers in the hall for the achievement assembly. I am really excited because I am going to share my achievement with the all the boys for the first time. When we get into the hall I sit down next to Alex my friend. Mr. Jones presents some maths awards followed by some chess awards. Finally he calls out my name. I receive my medal for being part of the winning team for the County selections. When I go up onto the stage I feel proud and happy to be representing Nottinghamshire for chess.

Joshua Lloyd, Junior School pupil

8.58 a.m.

The pupils slowly file into the already crowded player hall for assembly. Mr. Reid's hands can be seen dancing across the keyboard of the organ, filling the room with thick, viscous sounds. Eventually the hall is full and once Dr. Sibly has finished his speech the whole of Cutting Harmony stands up simultaneously and yet again the room is flowing with monastic music. Students can be seen craning their necks back to catch a glimpse of the group, but before long the ancient song has finished. Following this everyone is expected to sing the school hymn. The pupils' feeble effort, to create some sort of tune, deteriorates into a cacophony of sounds, but radiating from the back, Cutting Harmony's pure melody permeates through.

Jonathan Cutajar, Year 11

8.58 a.m.

An Australian motivational speaker comes to talk to Year 6. To start with, she introduces herself as Elizabeth Wright, a Paralympic swimmer. Elizabeth begins by taking us right back to the start when she was a toddler. She says that when she was young she went in the swimming pool quite a lot with her armbands on. This continued until one day there her brother picked her up and threw her in the pool at the deep end and she hit the bottom. This was where her Paralympic career slowly but surely began.

Simon Batstone, 6G, Junior School

8.59 a.m.

I line up for assembly and go to the hall. It is the squirrel assembly. Boys get to take the class toy squirrel home if they have done something special. There is also a swimming award and a boy from each class gets a star certificate. We sing a song at the end. Everybody claps the boys who get certificates. All the teachers are here too.

Zayyan Guri, Reception Class, Lovell House

8.59 a.m.

Paralympian swimmer, Elizabeth Wright comes to introduce herself to the Year 6 boys of Nottingham High Junior School. Her disability is that she was born with missing limbs because she has only one arm and leg. Unfortunately she has one missing finger and her thumb and index finger are joined together. Although her disabilities are hard to cope with, she says problems are not there to be moaned at, they are there to be solved.

Charan Mandeir, 6S, Junior School

9.00 a.m.

The boys walk into our weekly Achievement Assembly, while a Year 2 boy plays the piano. There is a sense of excited anticipation as they sit in their classes waiting to hear who has won the Star Certificates and the Squirrel Awards. A treasured part of the week, as I listen to all the class's news and celebrate with the boys their achievements. We sing our hymn, with actions and enthusiasm, before leading out, one class at a time, back to lessons.

Anne Cummings, Headteacher, Lovell House

9.00 a.m.

In Assembly I describe the feast of Candlemas as celebrated in around 1500. Christian Cummings [School Captain] reads the gospel for the day, a passage describing the presentation of Christ in the Temple, and I draw from this that finding truth and growing in wisdom are two keystones of a worthwhile education. Cutting Harmony sings 'Veni Sancti Spiritus', words and music stipulated by Dame Agnes for the opening of each school day. I outline some of the content of the earliest lessons [all conducted in Latin] and add a few thoughts about the extraordinary expansion in knowledge during the 16th century.

Paul Sibly, Deputy Headmaster

9.01 a.m.

I am in the music school right now; I am rehearsing for a school concert. I play classic guitar and I am practicing with a group of other classic guitars. I am playing two songs, one is called 'yellow bird' and the other is called 'trio for 3 guitars'. I have the highest guitar part, I always get this part. I am very excited about playing in the school concert; it will be the second time I have played in a concert. We will be playing in the music school again.

Reuben Amoaku, 7H, age 11

9.01 a.m.

On Friday we have Achievement assembly Mr Jones tells us we have to write 100 words about Friday. Then we sing happy birthday to the school because it is the school's 500th birthday wuhooo! Now the real assembly begins. First of all we have maths times tables certificates .One person in my class gets one! Next we have gold certificates lots and lots people get those. Five year three's get them and I am glad they did. Then we have student of the week. Tension is all around. "I hope it will be me", I say in my mind, "I hope it will be me!" But it isn't. Never mind, I'll try again next time.

Oliver Harcourt, Junior School pupil

9.02 a.m.

I am sitting in a Concert Band rehearsal in the Music school and I am playing the role of 4th Trumpet. I have forgotten to bring my music and have left it at home so I have to borrow some from the folders inside a clear box at the corner of the room. Once everyone has arrived, we begin rehearsing a piece called 'And The Multitude With One Voice Spoke'. I am struggling to keep up with the rest of the band because I have just joined Concert Band. Then the school bell rings and we pack our instruments away in the music cupboard and my class head off to a double period of German. Whilst walking to E2, My friends and I discuss what we are going to be doing over the weekend once school has finished. Once we arrive, we apologise for being slightly late and get out our German books ready for the first period of the long day.

James Bellamy, 9L

9.03 a.m.

Assembly sometimes seems like the most pointless thing in the school day; all it is a song and a story that gives us an extra lesson added on to the eight we already have. Next there are the rugby results, where my team losses 50-0 every single week. Then worst of all it takes away ten extra minutes of sleep I could have in my nice warm bed on a cold Friday morning. Sometimes we have performances which make the day a bit more interesting, but these are very rare.

Thomas Henley, 10L, age 14

9.04 a.m.

Today's assembly is definitely one which will be looked back on with great joy and pleasure. This is due the fact that we look back at the history of the school; how it all began and how far we have come since 1513. The assembly is led by our deputy head teacher Dr Sibley and the schools house captain, Christian Cummings delivers the Latin speech which was recited 500 years ago. In addition we listen to the cutting harmony perform before having the whole school sing the traditional school hymn. Overall it is a great way to commence the school day.

Will Atiomo, 7L

9.05 a.m.

I'm proud to be a part of this school to be able to celebrate the 500th anniversary of the Senior School. I am going to talk about a special visitor who came into school: Elizabeth Wright. She is an Australian Paralympic Bronze Medallist in the Atlanta Paralympic Games and Silver and a Bronze medallist in the Sydney Paralympic Games. I think that it is a great way to celebrate the anniversary because she gives us an incredibly motivational speech to teach us about attempting to achieve your goal, no matter what.

Akhilesh Huria, 6, Junior School

9.06 a.m.

The part of my day I choose to describe will be Elizabeth Wright's, the Australian Paralympic swimmer, inspirational talk to the Year Sixes.

Elizabeth starts off talking about her life growing up with missing limbs. She explains that it was hard to crawl when she was a baby with half of her right leg and arm missing. She then talks to us about the road leading up to becoming a Paralympics swimmer and what was in store for her along the way.

After she finishes her speech I felt truly inspired and feel lucky that I have all my limbs.

Barnaby McNamara, 6S, Junior School

9.07 a.m.

Me sentaba en el salón de actos y miraba mis alrededores. Las ventanas enormes que permitían que el sol impregnara el espacio vasto, hacían que cada uno de los cientos de caras parecía lucir con delicia. Yo, una extranjera en este mundo de riqueza en términos académicos y culturales me sentía en seguida aceptada. Más lejos todavía- me sentía *orgullosa*. ¿Orgullosa de qué? Orgullosa de ser parte de un mundo en lo cual tantas oportunidades se esperaban, en lo cual sueños y proyectos y futuros innumerables hay. Orgullosa de ver la próxima generación de líderes delante de mí.

Thea Williams, PGCE Student Teacher

9.08 a.m.

Assembly finishes and I walk back to the classroom. I sit down on the floor we order the pictures of the Billy Goats Gruff. I like the Billy Goats Gruff but I like the Seriously Silly stories best. My favourite is 'Rumply Crumply Stinky Pin', by Lawrence Anholt.

Josiah Ibrahim, Reception Class, Lovell House

9.09 a.m.

In the morning year 6 are privileged to listen to a motivational speaker named Elizabeth Wright. Elizabeth is a Paralympic swimmer and her disabilities are that she is missing her right arm from the elbow down and she also has lost part of her right leg.

She talks to use about her life and growing up and how when she finds something she can't do she tries and thinks how she can do it, this shows her determination and courage. One example of this in her childhood was when she couldn't crawl and observed her brother on his skateboard and when he came in she borrowed it to push herself around. The next thing was because of her brother getting revenge on her for taking his skateboard. Her brother told her to swim in their pool without her floats and how he threw her straight in the deep-end. At first she was scared and was sinking but when she touched the bottom she sprung back up and started swimming doggy paddle to the other end of the pool.

This speech encourages me to not give up until I have tried more than once and believe in myself. I am very grateful we have been given this opportunity as a pupil at Nottingham High School.

Noah Hughes, 6, Junior School

9.10 a.m.

It is time to start another Friday morning with a forty minute session of everyone's favourite subject - Maths. The weekend is already starting in my head as I arrive at the lesson with books in hand, only to find that, as a result of assembly running over (again), I have a wealth of diagrams on the board to copy up. Before I pull out my chair I take a moment to look over the room, wondering what everyone's thought process is. With a click of my back and a deep sigh, I sit down and continue my academic journey.

James Purchase, 11Y

9.10 a.m.

I walk to my first lesson which is English and I am writing notes on poems from World War 1 for our upcoming essay on conveying emotions using language.

Lucas Wilcock, 10S

9.11 a.m.

My personal highlight of the closest day for the 500th anniversary is when Australian Paralympian, Elizabeth Wright, gives us a talk about her life story and her 'hurdles'. I am absolutely inspired by her influential talk, as she won Paralympic medals without her right leg and half of her right arm!

I am stunned at how well she speaks, making us understand how it would have been like to be handicapped. After her speech, I am thoroughly motivated to believe in myself and others with full belief.

To sum up, I really find this day important for the near future!!!

Vignesh Bhanu, 6L, Junior School

9.12 a.m.

Today, I am expecting a guest to speak to our Y6's. There is always a little anxiety, will the person turn up, will they engage with the boys? I felt that all would go well within minutes of meeting our speaker, Elizabeth

Wright, a Paralympic Swimmer from Australia. She engaged with the boys immediately, explaining her disability and how she copes with it. Her advice was inspirational and backed up much of what we try and tell the boys – aim high, persevere and always try your best. I feel really proud that the boys asked sensitive and thoughtful questions. Great!

Karen George, Acting Deputy Head, Junior School

9.12 a.m.

No matter if I'm early or late for assembly I am always the last out. If I'm at the back, or the front, or the middle, it doesn't matter – my row is always last to leave. Finally I'm leaving but the 100s of students rushing through the same corridor next to the player hall is a complete nuisance. I'm trapped amongst them, with my only option to go forwards… Every Friday I'm late for period 1.

Raphael Charles, 10T

9.13 a.m.

It is nearly time to be doing something, despite the fact that I have been here for nearly an hour now, just dwelling around school for a bit in form period and in the dining hall. Right now I am listening to an assembly on how the first ever lessons at the school might have gone. I am mentally preparing myself for an equally dull-sounding first three periods with maths and chemistry that will probably seem equally pointless in the future as the first lessons 500 years ago do now. I've realised assembly has finished and am ready to sleepwalk my way through the rest of the day, maybe with some laughing at the kid that always falls over in the playground and gets hit in the face with a football every break.

Sam Kirkby, 11Y, age 16

9.14 a.m.

after coming from assembly I am thinking all the way about it and how dame Agnes Mellors went to King Henry the 8th to get permission to open

the school. As we enter our class we find out some exciting news. We are going on a history
Trip to Lincoln we are very excited about the whole prospect of it all then Doctor Colman
Tells us do the rules it is a curriculum trip a not to be messed around with that makes the class slightly less exited but it will still be fun.

Will Harte, 7H

9.15 a.m.

At 9.15 on Friday I have Learning Support. As always I go up to the Learning Support room, but today we go into Mrs O'Brien's room as Mr Kilby is using the normal one. I usually have Learning Support with Mrs Hubbard. Today we practise typing (because my handwriting is poor, so we are planning to get a computer for me to do my work on). Because today I am missing English, we type up my English homework. I really need to learn to touch type, which is what I have been working towards for a while now, but I am beginning to remember where all the keys are, so I am making good progress.

Jackson Sparks, 7Y

9.15 a.m.

As we sit down to start our geography lesson we are all in a good mood after the talk from Paralympic swimmer Elizabeth Wright. We discuss the talk all the way from the Founder Hall and then line up outside Mr Caldwell's room. As Mr Caldwell runs into the corridor he tells us to go into the class and sit down. We all quickly dash to our seats and wait for the lesson to start. He tells us that we will do an end of unit assessment to show what we have learnt on the topic. He will first let us revise for a few minutes so our minds are fresh with all the knowledge.

We are handed out some reference books and geography books. We all crack on and look through our books for useful information that we can write so we spend the next 10 minutes revising. After 10 minutes has passed, Mr Caldwell collects all the reference books and geography books. He hands out some paper to write our essay on and starts the timer. We have 10 minutes to show what knowledge we have picked up on the topic. We also have to show what skills we have improved in the lessons.

After our time is up, we let out a sigh of relief as we file out the room and run outside for break.

Adi Das, Junior School pupil

9.16 a.m.

I walk into the Waiting Room. Expectant faces look up at me. Who will I be calling next? Mum looks worried. Dad checks his phone for new messages. A boy fidgets nervously. I smile and try to look encouragingly at a little lad who has gone very pale. *"Would you like to come with me...?"* Is he ready to talk about himself; to talk about his hobbies, his school, his hopes for the future? He's made it through to the interview stage of the 2013 Entrance Examination. He's ready to take on the world. He's a future *Old Nottinghamian*.

Helen Bowen, Personal Assistant to the Headmaster

9.17 a.m.

The decaying wooden doors burst open, releasing a sea of black, fleeing the ice cold assembly hall into the rain. Attempting to turn *just another day at the office* into something remotely interesting is hardly going very well, looking at the world from a gothic perspective just isn't fitting for a boys' school in Nottingham. As I weave my way through the usual stampede to Friday morning Latin, I settle on seeing the world through the mind of Lewis Carroll.

"We are all mad here."

Much better, for some reason that I cannot explain that is more suitable. And as I enter the classroom to flee the downpour, I find that safety from the elements leads me only further down the rabbit hole.

Robert Myers, 11L

9.18 a.m.

I put my saxophone back into the cupboard, after having just played in concert band. I then walk upstairs into one of the class room, and my class mates and I play on the piano and sing until our music teacher comes in. I then sit down and listen to him talk about harmonizing and singing 'In the jungle' for a practical we have to do. After around ten minutes of this, myself and two other class mates walk into one of the practise rooms and start to work on our own version of 'In the jungle'

William Underwood, 9Y, age 14

9.19 a.m.

I walk into the geography room and instantly wish I hadn't. There goes my geography teacher, blah blah blah blah, you've got a test tomorrow, blah blah blah blah. I miss it completely and when he stops talking, I realise he's asked a question. Everyone in the room has their hands up but then he looks at me. I have a sinking feeling that he's pointing at me. "Well," I say staring at my unopened textbook, trying to buy as much time as possible as every boy does in these situations. Everyone is staring at me, I'm sinking in my chair. "Umm…is it…." somehow I manage to mumble out. Then my saviour - the bell rings out. I smile, gather my books and walk out the class. One lesson down, 7 to go!

Rohil Shah, 8S, age 13

9.20 a.m.

The assembly commemorating the schools 500 year anniversary and how teaching methods have changed has over run. I swarm out of assembly with the other year 10s' dreading the up and coming test on quadratics. I pick up my bag from outside the assembly hall, and head toward my math classroom, aware of the shortened time to do my test, as a result of the over running of the assembly by the deputy head. As I enter the classroom under the glare of my math teacher, I see the table arranged separately, and then I sit down, at the corner desk, ready for the approaching test.

Joseph Waplington, 10Y

9.21 a.m.

After Achievement Assembly, I have a double history lesson where I learn about Sutton Hoo. I log on to the computer and through internet explorer I search for information on work and clothes in Anglo-Saxon history. I spend ten minutes learning about the daily working life in those days and find that men cut down trees, women worked on the farm and children also helped. After history I have M.F.L where I planned my own "oso pardo" story, which means brown bear in English. I write the planning in Spanish.

Vihar Chikanna, 3W, Junior School

9.22 a.m.

We are in the Player Hall for the 500th anniversary of the school. It is an assembly for a special occasion being held by our deputy head, Dr Sibly. He is going through most of the school's key moments in history and what it might have been like when it was first founded. The assembly finishes later than usual as it is for a one off occasion. This sadly causes us to be late for our next lesson... P.E. - one of my favourite lessons.

Haris Khalil, 8L

6. The Morning's Lessons

9.23 a.m.

In PSHE we are studying teaching and learning. We have already done our lessons the previous week. I taught Arsh how to play table tennis; he taught me how to draw a dragon. This week we are doing a review of our lessons. I start by reviewing my lesson. I am the teacher; I do not think that this lesson went quite as planned. It was mostly successful with a few problems throughout the lesson. The problems are mainly like the ball being damaged or the net being tangled up. I am not naming any names...

Sam Bolton, 5, Junior School

9.24 a.m.

I am in English, it is the first period and I have just got back from choir with my music teacher. I can hear some giggles as people read their books and I can't help but smile when they do. We are doing something called the reading challenge at the moment; this is a competition to see how many books you can read in a term. Most of these are very short, about one hundred and fifty pages long. I like the library because it is so relaxing and whenever I leave it I feel as if I have been sleeping. Overall a good start to the day. I must stop, I have got to get to D.T!

Luke Aungles, 7S

9.25 a.m.

It is time to do busy jobs. Busy jobs are when you choose to do different jobs. I go and play with the playdough. I make some Halloween cakes because I am pretending it is Halloween.

Matthew Moran, Reception Class, Lovell House

9.26 a.m.

Assembly has run over; my lesson plan lies in tatters. How can I salvage something from the remaining twenty-five minutes? Fumbling with my jacket and scarf, I shuffle past the impatient ranks of blazers and haircuts, squeezing my way outside where I am unceremoniously frisked by the wintry air. As I weave through a crowd of desultory sixth formers, past noticeboards and portraits of former headmasters, I contemplate the options before me: should I simply speak faster and hope for the best? Hold an impromptu quiz? Admit defeat and put on a video? Before I can decide, I arrive at the classroom where I am greeted by the expectant eyes of pupils. How did they get here before me? Copies of *Henry V* lie open and ready. Once more unto the breach….

Ben Burton, teacher of English, age 31

9.27 a.m.

The marquee company arrives to build the kitchen for tomorrows Anniversary Party. A kitchen on the playground in a tent! I present a health and safety induction for the three operatives in my office using my picture frame presentation device. I give instructions on what to do in the event of a fire or emergency, and when to stop work during boys' morning break for their own safety! I advise them on the location of all the gas, water and waste pipes beneath the playground before they put in their 600mm steel pegs to secure the marquee.

Chris Scott, Estates Manager

9.28 a.m.

My Friday maths lesson begins at 9.15 in the morning.

I am learning about temperature in my junior maths book and I am working with Rio Gill. Rio and I enjoy working together. We have nearly finished all the questions that have been set. We are the best partners in the class.

We learn how to put numbers onto reading scales so we can see what the temperature is. The temperature is measured in Centigrade. I enjoy looking at scales that go up in two's.

Maths is my favourite lesson.

Alexander El Khoury, 3W, Junior School

9.29 a.m.

Were fifteen minutes into Spanish now and to be honest I'm kind of interested for once because our teacher has said we are allowed to write what we liked about just to make grammatically perfect Spanish for ten minutes. So I get out the dictionary and get on. I actually manage to get about three sentences done before Sir tells us to stop which for me is pretty good. I then am told to tell my sentences out loud to the class, luckily sir doesn't find them to offensive and just laughs. That is what I like about Spanish it's always something to look forward to.

Will Staton, 9L

9.30 a.m.

I am making a troll. I am colouring his body and his legs and his arms in lots of colours. I cut around the lines and am using split pins and a hole-punch to put him together. His arms and legs can move.

Marley Parejo, Reception Class, Lovell House

9.31 a.m.

The winter sun streams in through the large windows, lighting up the whole room. There are thousands of books arranged neatly on shelves all around the room. We have English in the library, where we are reading our reading challenge books, when our teacher announces we have homework. There is a big groan from the whole class. No one likes homework! Everyone is reading in silence – no one makes a noise. I go and change my book for a new one. We carry on reading just waiting for the bell to go and then it will be off to DT.

William Baker, 7S

9.32 a.m.

We're halfway through drama now. We're listening to 'Stan' by Eminem to help us use music as a stimulus and even though our teacher claims she hates every word of the song, no one is surprised when she sings the chorus word perfect. Someone has just given a brainless answer to a perfectly simple question, how difficult are they making this for themselves. Second run through of this fantastic song, but this time for different search criteria. It's finally finished, now we wait in anticipation of the bell.

Amarni Saunders, 9Y, age 14

9.35 a.m.

I get my books ready for the school day and head into my form room seeing all my friends as I do so. I go to my seat and talk to my friends only for a short while because I've got to get to maths so I get up put my bag on my back and go to the staircase up to W13, my maths class. The teacher's in so I enter and sit down. It's now 9.45 and my lesson begins.

Joshua Clarke, age 11, 7T

9.37 a.m.

I am sitting in the cold, cramped computer room. Double French? Just what I need. I was just thinking what a great idea it would be to write the number '500' on the screen to show how learning has developed over time. Yet, like most technological devices these days, my keyboard and screen have decided to take a nap. So, being a high-school student, I have decided to make the most of the materials I have to hand, and be creative. Eye-catching? No. Creative? Most definitely.

Douglas McConachie, Senior School Pupil

9.40 a.m.

At 9.40 I am just finishing my P.E lesson (in which I'm doing basketball) and I'm playing my final match. I'm now going back to the changing rooms and I'm getting changed for period 2 which starts at 9.50. At 9.50 I am heading towards the art and D.T block for my double art lesson. At about 9.55 I go in and get reminded how to use the clay properly (this is our third lesson on clay) at 10.00 I just just be finish off my clay goose that I have been making in the previous lessons.

Harry Fogelman, 8L

9.41 a.m.

I am playing with the playdough. I am making a big cake because I am pretending it is someone's birthday. I go to the role play and am acting out the story of the 3 Billy Goats Gruff. I am the small billy goat.

Sahib Thiara, Reception Class, Lovell House

9.42 a.m.

The bell has rung and I head out of the classroom towards the Design Technology block, which is, typically, in the yard, about as far from the library as can be. I sail down four flights of stairs, through the door in the North Entrance, and across the yard, and stand outside the door, panting like a labrador.

Seconds later, our D.T teacher emerges in doorway, and ushers the line of fourteen boys into studio one. Having collected my planner and pencil case I sit at a desk, at which we all discovered last week, has a drawing board underneath, which can be revealed by flipping the table over in a James Bond style manner. As you can imagine most of the year sevens had a fantastic time flipping the desk back and forth and back and forth.

I then complete my self-evaluation sheet for the boat which I made last term.

Ben Bedforth, 7S

9.43 a.m.

At Lovell library. Class 1B arrive to have a reading session and change their library books. Chris is reading to me. He reads to page 5. The other nine boys are sitting on bean bags reading or choosing a book to take home. Now listening to Kapil read. Am putting books back on shelves. The boys are showing me the books they want to take home. I scan their school admission number into the computer, then scan the barcode in the book. They line up to go to their next lesson. 1S arrive in the library.

Christine Martin, Library assistant, Lovell House

9.44 a.m.

I am currently sitting in English, thinking of what to write for this assignment of 100 words talking about a part of your day. I am finding it extremely hard as I find it extremely hard to concentrate when I am not listening to music, so my mind keeps wandering......it's fish and chips for lunch today, my favourite school meal of the week...behind pork and chips on Monday. But today is battered fish, the battered fish is nowhere near as nice as breaded fish, why do they alternate? It makes no sense to me. Why would you alternate between a good meal and a bad meal? You should just stick with the good breaded fish. Now, what to write?.......that's a really nice poster on the wall...

Alex Manterfield, 11S

9.45 a.m.

The clock ticks. The sharp winter breeze slices at the faces of the jaded pupils - through a small crack in the window and a slow whale-like drone drifts across the room from somewhere near to the teacher's desk. Pencils gently drum on desk tops and the scratching sound of biro to paper can be heard. I look over my shoulder. The looming shadow of the teacher is approaching. In a frenzy of horror, I snatch at my pen and scrawl down sentences swiftly. The shadow overbears me as I frantically hope that my scribbles will suffice.

Usman Rana, 11L

9.46 a.m.

I count all the cash, the coins are put through an automatic counter and the machine is loud. I have my photo taken for the photo records of the day. I add it all up to make sure it balances before bagging it up to go back in the safe and wait for collection.

Catherine Scholes, Finance

9.47 a.m.

I am playing in the sandpit with 2 of my friends. I am building a castle. The castle is for a pretend breakfast for the toys. Lots of guards live in the castle. The sandpit is in my classroom in the conservatory, so it is nice and bright.

George Turton, Reception Class, Lovell House

9.48 a.m.

I go to a double period of physics and this lesson we are in the fitness suite and we have to measure our power on each resistance machine.

Lucas Wilcock, 10S

9.49 a.m.

I briskly walk out of the language lab from my French lesson, I remember the depressing thought that I'm only one lesson through the day. I slowly walk up the stairs and dread the double period of English that awaits me. I discuss with a friend how boring essay writing and analysing texts is when as i walk down the corridor I see our English teacher walking towards us from the classroom. Hallelujah! We are in the ICT suite!

Alex Davey, 11H

9.50 a.m.

The bell has just rung. I sprint out of the Geography lesson, but on the way to the Art department a teacher opens the door on the other side. I sprint past her without saying anything. She stops me and says, 'excuse me, I opened the door and you ran past me without saying anything, what should you say?' Now I was definitely late for Art, so I quickly respond and reply, 'Sorry, I meant to say excuse me', and sprint all the way upstairs into the room and it is all ready 5 minutes into the lesson. I tell the teacher, 'Sorry I am late I just went to the toilet.'

Esam Shahid, 8S, age 12

9.51 a.m.

I walk into my English classroom, w16, I greet Mrs Wheeler, with the usual 'wagwarn' she ignores me, and as usual … I think "what is life?" I sit down and she explains this task. 100 words about 10 minutes of today. As usual I refuse. Back up against the radiator, sat next to Mark Needham, it was just a normal Friday. Over the next few minutes I talk to Mark and Mrs Wheeler continually tells me off. I work for the rest of the lesson taught by the lovely Mrs Wheeler.

Nathaniel Day, 11H

9.51 a.m.

Year 13 leave my classroom, W16, and as they do I wish them a good weekend. I go into the English Office next door and run over in my mind what I have planned to teach Year 11. I can hear them laughing and joking through the wall as they arrive and so I walk into the classroom. Tom asks if he can take a picture to commemorate the day and I agree. Nat asks, "Wagwan?" as usual – I still don't understand what this means. I ask the class to settle down as they are excitable. I talk to them about writing 100 words about today. They gradually settle and quiet descends on the room. Outside it is very sunny; inside it feels calm.

Rhian Wheeler, English Teacher and Deputy Head of Sixth Form

9.52 a.m.

The bell has just going for the end of period 1 (Spanish), English is next and to get there I am going to have to climb two flights of stairs. Walking through the door and the first thing I notice is how cold it is in the English classroom, my eyes turn to the half open window and I inwardly groan. It is going to be another cold double English. I am not the first to arrive but I am there before James Mellor and sitting there, waiting, I ponder what will happen in today's lesson.

Tommy Radford, 11S

9.53 a.m.

I have just finished a thrilling Spanish in which I prepared my controlled assessment. I gently stroll up the west side stairs to my English class where I find my teacher leaning against the wall. She tells me that we are going to art ICT. William Sanderson then is eating in front of her and I get revenge by telling her to take the sweets off him. At this time Mr Burn is walking past and takes the sweets from him. At this I chuckle uncontrollably to myself.

Tom Banks, 11L

9.54 a.m.

In my History lesson we have just finished our Roman topic and move on to an Anglo-Saxon topic. We read non-fiction books about the Anglo-Saxons. Mrs Mays sets us a task to write at least three sentences about what we know and at least five sentences about what we want to learn.

I enjoy reading about the Anglo-Saxons gods. Some of the punishments from the King were having to hold a scalding hot heavy iron bar or being thrown in to a very deep pool!! It was very dangerous!

A King called King Offa hated Wales and built a dyke to stop Wales attacking!

Arrandeep Mann, 3M, Junior School

9.54 a.m.

I have physics now. The lessons are never dull and I am usually focused, but it's a Friday, so that's out the window. Just thinking that this time in four hours, there will be two hours until there are only ten minutes of the day left makes me feel as if I am already at home. After physics I have chemistry, good, then I have break, better, then I have art, not as good but never the less, good, then maths, very good. I will, inevitably spend most of those lessons gazing deeply and thought provokingly out of the widow, or trying to clap quietly at the exactly the same moment as the clock ticks so that nobody notices, but these time wasters will have lost their novelty and after about ten minutes of these games, I will have decided that instead of wasting my time I should really pay attention to something that will be on my GCSE's.....Maybe.

Cameron Stumpf, 10S, age 14

9.55 a.m.

At 9.50 we in 8S split up and one half goes to art while the other half goes to DT. In art right now we are working on our clay projects. My teacher is really nice but sometimes we do get on her nerves. Our clay project is on a fairground ride. Some of us have finished while others are still working on it. In DT we are making a moving object on a box which has an item on top that moves. Some are making simple projects, such as animals. Others are doing a running man which is one of the harder projects. I am doing a wooden plane which has a spaceship on top. The teacher is a really calm and nice teacher and rarely gives us homework. This is a good quality as we have quite a busy weekend doing homework and other personal activities.

Jay Vachhani, 8S, age 13

9.56 a.m.

I ask Mr.Hayton if I can take part in today's physics lesson, as my shoulder is broken and in a sling. He says, 'you can do it! Just try your best, Michael'. I get changed into my slightly unconventional gym kit; consisting of a black school rugby top, a pair of blue Tottenham Hotspurs shorts and some grey vans shoes. I walk upstairs, knowing my strange kit will cause a wave of jokes. As I reach the top of the stairs leading to the gym I heard a faint laugh come from Mr.Hayton. 'Tottenham shorts', he remarks wittily.

Michael Parkes, 10H

9.57 a.m.

I am now approaching 10,000 days at the High School.

After the usual 15 minute bike ride from home down Woodborough Road, dodging and overtaking traffic, I arrive at school at about 9 a.m. Having made use of the school fitness room and changing facilities I get to the staff room awake and refreshed (?) by 10 a.m. After checking my pigeon hole, collecting my appointments folder from Reception, I go up to my room and prepare for my 'clients'. Seven today, a cross section of boys from school with various issues and problems. Hopefully I will be of some help to them.

The appointments keep me busy until 4 p.m. Another hour is spent writing up notes and reminders. Then it's back on the bike and the challenges of Woodborough Road.

Martin Jones

9.58 a.m.

In our PE lesson today, basketball . I always find basketball to be exhilarating and exciting . Our initial routine comprises a set of routines to improve skill and technique – we are required to improve skill and technique – we are required to aim in the inner ring of the basketball board . By doing this, you increase your chances of scoring a goal ! Finally, we are placed into teams- initially three people per side, and then six people . Each game is fast and furious, and by the end, we are all quite tired.

Nathan Lazenby, 8Y

9.58 a.m.

On Friday the first of February I am ill so I cannot go to school. I have a stomach bug and it is very bad. So I stay at home and watch TV and read my book. It is about ten o`clock and I am watching television and although I am felling awful I am in a good mood I am watching my favourite TV program with my dogs and some water and I am beginning to feel a bit better.

Joshua Mc Culley, Junior School Pupil

9.59 a.m.

I am playing in the sand. There are some toy bugs in there and I am playing with them. It is now tidy up time. I am helping to sweep the sand from the floor.

Saad Jadoon, Reception Class, Lovell House

9.59 a.m.

On Friday 1st of February 2013 my favourite 15 minutes of the day are in I.C.T. We are doing programming on Terrapin Logo, we are told to make the shapes on the board. Euan, Adnan, Yuvraj, Amran and I work together and are some of the first people to finish the first one. I enjoy this because when we work together we soon do it another reason is that it is fun. I like programming because it's fun and you can work together. I like working in groups because we can learn about other peoples ideas/beliefs.

Joe Card, Junior School pupil

10.00 a.m.

Just finishing off my clay project. Absolutely terrible, and I mean terrible. Luckily, I am good at other things. It's a good job that the other art lessons aren't this tedious...we used the slip to attach the clay together and make sure it sticks – something I'm good at with this clay at least. We used a metal kidney to smooth it down and a weird wooden tool to seal it. This is clay at Nottingham High School. Not too complicated, which is good. Hopefully mine will be alright, but I really doubt it to be honest.

Oliver Hopkins-Burke, 8L,

10.01 a.m.

In History we are learning about what we are going to do in the Lincoln trip and how we are going to see the castle and a cathedral. It will be quite fun because our history teacher told us that last year That they saw some American soldiers and you never know quite who you will meet on the trip. It is also an educational trip not just for History but for R.S. as well so we will be completing a worksheet (which we all groaned at) But I hope it will be a good trip all the same.

Donald Flynn, 7H, age 12

10.02 a.m.

YIPPEEEEEEEEE!!!!!!!!!!!!! Geography is over and I am ready for my favourite lesson, PSHE. I pick up my pencil case and get my water bottle. I get my reading book (which is The Austere Academy by Lemony Snicket, what a name!) and line up. When I get to the line I am quite near to the back. Ms Able doesn't arrive for AGES! Some boys go off to scout ahead. I just wait. Suddenly Adnan arrives and says, "Ms Able has forgotten she had a lesson with us"!

Hugo Bonney, 4S, Junior School

10.03 a.m.

Aah. Finally I've got P.S.H.E. a once in a week lesson; the best lesson on Friday.

Firstly we have a debate on what we think is a global man-made environmental issues. I think endangered animals but there are lots of different options such as global warming or poachers trying to capture animals. Then we make a mini mind map in a group and secretly vote for the topic we will like most. Lastly we are set the most interesting homework of writing a report in a group of what we chose. When we finish our work we are dismissed at last.

Arsh Dhange, 5S, Junior School

10.04 a.m.

Today at period 3 I am in D.T. I really enjoy D.T because when you finish a hard project such as a boat you feel really proud also you learn lots of new skills. Today in D.T we are evaluating our boat. I think my boat is really good and I am looking forward to seeing what my teacher thinks. Also in

D.T we are writing about the skills we have learned in D.T my list is almost endless. I write about all of the different drills I have used how to solder and how to make a circuit board. As we all work on this the teacher calls us up one at a time so that we can go through our work and give us a grade. I am nervous but I shouldn't be, I get an A*.

George Gray, 7S

10.05 a.m.

I unpack my school bag getting ready for a Spanish lesson. Once I get my red, broken folder out, I instantly go into my own world by reading poster by poster on the left wall. I do this until I am asked a question by the teacher where I listen to the boys around me telling me the answer. I use their answer. After that I switch on and listen to the teacher. I learn that we are talking about school and slowly flip to the right page of my textbook, losing concentration as I do so. I read through the exercises labelled in colourful blue circles as the teacher gets mad at a pupil. Finally I start paying attention to the lesson as the teachers face goes red.

Brandon Lim, 9L

10.06 a.m.

Spreading rapidly across the room, a low rumble of discussion signals the start of four minutes of sharing ideas, identifying global environmental issues. Examples flow thick and fast, almost too quickly to be recorded. The occasional voice rises above the general hubbub, as one group member becomes especially emphatic, requiring acknowledgement of his particular contribution. In the next eleven minutes, each team contributes to the whole class pool: deforestation, endangered animals, nuclear accidents, pollution, oil spills, vehicle fumes and more.

Now, each group is ready to select their topic to research and later present to their peers.

Jenny Abell, Head of PSHE, Junior School

10.07 a.m.

I sit waiting at the back of my History classroom, as my teacher puts in a video on the battle of Passchendaele in World War 1. The figure of Richard Holmes sprung up onto the screen, describing in vivid detail the dreadful horrors of the bloody battle. The sound note writing as Holmes tells exact figures and details that will come in handy in the inevitable long essay that is going to follow this video. The voice of Dr Swain is heard as he fills in more information on something that surprisingly Holmes has missed.

Luke Fowler, 10H

10.08 a.m.

Thoughts in my head. Lots of 'last times' this year. But this one is, for some reason more striking. Will I ever demonstrate the practical technique of 'titration' ever again? These Year 11's don't realise that their generation is the last to witness this spectacle delivered by yours truly. Must ensure that I give a first class 'performance'. Can I release a single drop of acid from the burette in order to give the desired colour change in the methyl orange indicator? Do I have the dexterity in my aging fingers to impress? Of course I do! Another cohort converted!

Mr.Mark Cleverley, teacher of Chemistry

10.10 a.m.

I am in my phonics group. We learn about the sounds the letters make in phonics. I am very good at learning the 5 vowels. They are a, e, i, o, u.

Ahmed Hamad, Reception Class, Lovell House

10.13 a.m.

Jetzt an einem typischen Freitag befinde ich mich im Sprachlabor für die Deutschstunde. Wir haben einen Vokabeltest gemacht und natürlich schon wie immer habe ich nicht dafür gelernt. Freitag hat sowohl meinen besten Stundenplan als auch meinen Schlechtesten: ich habe eine Doppelfreistunde aber ich muss zurück in die Schule für meine letzte Stunde: Physik. Und ich muss zugeben, dass Freitag abends kann ich mir die Mühe kaum aufbringen, mich zu konzentrieren. Heute ist schon schlechter und doch gleichzeitig viel besser: morgen beginnt die

Ferienwoche und deshalb hoffe ich, wir schauen in der Physikstunde einen Video. Sonst ist die Zukunft nicht so aussichtsvoll.

George Millington, 6M2

10.14 a.m.

Literacy is over and yes, at 10.15 the boys are working hard. Now it's time for snack. I ask who my classroom helpers are and two boys spring into action to hand out the milk and fruit…how responsible of them! As you expect 6/7 year olds love to talk but I feel setting them a daily challenge question to discuss with each other lets them use their brain in a more constructive way, and allows them to channel their thoughts with some surprising yet entertaining answers! Now, role on play time!

Richard Miller, Year 2 Teacher, Lovell House

10.15 a.m.

It is 10.15, I am 25 minutes into my DT lesson. Our teacher told us we are marking our boat and moisture sensor projects. We are in the classroom and I am logged onto my computer. The DT teacher has told us to write a word document, about what we have learned and enjoyed about the past term. We are going individually to get our projects marked. I am just about to get my project marked, I am really nervous. I have finished the document and checked all the points that he told us to write. Then I am called up by the teacher. He anylyses my boat and afterwards I am happy because I get two 1's and two 1*'s.

Shraavan Chilamkurthi, 7S

10.16 a.m.

'Run!! We're going to be late for the bus!!' I say as we are late for the games bus. And this isn't any regular games session either; it is House Rugby. As my friends and I turn the corner we see that the bus hasn't left yet and that we are on time.

On the bus there is a buzz about who will win the first matches.

At the games field we see all the houses allocated with separate changing rooms which only creates even more excitement about the seriousness of the occasion.

Everything is set for a fantastic match of rugby.

Sacheth Menon, 7T, age 12

10.17 a.m.

I am about to start my individual medley, knowing that if I manage not to drown I will score no more 1 point – which I know will is a 'huge' contribution to my house. However I placed myself in the last race so hopefully I will not be the only one drowning. Since this is the last race and we are most likely the worst swimmers in the class, only two people bravely attempt to dive in. The other two swimmers and I try our best to keep our heads above the water until the teacher shouts go! Then in a flurry of kicks and one belly flop, we all squirm our way to the other side using butterfly stroke (which ends up looking more like a drowning caterpillar)! I really don't like swimming…

Isaam Anwar, 9H

10.18 a.m.

"Thank God Almighty we are free at last!", words of Martin Luther King in 1963 in front of the Lincoln Memorial ring out in E6 during Y12s consideration of the Birmingham protest and the Civil Rights Era. King is the sort of hero I like, namely human and flawed, at the same time impressive, articulate and prepared to sacrifice himself for the cause should that be required. He knew exactly how to address a multi-racial audience of 250,000 and place before them his vision of a better, freer, fairer world. Inspiration for the 500!

Simon Williams, History teacher, age 49

10.19 a.m.

I ask the boys to line up quietly outside the Junior School Science Lab. They are chattering, exuberantly about a motivational speaker they have just had the privilege of listening to in the Founder Hall. As I hear their conversations for a brief moment, I am quickly planning in my head how to condense a 70 minute practical science lesson on bread mould growth into 40 minutes. The thought does not concern me as flexibility is a key quality needed by many working at the 'Prep School of the Year 2012'(Sunday Times 2012). With this quality the boys receive a great spectrum of wonderful opportunities that they revel in and enjoy.

Mrs Gunmeet Sethi, Head of Science & Assessment, Junior School

10.20 a.m.

I am asked to chat with the Australian Paralympic swimmer, Elizabeth Wright. Elizabeth won two bronze medals (Atlanta 1996) and a silver medal (Sydney 2000) in the Paralympic Games she is here to speak to our boys in Friday Forum. She is so easy to talk to and such an inspirational woman. She explains how from a very early age she embraced her abilities and worked through her difficulties, enabling her to connect with others in her mainstream school. Elizabeth really touches me with her enthusiasm for her sport and life and I am sure she will continue to inspire many others with her story.

Clare Lawrence-Forbes, Administrator, 49 years old

10.21 a.m.

Hallo aus der Vergangenheit,

Heute ist der fünfhundertste Geburtstag der Schule und wir müssen einen Brief an Sie schreiben anstatt unsere eigenen Aufgaben zu machen. Heute hat die Fahrt zur Schule zweieinhalb Stunden gedauert, da es einen kleinen Autounfall gab. Meiner Meinung nach passiert das zu oft heutzutage aber hoffentlich ist am Nachmittag alles in Ordnung. In der Pause essen wir Kuchen und Kinder aber mein Freund, der Matt heißt, glaubt, dass es möglich ist, den ganzen Kuchen auf einmal zu essen. Leider ist es nicht möglich und jetzt sieht er sehr lustig aus.

Peter Horton, 6M2

10.22 a.m.

I am in my D.T lesson as normal and the project I am working on is fascinating and ingenious. I really like D.T because it is different from all the other subjects and I aspire to do it in year 9. In this lesson my goals are to finish joining all of the cogs together, gluing the box and sanding down the side of it make it nice and smooth. By the end of the lesson I have managed to complete all of my goals and this pleases me very much.

Hugo Marchant, 8L

10.23 a.m.

I am tidying up the classroom. Ready for fruit and milk. After, it will be playtime!

Jai Sharma, 1S, Lovell House

10.26 a.m.

Straighten tie, tuck-in shirt, fasten blazer. The three steps I am happily performing –for a change- as I climb the staircase with the weight of the school's reputation on my shoulders. I casually, yet coolly, stroll into reception whilst battling against the nervous tremors that are gripping my body. Little do I know of the sheer humiliation, rejection, I am about to face.

"You're not required for this tour."

Crushed by rejection, I trudge back to period 3.

Chris Carty, 11H

10.27 a.m.

Maths is good. We do our assessment and we do our times tables, 6, 7 and 8 times tables. I find it ok. I do 71 questions, I just need 6 more to go onto my next set of times tables. After I have done my times tables we do another assessment to find out what I know and what I don't know. We also do some brain academy. Maths is fun, it makes my brain go hyper! There are some questions you do know and some you don't but if you get it wrong you learn from your mistakes.

Daniel Mok, Junior School pupil

10.28 a.m.

In period two on Friday 1st February Mr Shaw gives us our maths assessment results for this term. Although I am confident that I have done well, still my heart is pounding very fast, almost like a cheetah. I hurriedly calculate my score and gosh!! I have achieved full marks. I become so excited that I almost leap out of my seat and nearly shout it out aloud. Fortunately I don't, as it is bad manners to boast about these things but I cannot wait to tell my parents about it. I am happy that my hard work has paid off.

Rohan Tandon, 4S, Junior School

10.29 a.m.

Ouch!! The ball smacks me in the head: another reason to complain about House Rugby and the pain it brings to the less talented players in the house team. At least we're winning. Another scrum, and another opportunity to be mortally injured. Apparently our team is a favourite to win the tournament. To be honest, I'm just looking forward to securing the hopefully positive result and enjoying the fish and chips being served at the canteen for lunch. PUSH. Yes, we've won the scrum, get it out get it out. I'm trying my best to do my job, but it's difficult when you are running around the pitch half dazed. The whistle's being blown and we are forming a tunnel to console the opposition. One down, two to go.

Hari Solomonides, 7T

10.30 a.m.

English starts, my favourite lesson. My teacher, Dr.Burton, is really kind. We are in the library and having a good time. We are supposed to be quiet but the atmosphere is being ruined by the extremely loud radiator. Later on we have games: House rugby. I really dislike rugby. I wish in games we would do something different for a change like cross country or football. After we have rugby we have ICT then my favourite language, French. There are three minutes left so everyone is clock watching especially one boy who always clock watches and thinks no one notices.

Archie Norton, 7L, age 11

10.31 a.m.

As the half ten bell sounds a slight feeling of relief is quickly subdued by the realisation that there is yet another period of Chemistry to endure. As I struggle to absorb the information being thrown at me by my teacher through the thick fuzzy cloud of boredom that fills the classroom, I begin to become distracted by the smallest of things, as though my mind is disparate to spare itself from the torrent of facts and figures. I sit there as the faintest hope of there being practical work this lesson slowly fades away and my head slowly sinks until flat on the desk wishing that the ground would swallow me up whole and rescue me from my misery.

Ben Butler, 11Y

10.31 a.m.

On Friday we have a maths lesson with Mr Shaw and we do temperature.

I get on to the last bit of work and nearly finish it. Alexander and I are the only ones who get on to the second bit of Junior Maths book that we have to do. Mr Shaw says that we have worked really hard to get to the last bit of Junior Maths. It is near the end of the maths lesson when Mr Shaw asks us to mark our own work. I get them all correct except one.

Rio Gill, 3, Junior School

10.32 a.m.

On the 1st of February at 10.32, I have just started our second half of our double lesson. We are studying Spanish at the point and learning how to say different rules in the fascinating language. We are having a brief discussion on people's homework, and picking out good points from the homeworks. Then, Mr. Allerton will give us all points on how we can improve the quality of our work, and also tell us some new, interesting, vocabulary.

Arjun Narula, 9L

10.33 a.m.

Me and my classmates are listening to our DT teacher. I'm just sitting on the table trying to entertain myself. I start messing around but eventually I get caught. I'm just logging on the computers, I'm boiling here I immediately take off my blazer and jumper I feel so much better. I stand up and walk to the little dices also known as Genie 08. I grab a few wires and plug them in the computer. I look at the person next to me because I wasn't listening properly, I copy him closely and my program succeeds. I breathe a breath of relief.

Brooklyn Chan, 7S

10.33 a.m.

Amun strides confidently into the percussion room. A year 4 boy from the junior school he is a recent newcomer and my only pupil for this lesson. I make preparations for him to play a piece conceived at his previous lesson the week before.

There is a faint knock at the door and I shout to come in. The knocking continues so I shout louder.
Eventually the door opens to reveal a small boy looking rather pleadingly towards me. He is clutching a pair of snare drum sticks. I begin to question him.

His name is Matthew and is a member of the same class as Amun-4S.

He tells me he has come to start his drum lessons. I've had no notification (as is the usual procedure). I tell him that if possible I should be able to find a time to teach him in the near future, or possibly to have him share his lessons with Amun if this can be arranged. He looks into my eyes with a sorrowful stare and begins to cry.

I've experienced this response before from a junior school pupil-very infrequently and many years hence. This puts me on the spot a bit. Amun's lesson time is ticking away as I ponder the situation.
For them both to share a lesson I have to have their parents' consent.

I hear the door being opened to reveal the junior school class music teacher coming to see why young Matthew is taking so long to return.

We tell Matthew it will all be sorted out within a couple of days.

Still a little weepy he returns to his class with his teacher. I then proceed to continue with my teaching.

As Amun leaves at the end of the lesson my next pupil arrives walking unsteadily with a pair of crutches clasped firmly within each armpit. His Injuries are due to an overactive tussle on the rugby field.

Michael Sillitoe, teacher of Music

10.34 a.m.

Today it is my 8th birthday and I am glad to be spending it at the High School, as it means that I see my friends.

I am in my Maths lesson, which I enjoy because I like doing practical work and multiplication. Mr Shaw is a great teacher and he makes the lessons interesting.

Straight after Maths it is lunchtime and we are having my favourite meal of fish and chips. The school meals at the High School are perfect and much nicer than at my old school and sometimes my Mum's!

Jake Douglas, Junior School pupil

10.35 a.m.

It is now 10.35 and I am in Design & Technology with my class mates. Lately I haven't enjoyed D.T lessons as much as at the start of the year when we were in the workshop. Now, we have been drawing blueprints for an electronic dice that we are going to make next term. However Friday 1st February's D.T lesson has been particularly disastrous as I left my boat at home and my teacher wanted to mark it. Unfortunately, I was informed in the lesson that as well as my teacher marking my work, I had to do a self-evaluation so I had to imagine it.

Amit Gosal, 7S

10.36 a.m.

I'm glazing 10 little coiled clay pots that boys made during enrichment club with a watered down PVA mix. It's really very watery and I've managed to glaze the pots, my hands and my dress. Oh, and now my boots. Suede boots.

Mrs Julie Ockelford, Teaching Assistant, Lovell House.

10.37 a.m.

1So it all starts when my group and I (Joshua Bolton, Dhruv Gupta, Archie Symes and myself.) are starting our science experiment on bread mould growth in the Science lab. We work impeccably together, getting the box ready, dabbing the bread with water and positioning the bread in the box. When we finish we are ready to start the test. We place the box in the boiler room and leave it there. Now we have to check it every day.

Matthew Nettleton, Junior School pupil

10.38 a.m.

I am putting my coat on to go out to play. When we are outside we have lots of fun!

Ben Harcourt, 1S, Lovell House

10.39 a.m.

What an interesting day.

It all seems like a regular day till we finish our English lesson. The Math period is full of action. We are challenged to take a test on the 6, 7 and 8 times division facts tables which is followed by a puzzle solving exercise that has similarities with Sudoku.

Unlike Sudoku the puzzle has to be done using coloured counters instead of numbers. There are five groups 6 circular counters coloured red, purple, blue, orange and green. There is also one group of rectangular counters coloured red. The game requires the colours to be put in sequence in a square grid without repeating the colour in the vertical, horizontal or diagonal rows. This challenge is a step too far for the mathletes of year 4 group 2.

The whole group heaves a sigh of relief when the period is over. We realise that the significance of the words:
>The great heights reached by men and kept
>Were not attained by sudden flight
>But they while their neighbours slept
>Toiled upwards through the night.

Rohan Bhattacharjya, 4C, Junior School

10.40 a.m.

It is only twenty minutes away from the house rugby matches, I cannot wait. We are going to play Mellers; I know we can beat them. I am still stuck in Chemistry carrying out solubility on potassium nitrate. It dissolves quicker in boiling water - obviously! I never really look forward to the conclusion questions at the end of the experiment. I dream about making that dream tackle as a forward and it's really starting to bug me and it feels like forever! We have to turn the Bunsen burner on and off so the beaker doesn't break, it's pointless!

Charles Harte, 7T, age 11

10.41 a.m.

There is nothing for me to do but follow the teacher pleading for his assistance on what to do next, but the question is always answered by another question such as, 'What do you think is suitable?' or 'What would you like to do next?' This is why D.T is such a boring subject, but now and again the teacher's assistant comes to my longing help by showing me what to do but instead doing it for me.

The only thing that is keeping me going is that in a mere half an hour the bell will ring in its usual deafening tone, and after that I can spend 20 minutes playing football outside before I go to English and due to the topic can gently rest my head behind my book without the teacher noticing.

Rohan Chauhan, 8L

10.42 a.m.

I like apples very much. We sit on the carpet while we are drinking our milk and eating our fruit.

Isaac White, 1S, Lovell House

10.43 a.m.

I am sitting here (in the library) listening to chatter and the radiator rattling on its metal hinges. I am trying to do work but I am being distracted by my friends talking and joking. The atmosphere in the room is joyful but I am getting angry and annoyed. I try to focus on my sheet of paper but I cannot block out the block out the hideous noise. Finally the bell goes for break and I walk downstairs to pick up my games bag. I then grab a coco-pops cereal bar from my locker and walk out to the playground.

Will Stewart, 7L, age 11

10.44 a.m.

On Friday, in maths we are asked to write our names on the test sheet. Then we do the practice question together and we are asked to show how we have worked it out. We are asked to do the questions by ourselves. I have a wobbly tooth which is hanging out. I am then reading in my head when our teacher asks if we have all finished and everybody says yes. Then she comes over and collects all the test sheets in. My friend says to me," Twist the tooth and it will come out", but I just push it a little and it comes out.

Rohan Sivakumar, Junior School pupil

10.45. a.m.

History is not going well. As much as I enjoy the subject, a thirty minute presentation on the Boer war is enough to make people want to kill themselves. As I rock back and forth in my chair, my mind ponders the mysteries of the Universe, and I ask the question, 'why am I here?' Not here in a philosophical sense, but more literally, what got me to this point? There must be a logical explanation for why I chose History, both at A-level and for my future university course; otherwise, no-one would ever ask, 'Why did you choose History?' The answer eludes me, but when it comes to looking at the Boer War, I question my judgement.

Sam Pendleton. 6F2

10.46 a.m.

3W pupils are on safari. They arrive in that well-known savannah a.k.a. the Junior School yard, eagerly grasping their 'to find' sheets. From the prolific *cocodrilo verde* to the endangered *pájaro rojo*, teams must find each animal on their list. The whistle blows and they are off. Both pupils and *animales* join the stampede. An *elefante* is taken back to base but, disaster! It is *azul* and not the required *amarillo* so it must be set loose back into the game park. The whistle blows again, the *ganadores* celebrate, and the savannah is peaceful once more.

Miss Victoria Walster, teacher of Spanish, Junior School

10.47 a.m.

It is twenty minutes before the end of the Chemistry lesson and my class cannot wait for break. Most people in the class decide, one by one, that enough is enough and their plans for the weekend are a more interesting subject for conversation. The teacher attempts to regain our concentration by carrying out the experiment to neutralise acids and alkalis. The class nod their assent with one and a half eyes on the clock; there are two minutes to go until our small reprieve. At last the bell calls out its tune and the teacher dismisses us. Hoorah!

Reece Wood, 11H

10.55 a.m.

A parent calls in to drop forgotten football boots in for their son and also wants to pick up his Oboe which has been left in the Music Room. I accompany the parent to the Junior Music Room in the Music School, meeting Mr Douglas in the corridor on the way. All is now quiet for the time being however, it is now only 5 mins before breaktime for the boys. Stan has delivered the Junior School mail in for me to circulate and I have just answered the telephone to a query for entry into the Senior School for 2014 which I transferred to Admissions for them to register interest. Ed, Interim Headteacher, is submerged in budget submissions for the day and, in the absence of the ex Headmaster, we are trying to understand the various sub-headings etc. It is now breaktime and the noise generated is getting louder and excited boys rush to get outside into the fresh air!

Mrs Michelle Cartwright, Junior School Secretary

10.59 a.m.

I am in the line going in for my lesson. We have a lesson with Mr Fowkes, who teaches us about safety

Alfie Armson, 1S, Lovell House

11.00 a.m.

On Friday at 11.00 a.m I am busy working on my D.T project, which is a running man that is made of cranks that move the man up and down. I have just finished my box and now I have to make the man on the laser cutter, then, at 11.10 the bell goes and I go back to my class where I do some homework and make my way to the English lesson which is my 4th lesson of the day

Reeve Ganatra, Senior School pupil

11.01 a.m.

Today I am attending the National Conference for Directors of Sport in Independent Schools. The key note speaker is Baroness Sue Campbell CBE, Chair of the Youth Sport trust and UK Sport. She has delivered an inspirational talk looking at the lessons we learnt from the London Olympics and how we can use it help engage young people in our schools. As well as other inspirational speakers, it has been nice to have had the time to speak to colleagues working in similar schools and be able to share thoughts.

Martin Smith, Head of Physical Education

11.02 am

On Friday at break time I am playing with my friends Ryaan, Aamar and Fareed.

We are playing a game of dob. To start off with Aamar is 'it'.

There is lots of wood lying around so I just pick one up.

After break time I have a lesson of double ICT.

We are doing logo programmings but Mr.Simpson isn't in school so we have to do our lesson with Mrs.Whittamore.

Adam Khan, Junior School pupil

11.03 a.m.

It's the English library lesson. I have just finished the assignment and am just watching the clock, waiting for first break when I can jump on to the games bus and go off to rugby where I can play in the first game in the year seven house rugby tournament! Finally the bell! I am walking out of the library and race down the stairs to my locker to get my rugby games kit while bursting with excitement! Finally! I have been waiting for this moment all week! I am racing out to the main yard where the rest of the year sevens are in a big group with a nervous but exited uproar while they wait for the buses to arrive….

Daniel Smith, 7L, age 12

11.04 a.m.

Playtime is at 11:00 am and it lasts for twenty minutes. I like playtimes because we are allowed to bring snacks. My mum often packs me an apple and a bag of mini cheddars. My friends let me have their snacks every day. Pepperoni is my best snack.

I enjoy playing on the adventure playground and climbing on the monkey bars. I can jump on the skipping rope and my record is twenty jumps. My favourite thing is that we are allowed to bring in our own diabolos. I am good at playing the diabolo because I can throw it high and catch it. I can do lots of tricks. I am one of the best players in my year.

That's why I love breaktime!

Ben Ong, 3M, Junior School

11.05 a.m.

I am sitting in W10, attempting to visualise shapes to draw on isometric paper. The questions are easy so I fulfil my mind by finding some real world application for this skill. I can't think of anything, nothing applicable to my chosen career however. More importantly it is Friday, looking across at the founder hall I realise that today I will be preforming my long awaited Drama assessment. I will be doing lighting and sound as opposed to acting, something that my classmates struggle to comprehend. Back to maths, I am pleased to have plotted all of the shapes correctly. It is such an easy topic but still I fail to be bored by it.

Nathan Hancock, 9L

11.06 a.m.

Our wet feet slapping on the wet tiles, preparing for the final competition of the swimming lesson. I line up, last to see what distance I have to beat, which was made by Joseph Geldman. "Go!" a voice shouts so I dive in, keeping low near the bottom, so as not to be tempted to take a breath. Kicking with my legs, I propel myself forwards until my lungs burn and go up for a breath. I open my blood shot eyes and splutter for air. I have failed. I always preferred sports on the land than in the water.

Christopher Cutajar, 8H

11.07 a.m.

I arrive to do a cover lesson in the Junior School ICT suite. I have 10 minutes to set up whilst the boys are out at break and still time to leg it back to the staffroom for birthday cake (YUMMY!). I decide to be really organised, log on and set up all the instructions for the boys and display them on the inter-active whiteboard....then TRAUMA! As soon as I log onto the Activ Primary programme-the computer freezes and will not accept any command!! The overhead projector is not working either! Dilemma-miss out on cake and sort out ICT?!

Helen J Whittamore, Junior School Teacher

11.08 a.m.

It is a very boring lesson of Physics. I try to do an experiment but I guess I ruin it! My teacher looks at me in sympathy, trying his best to keep a straight face and say I am actually doing well in the practical. Breaking the hi-tech equipment, however, is not what I would say is 'doing well.' I just hope I get better at this!

Aadel Afsar, 10L, age 14

7. Break, and More Lessons

11.09 a.m.

The bell rings" Bring ," all the children get their snack head off straight to the yard and take equipment to play at break.

"Pan au chocolate," I screams in my head. Go into the yard and realize my friend he has got the best bat and ball. I go over to congratulate because it is very hard to get the best bat and ball.

"How is that" I shout to the umpire

"It's got be out," I think in my mind

The finger is shown by the umpire

"Yes," I say to myself and then take the bat and am ready to hit the ball hard.

Nabeel Khan, 4C, Junior School

11.10 a.m.

A sigh of relief drifts through the classroom as we realise that third period is over. I storm through the corridors running to the football. Everyone seems to find a certain joy in attempting to head the ball or kick it towards the unsuspecting goalkeeper's face. The ball's condition is quickly deteriorating and we soon find ourselves knocking a balloon around the ground. My face is now pouring with sweat, I do not know why; it is still a frosty morning. A look of disappoint befalls the players that as the bell goes again. My heart sinks I haven't scored again. It must have been months by now

Fraser Lim, 11T

11. 11 a.m.

As is the custom for so many at the start of first break, I head out into the playground for a brief kick around with the football: to be more precise, with my football that I had brought in to school only three days before on the Tuesday. Yet in that time it has suffered much ignominy, stripped of its outer casing, and left with a boil-shaped projection on one side. It no longer bounces in any dependable way and merely balloons upwards when struck with enough power. It is gone by long break.

Max Bowling, 11L

11.12 a.m.

As we gleefully depart from yet another tedious, nonetheless informative, lesson on the Atomic bombs dropped on Japanese soil, (Hiroshima and Nagasaki) we await the next lesson after break. However, my two friends have other ideas. They decide to sneak craftily sneak away and leave me on my own. After five, long, hour-like minutes stampeding round corridors searching for my elusive friends, I eventually decide to give in. Moreover, it appears that they have taken my next lessons equipment. Suddenly, I feel a light tap on my shoulder and slowly turn around. I then see my two friends who stand there, holding out my books. Finally, after a lengthy pause, my friend says: "Yeah…we found them in your locker. We have no idea how they got there!" There is something deeply untrustworthy on his leering face, which was frankly unnerving. They then bound off to the maths lesson, which succeeds break, and leave me flabbergasted and bewildered beyond belief.

Will Lowden, 9T

11.13 a.m.

The day looks like it is going to be like a normal day until my friend josh runs up to me and shouts that I have got student of the week. First I think he is joking and just trying to trick me. He takes me around the school looking for Mr Shaw who is also trying to find me. As I go around other people come up to me and say I have got student of the week and when I find Mr Shaw I find out I really have won student of the week. I am stunned.

Colin Mok, Junior School pupil

11.15 a.m.

I line up 20 reception boys for a visit to the school library. Marley is the leader and George Akins is at the end of the line. We call it our snake line and we move at a slow pace upstairs. I walk in the centre of the line to control the speed! When we arrive at the library the boys sit cross legged on the rug and I read them a story about a polar bear in the Arctic. They listen attentively and then I ask them to choose a library book to take home.

Julie Faulkner, Reception Teaching Assistant, Lovell House

11.16 a.m.

On Friday at break I am playing football with my friend Isaac and our team are winning 7-0. I score 6 goals then Jake scores one goal. The scores are level. Then we have a lesson. After that it is lunch. Then we play dob. Next it is Games at Valley Road. We are playing tag rugby. When we return from there, I go to after school club. I play table tennis and we even get onto building some Lego. We then stay and do some exciting chess matches and I win all of mine.

Ameer Khan, 3, Junior School

11.17 a.m.

It is 11.17am on a Friday. It's a sunny afternoon, which is classic England because the week before we had to go into the sports hall because of torrential snow. Our teacher (Mr Robsinson) finally lets us out of the black, metal gates and we approach the bus. We all rush onto the bus with our friends and sit at the back, the pick of the seats...After and entertaining journey we eventually arrive at the lush, mown grass and stumble of to get changed for rugby. When we change we are ready to play.

Joshua Williams, 7Y

11.18 a.m.

Having already endured an hour of Latin, I power on to try to get to lunch, but the Latin literature hinders me. We try to work together to get past this lesson once again, by writing on the board, or at least trying. As we are ahead of our course we are able to write on the board to waste time and it is fun as well. With one of my friends, trying to write but failing completely we power on till the end of the lesson. But we dread the worst part of the lesson homework

Nisarg Shah, 11Y

11.19 a.m.

Friday! The busiest day of the week for me. Biology with years 9, 10, 12 and 13….. luckily, all in my lab today in B1. I've just finished a test with Year 9 on the heart (we dissected one last week). There are some fantastic scores at the top end: Tom Walton, Matthew Croft, Richard Smith and Arjun Narula all over 90% on a tough test. Do you know what the function of the chordae tendineae (valve tendons) is? Year 13 also seem to have finally grasped Genetics. Good ….. five of them are sitting the national Biology Olympiad examination next Tuesday, and genetics problems don't get much harder than that!

Jim Cook, Head of Biology, 1979 - present

11.20 a.m.

A few minutes ago, the sweet sound of the bell ends my DT lesson, which was boring me to death. After I am excused from the classroom I run with a group of others to the bag rack. After snatching my games bag it is time to go to the bus. Now I am at the back of the bus trying to talk over the shouts and screams from other people. No use. No one can hear me, not even myself! Therefore I'm sitting here on my phone while other people do the exact same thing. Suddenly I fall to the back of my seat and I notice now we are moving. Off to games!

Robbie Heath, 7S

11.21 a.m.

I'm playing basketball with a few of my friends; it is a bitterly cold morning. We play basketball until the end of break at 11.25, and I am going to my form room to collect my school bags. I am going to the top floor and I go into my English lesson just on time at 11.30. In English we're read the class book Coram Boy. In turn we all put our hand up to read, English is my favourite lesson.

Nathaniel – Edouard Davidson, 8L

11.22 a.m.

CASE is happening right now. We are having a good time.

Ryan Mannion, 1S, Lovell House

11.23 a.m.

We know where to go and where is safe because of Mr Fowkes lessons. He used to be a policeman, but he is retired.

Harry Goonan, 1S, Lovell House

11.24 a.m.

Part-time, it's my day off. But I'll be going into school in a bit to sort out paperwork for Monday, and lap up some 500 year old atmosphere. Every Learning Support lesson requires four pieces of paper to be generated. This takes some time.

Sitting at home with my coffee, I think of my colleagues, and I miss them. I think of my students, past and present. Some of them I don't miss, but some have touched me profoundly. Without them, my life would be different. And I'm quietly thanking all of them

Marion Hubbard, Learning Support teacher

11.25 a.m.

When Lorraine, my assistant arrives, we have a visit from Chris Scott to take photographs. It is all very exciting and it's great to see how many of the staff want to be involved with all of the hype. Chris has been to various areas of the school and taken more photos of some of our cleaning team, all of this is making sure that they are part of it too.

Quite a few of the cleaning team have taken a copy of the request for taking part in the 100 word summary of a day in the life of a member of the support staff. It will be nice to see how they feel about it all and what they get up to apart from working here.

We are honoured with a visit from Richard Willan, who wants to request that the white boards have a good clean and some cloths for the boys to use when they have written on some cards. (Would like to be a fly on the wall in that lesson)

Now I will get on with the references that I need to check from the applicants for the cleaning positions.

Susan Ford, cleaning manager

11.26 a.m.

I have double maths and I myself think I am doing very well that day. Firstly, I finish off a piece of work from the day before called C2 temperature. Then I move on to Junior Maths. I finish that pretty quickly and what I have to do is use a ruler and write out the number of centimetres in our books for sections A B and C. Finally I move on to exercise eleven point two. I only do two questions on that because it is a bit more complicated.

Joseph Mannion, 3, Junior School

11.27 a.m.

The kick off for the Year 7's House Rugby commences in 15 minutes. The bus is 10 seconds away from the Valley Road Playing Fields and you can feel the excitement amongst the boys. Rugby kit has been neatly folded in bags the night before. Gum shields, head guards and water bottles all packed. And then, the bus driver opens the doors, bags are thrown everywhere, and boys rush out. They run up the stairs of the pavilion to get ready before battle commences. The question is – which House will win the Year 7 House Rugby Tournament?

Chris FARMAN, Teacher of PE and Games, age 27

11.28 a.m.

I remember we have a fantastic ICT lesson! Following a break we rush to the I.C.T. suite. We work with Mrs Whittamore on software called 'LOGO'.

As a class we are good at many things except 'estimation of angles '. We need help. After quickly completing the easy first challenge everyone is soon on difficult challenge2.

By using trial and error method, I examine the shape and quickly realise that it is lots of squares overlapping. I get it! I am one of the first one to finish challenge 2. I feel very happy and confident.

Viraj Deorukhar, Junior School pupil

11.29 a.m.

The boys sit on the bus on the way to their games session. There is no seat for me so I perch in the stairwell. There is a buzz of conversation. House rugby is the topic today. Who will be in the team? And in what position? Some are less interested; they sit and read, listen to music or play on their phones. The bus arrives and the boys hurry past me as I stand at the door, they are eager to go and get changed for the matches.

Andrew Miller, Chemistry teacher, age 25

11.30 a.m.

I am walking towards Drama with my friends, they are talking yet I have no idea what they are saying as I am too busy thinking about the performance I have to do in the lesson. Many questions are going through my mind; will I get a good mark? What if one of my workmates make a mistake? What if I make a mistake? Queuing up waiting to go into the lesson I am trying to put my mind off things by talking to my friends. But this is not working. We are getting sent in, I can feel my palms are sweaty. We are getting changed and sat down ready for the register.

James Hallam-Allsop, 9L

11.31 a.m.

I am nervous very nervous because today is the house rugby I am dreaming about scoring that winning try. I look out the bus window to see lots of shops- carpet shops, restaurants, grocery stores and barbers. Most of the people on the bus are talking but I am silent and thinking about the game ahead .at last the bus stops and I know we have arrived. As usual there is a huge crowd trying to get out of the bus through one tiny door after a few minutes I get out the bus and into the changing rooms. I open my bag and start to get changed skins- check, shorts- check, socks- check, shin pads- check, boots- check, scrum cap- check and shirt- check but where is my gum shield? oh no! i won't be able to play and we might lose! But then I remember: it's in the side pocket of my bag i put it in and join my team mates on the playing field. We are ready! The whistle blows and we run after the ball. Game on! And then as soon as it all starts it is over and we have won. Unfortunately I do not score the winning try but there is always next time.

James Payne, 7S

11.32 a.m.

We are walking up to the Junior School. We are going to see a Fire Engine and the Firemen.

Seth Dineen, 1S, Lovell House

11.33 a.m.

Break finishes. Year 7 appointment. Problems with learning vocabulary so use coloured cards and devise a game.

Carla O'Brien, Head of Learning Support

11.34 a.m.

As the paintbrush touches the paper, I know this is going to be a thrilling and exciting lesson. I am painting a jungle picture by a French Post-Impressionist painter, Rousseau. I make a considerably lighter blue for the rain which is pouring down on the jungle picture. My friends and I are talking as it is my birthday as well as Nottingham High School's 500th anniversary. I am so engrossed with the work (which is either painting/drawing our jungle pictures or drawing pictures of parrots in your book) that I don't hear the bell signalling the end of the lesson.

Abhishek Sama, 5A, Junior School

11.35 a.m.

We leave school; it's lunchtime. We really want something delicious inside us. We decide to walk into town so we don't have to spend any money on the tram. We arrive. Plunged deep into the darkness of the basement, a whole new world of pleasure opens up before us. Filling ourselves with the sensations of wonder and in awe of the atmosphere down here, I feel ready to burst, but there's always room for more. It's just so good. By the time we leave we are almost in pain. Red hot buffet is amazing! School dinners just don't do it for me now.

Luke Framji, 602

11.36 a.m.

We are visited today by 5 firemen and have a talk about fire safety. My class of boys aged 5-6 years old, learn how to stay safe at home by using fire alarms and are told what to do if a fire starts at home. Boys are told about the dangers of matches and what to do if they find some. I then walk my class and the other Year 1 class up to the Senior School playground and boys are shown around a fire engine! We have to hold our ears when the sirens go off.

Mrs Baker, Year 1 Teacher, Lovell House

11.37 a.m.

I am having Art. I am going to paint a parrot that I drew in my sketch book with the colours of red, purple, green, yellow and two different shades of blue. I collect my pot of water, mixing pallet, brush and paint. Firstly, I paint part of the tail blue. Above it, I paint a lighter shade of blue to make a fading affect. After that, I paint a red next to the two blues. Next I paint green above the blues, making the picture lively. I then paint a yellow above the green, joining on to the green.

Rohan Acharya, 5A, Junior School

11.38 a.m.

Maths period 4, one very grumpy teacher and a class full of dogs. Dogs enter classroom as grumpy teacher says letters in the names of members of class. 'Pupil regrets forgetting calculator and is forced to use ancient slider.' The teacher remarks "the kennel is full". Last, teacher thinks of picture with quote for 500 years of teahcing. Pupils line up against wall with open window. Teacher with head out of window. Quote: 'Grumpy teacher lets pupil hit the ground before throwing out the next.'

Alex Firth, 9H, age 13

11.39 a.m.

I struggle to stay awake as the French teacher drones on about French verbs. Our class is told off for the 6th time because my friend pronounces 'c'est' wrong again. Then we study the regions in France which are most popular with tourists. No one has done their homework. There are excuses such as: "It wasn't on frog", "I wasn't in the lesson", "I've only done half of it" Our class really need to improve the standard of our excuses! After an intense French lesson, we receive a 500-page essay homework for the day after. Everyone groans. I hate French.

Arun Sahota, 8S, age 13

11.40 a.m.

After break I go to chemistry and we learn about the chemical reaction of rusting.

Lucas Wilcock, 10S

11.41 a.m.

I am practicing my handwriting. It is getting much better! We write with capital letters and full stops.

Abdullah Ahmed, 1S, Lovell House

11.42 a.m.

It is period 4/5 and we are in ICT. Mr Simpson teaches our new topic. Our aim is to copy out the shapes that are on the whiteboard onto terrapin logo. I sit next to Amun Sahota and Adam Woodings. I accomplish challenge one and therefore begin challenge two. Amun and I are helping each other to accomplish all of the challenges being set by my ICT teacher. It is great fun as I find it very interesting looking at the shapes and examining them.

Aamran Ahmed, 4, Junior School

11.44 a.m.

I am sitting in English, reading the class book 'Coram Boy' by Jamela Gavin. Whilst everyone else has stopped reading and is discussing the book with the teacher, I plough on, not able to put the book down. I can't hear what is happening around me, all I notice is my friend telling me to stop reading and put my hand up to answer a question. After the rest of my class has finished the chapter, I am already a few pages ahead. My teacher has noticed I am still reading and has asked me to put my book down. The bell rings for the end of the lesson and off I am to German.

Jack Peirce, 8L

11.46 a.m.

Today it is year 7 house rugby tournament. We are on the school bus on the way to the games field. As per usual it is full of noisy loud boys. As it is house rugby today it is particularly noisy, many of the boys are discussing tactics. I sit with my friends Ben Welling, Josh Williams and Will ash. They are discussing tactics even though they aren't in the same house as me I make a few suggestions as to how they can improve our team. At around 11.50 we arrive at the games field. There is a huge rush to get off the bus and into the changing rooms. Every house has an assigned changing I am in changing room 6 which is Whites house changing room. I quickly get changed with my friends Tommy Fisher and Ralph Wills and we quickly discuss a few tactics. I begin to panic as our star player Will Atiomo doesn't arrive till around five minutes after us. Fortunately he does turn up and then we run on to the games field.

Samuel Peters-Green, 7s

11.50 a.m.

3W están de safari. Entran en el mundialmente famoso parque natural "El Patio de la Junior School". Cada equipo agarrando con entusiasmo a su tarjeta de juego, cada uno con la esperanza de ser campeones del día. ¡Y comienzan! ¡Encuentran un león! Desgraciadamente, es un león azul y no el león púrpura que buscábamos. Tiene que ser devuelto a su hábitat natural. Capturamos un cocodrilo rosa, el siguiente es un pájaro blanco...Y demasiado pronto, todo ha terminado. El equipo vencedor se alegra y nuestros fanáticos de los animales salen del parque natural mientras que el sol se pone sobre las llanuras.

Miss Victoria Walster, teacher of Spanish, Junior School

11.51 a.m.

I am getting ready for lunch. I put my red apron on and wash my hands. My favourite lunch is jacket potato with beans.

Cholan Sundar, 1S, Lovell House

11.52 a.m.

The clock ticks steadily, never quickening nor slowing, as twenty eager eyes spur it on. The pen is heavy in my hand and my eyes are drifting, searching for a distraction. The teacher reaches for some expensive looking equipment and we all glare obediently, eager to see what may follow. His quirky, slightly eccentric demeanour encapsulates us, as we try to predict his next move. We all gather round his boiling tube, filled with a liquid of some sort. He then explains it and suddenly everything is understood. It is moments like this that remind me why I love Physics.

Will Stevens, 11S

11.53 a.m.

The boys have washed their hands and are now lined up in their red aprons ready for dinner. They chatter excitedly about what they have chosen today. The choice is chicken nuggets, vegetable nuggets or a jacket potato. Most boys have chosen nuggets today. The boys collect their dinner from the cooks and they sit down at the tables to eat. I have a jacket potato today with tuna and salad. I sit with 5 boys and they chat about what they will play outside after dinner.

Lesley McCluskey, Reception Teacher, Lovell

11.54 a.m.

It is a lovely sunny day today, Tara and I walk down to Lovell House to supervise the infant boys outside. The boys are out slightly later today, not sure why. They love playing with the scoops and a tennis ball, they play "hockey" as they are not allowed to play football at lunchtime, this always turns into football as they get into it From there we walk back to the Junior school to supervise the boys there whilst they are having their lunch. They have Chicken Chow Mein today which they enjoy, especially eating with chopsticks.

Mrs Katrina Ritchie, Lovell House

11.55 a.m.

As I exit the Junior School, I cross over the tram lines, making my way to Lovell House as I ponder which toys to get out for the boys. Out come the Year 2 boys, ready for some fun. They soon get stuck in with scoops and balls. Year 1 and Reception start to trickle out, "Mrs. Bashir, can you help me with my zip?" "Mrs. Bashir, can you help me with my gloves?" A short queue forms. At this precise moment, I really do wish that I had another pair of hands!

Taheera Bashir, Midday Supervisor, Junior School

11.56 a.m.

I lie in my bed, exhausted. My eyes look at the ceiling then close shut, sending me into darkness; I quickly fall asleep and begin to dream. I dream of the moon, of talking teacups and clowns juggling with eyeballs. I wake up soon, wondering what all *that* was all about. The bed creaks as I get up and put on my slippers. After walking downstairs, I look around wearily, flicking on the light. I see the table, piled high with homework. I see the television, old and still fun. I see the blue, broken sofa, and walk over to it, lying down. A little more sleep couldn't hurt.

Joe Brough, 9T

11.57 a.m.

On Friday in ICT we have to program a shape by typing in words. For example, fd 4 which means forward 4 and bk 21 which means backwards 21. We do this as we have to control a turtle on the program [which is not a real turtle of course] to make the shape.

In order to program the shapes they are in challenges. I do the first challenge but unfortunately don't have time to finish the second challenge because it is the end of the lesson and also because the first shape is very hard to program.

William Chang, 4S, Junior School

11.58 a.m.

Latin, it is the last lesson before lunch. If my teacher goes on, I don't think I will be awake for any longer, when he is talking about nominative and accusative endings. He goes around the class asking people to translate sentences, although, due to me falling asleep and not listening, I struggle to understand the task. The teacher has a rage at me, because my homework wasn't done in pen, so he hands it back to me and tells me to re-do it. The bell finally rings for lunch but he keeps us waiting, just to talk about who was thinking about taking Latin for our Year 9 options. Only two or three people put their hands up.

Daniel Taylor, 8S, age 13

11.59 a.m.

Teams ready, referees ready, pitches perfect, game on!

Coopers A start strongly v Maples, with Ali Samatar running 75m unchecked to score. Poor tackling by Maples, who are given a pep talk under the posts by Captain Ash. They regroup for the kick off and never look back taking the game to Coopers and running out victors by 29-5. The B team encounter is a one sided affair with the mighty Maples crushing Coopers 51-0.

Over on Pitch 3 Whites A inflicted another crushing defeat on Mellers 54-0, but on Pitch 4, the game of the day as Mellers B fought back to pip Whites 22-20.

Stuart Whitehead, Games teacher

12.00 noon

At noon, I am taking a prospective student and his mother for a tour of the school. They have just had their entrance interviews, the mother speaking to Mr.Fear, and Toby, the boy, has met Dr.Fletcher. They appear happy and eager to see more of the High School. As we go around the school, they become very impressed with the range of facilities on offer, and, after meeting a few members of staff, are astonished at their friendly and cheerful attitudes. They are feeling very honoured to be present on the 500th anniversary of the first lesson ever taught at the premier educational institute in the county.

Peter Hardwidge, Sixth Form Pupil

8. Friday Means Fish and Chips

12.00 noon

12 noon. It's Friday. Fish and Chip day!! Probably the most popular day in the School dining hall!! After lunch, a brisk stroll around the Arboretum with a colleague, admiring the sunny spring-like day and the hundreds of spring flowers starting to push their way through for another cycle of life. Who'd have thought that less than a week ago the Arboretum (and a lot of the entire country) was smothered in 4 inches of snow?

Back to work. Next job a CRB check for a new employee.

Ah well, it is Friday!!!

Christine Winter, P.A. to Director of Finance and Estates

12.01 p.m.

At this point, I am in my English lesson. I am being told to write about a time of the day on Friday. After I have written this in my planner, I carry on reading the Coram Boy. It's a great novel. I am trying to enjoy my lesson; however, a quiet humming exists. We stop suddenly and wait till it finishes. Miss now carries on reading. She puts emphasis on the right words. The bell rings. Everybody gets up and packs their things quickly. I try rushing out of the room, but miss says I'm going last. A minute later, I leave the room.

Bilal Haq, 8L

12.02 p.m.

I always get the 'Friday feeling', which is the great feeling you genuinely get when you know you have the weekend yet to come.

We have a double lesson of Drama with Miss Webster. My class and I are watching a play and my friend's group are presenting their own. Each of our selected groups has a play to perform, during the double lesson. My friend's group's play is incredibly amusing. I am watching the play, which will last 15-20 minutes, with the whole class. In the first ten minutes though, all am literally doing is watching a humorous video, while my back begins to ache, from sitting on the floor.

Azaan Zaki, 9L

12.03 p.m.

I am going into the dining room.

I like chicken nuggets the best!

Having chicken nuggets is yummy.

Aryan Kareer, 1S, Lovell House

12.04 p.m.

It's a rare occurrence to meet a Paralympian. It's an even rarer occurrence to blank this paralympian for the 5 minutes needed to finish off a game of table football. Australian Paralympic swimmer Elizabeth Wright came with Mrs Robinson into the sixth form centre to have a lovely chat with the students, and instead of a formal hello or handshakes, she was greeted by the grunts of teenagers more interested in the table football game. In all fairness though, it was a classic match. We did, in the end, have a great chat with the athlete.

Alex Fowler, 6M2

12.04 p.m.

I have never really liked playing rugby, but house rugby is different I feel it is more fun. My teammates scoring tries, and me taking the kicks. Now it is my time to shine as my teammate have just scored a tri and it is my conversion. I run up to the ball and hit it with all of my will, it is at such a tight angel as well. It is curving in and at the last second it curves too much and hits the bar. I feel as if I have failed my house as it was one of the last kick of the last kicks of the game and I have missed it.

Dylan Sandhu, 7S

12.05 p.m.

The bell rings cutting through the silence of the physics practical, everyone is nervous and I can feel the tension in the room. The pressure of the practical is getting to us and no one wants to do anything wrong. I am excitedly waiting for lunch and cannot wait to eat my well-deserved fish and chips but first I have to complete the physics practical or I will surely fail the homework. Sam turns to me and asks how long till break and that's when the bell rings releasing us from the intensity of the lesson

Robin Marshall, 11L

12.06 p.m.

The bell goes for the fifth lesson and with another late entrance by my Latin teacher we enter the usual E5 classroom. After the usual comments of 'Very drole Mr.Hurrell' the lesson begins. With the usual rivalries of who's wrong and who's right for the correct translation for our text (Virgil's Aeneid) being established the lesson continues with its normal not so intense nature and finally after what feels like a very long lesson the bell rings which signifies the best part of the day lunch! Most of us are hungry by first break and by now we just can't wait for that usual chaotic run to the dining hall.

Chris Hurrell, 11Y

12.07 p.m.

Oh, it is freezing cold today! I am still cold and I am wearing a black and white striped rugby shirt as well as a thick black rugby training hoodie. I can see my group all shivering. We have still got forty-five minutes to the end of the lesson. So far we have done the usual, tiring run around the massive, green field and I feel like someone has taken all the strength in me at the end of the long run.

We are now learning about how to tackle in rugby. The rugby teacher says that the perfect tackle is to bend low down and knock them using your shoulders. I am a bit bored but then the rugby teacher tells us that we are going to try tackling. We are split into two groups: the tacklers, and the people being tackled. My luck gets me into the "being tackled" team. I stand there, a little nervous as a person in my group charges straight at me, like a raging bull and knocks me over with a thud!

David Ding, 7L, age 11

12.08 p.m.

My mind is clear, not worrying about work at school (obviously I was thinking about my English coursework but that's always synced into my mind). My legs feel like jelly just as they would have done if I was in assembly and hearing the magic number 500 being spoken from our head teacher. I wish I was in school for the first time to witness this historical event. My heart thumps against my chest, reminding me of my illness. I get up, look at my school bag and begin catching up work that I have missed.

Jawaad Ramzan, 10T

12.09 p.m.

I am eating vegetable nuggets, I normally eat jacket potato. I wanted to try something new. I like talking to my friends Ben and Omar.

Harry Elwick, 1B, Lovell House

12.10 p.m.

Sitting down, ten past twelve, it's Physics.
Learning about pressure, minutes drudge by,
Slow, continuous, broken by banter,

A classroom affair, little to report.

Sitting down, twelve twenty, it's Physics.
An experiment now, spheres and a vacuum,
Attracting the crowds, gaping in awe,
A classroom affair, little to report.

Sitting down, twelve thirty, it's Physics.
Once again a vacuum comes to the fore,
A flask implodes, an audible bang,
A classroom affair, little to report.

Sitting down, twelve forty, it's Physics.
As the lesson reaches its dreary nadia,
Weary boys while the minutes away.
The great bell rings and all of a sudden
Boys jump to their feet in a thunderous surge.

It was a classroom affair, little to report.

Harvey Aungles, 11T

12.11 p.m.

I am running Puzzle Club for Year Two boys whilst marking their literacy work. I listen to boys enjoying themselves and forging new friendships or acting as referee! I help a boy with his questioning skills within a game of 'Guess Who' and despair about why some boys find it hard to copy a word that is already on the board! Now, that is more like it, a beautifully written piece about 'What is a non-fiction book?'- faith is restored. I am now making notes for a meeting for our 500th anniversary. Tidy Up! It's fish and chips for lunch.

Andrea Williams, Year 2 Teacher

12.12 p.m.

Year 12 student wants new strategies for learning Chemistry equations. We work on highlighting key elements. Have to do this off the top of my head. Brain hurts.

Carla O'Brien, Head of Learning Support

12.15 p.m.

It is 1215 and I am holding a rugby ball in my freezing cold hands. I am in Cooper's house and I am playing in the B team for house rugby. We are playing against Maples house and we are just going on an attack. Yes! We nearly score a try. Oh no! He just gets tackled about 5 yards from the try line. Maples house are on the attack now and they are about to score a try. Their player is racing through our forwards and he scores a brilliant try. Hopefully we will get back in the game after half time and we can win this game.

Gurvir Sidhu, 7S

12.16 p.m.

I sit here in period five as the frothy cappuccino travels down my throat. A warm, energising sensation swirls inside me as the caffeine boost kicks in giving me that much needed boost to revise for the Latin vocabulary test. As I get half-way down the page, I take another comforting slurp. It needs more sugar. I muster up the energy to trek down into the brasserie for the precious powder. But a decision must be made – white or brown? I go for brown. Enough distractions - Latin vocabulary awaits.

Faraz Ghani, 6F2

12.18 p.m.

I am in German in the language ICT centre with Mr.Brown and though I missed the German ICT session the week before, I am working hard and I catch up with the rest of the class. At the end of the lesson I remember that year 8 are 1st sitting and I am thinking of the fish and chips that I want to have at lunch.

Fred Tindale, 8L

12.19 p.m.

In Art, I draw a part of my Rousseau jungle scene composition which I will call Life is not long for the small!" In the picture most of the small insects/animals are being eaten by the bigger ones. I draw the last few animals so that I can start painting the horizon. The time of day in the picture is sunset. The sunset is red nearest the sun then getting darker towards the edge until it is black and there are stars. I only paint the horizon in the double lesson because I add more detail, animals and insects.

David Eatch, 5A, Junior School

12.20 p.m.

The ball is knocked-on, the whistle goes. The boys look confused, as if they have not seen this before, but they have. They see the arm raised; they hear the explanation again "ball knocked on black and white. No advantage. Scrum down, black put it." They run, they organise, they set their team up as best they can, remembering the teachers' instructions from day one of Year 7 Rugby. "Crouch, Pause, Set." The game re-starts, the moves are quick, the passes fly and with 10 metres gained, knocked-on again. "Scrum Down."

Benjamin HAYTON, teacher, age 28

12.21 p.m.

I am told what position I am playing in house rugby...Fly half. My favourite position at all. We start and I kick the ball as far as I possibly can. A Mellors player catches it. I am running in for the tackle but just before, he passes it. Luckily the ball drops to the floor so I run in and pick it up and sprint to around 2 meters from the tri-line just from the corner of my eye I see a different Mellors player coming in to tackle me. I sprint harder but eventually get tackled. I receive the ball again and this time I am sprinting as fast as I can. However someone comes behind me and accidently catches his boot on my leg. I fall to the ground in agony. I slowly walk off when I tell a White's player to swap with me. Luckily he does so I sat off for the last 2 minutes of the game.

Harry Mahal, 7L, age 11

12.22 p.m.

I take off my red apron and put it in my tray in the cloakroom. I put on my coat, gloves and hat and go outside to play in the garden.

Omar Amasha, 1B, Lovell House

12.23 p.m.

On Friday the 1st of February 2013 it Is maths (my favourite lesson). The Year 5 groups 1 and 2 have a test. Mr Caldwell is running my group and even though we have a test, Mr Caldwell makes you feel relaxed and confident. This test is the third test of maths and I'm sure it is the last.

I have never liked maths because it isn't a challenge. I absolutely love maths now because my super hero Mr Caldwell made it more of a challenge and I love challenges. I love to have a go at things and I won't give in until I solve something.

Kain Watts, 5A, Junior School

12.24 p.m.

I am walking back to the Whitehouse from the Sixth Form Centre, snatched lunch of Cornish pasty and chocolate flapjack in hand. One day I will make more healthy lunch choices. Here comes Henry Ellis to talk about the Macroeconomics paper. He did okay, he thinks, although the paper had tricky questions about countries leaving the Eurozone and UK austerity cuts. There are so many other things that I should be doing but it is nice to stop and chat on a mild sunny day. It will be good next year when the sixth formers will take no exams in January and teaching can continue without disruption.

Peter Cramp, Head of Economics

12.25 p.m.

I am sitting at my desk on the front row of the physics classroom. Our teacher is standing at the front trying to get an old engine working. It starts making weird gurgling sounds as she stares disapprovingly. We send for a technician who takes it away. It is very nearly lunch and I can't wait. As the machine fails to start again, we all get up and crowd around a large speaker hocked up to a sound generator. We then experience lots of high pitched sounds that scream inside our heads. This is supposed to test our hearing capabilities but I am sure it has just made us all more deaf! As the clock slowly rotates to 25 to 1, she asks us to do some work sheet questions on what we did. After this the bell goes and we all run to lunch.

Benji Hopkin, 8H

12.27 p.m.

My class and I have art we are either painting or drawing and I am finishing drawing my picture of a drawing similar to Henri Rousseau's surprise picture themed in the green jungle. When I start to paint I am told to start from the back of the picture so I decide to paint the sky pretty blue. So I start to get out my paint brushes and pots to be prepared for painting so I start painting and I get halfway. The bell rings, we have to pack up our belongings.

Dilip Krishanand, Junior School

12.29 p.m.

I am sitting in DT talking to my friends whilst designing a program on circuit wizard. I am doing the same design as my friend and we are trying to work out how it works and what to do next. I am going to take the 500 year anniversary photo using the panorama feature on my Iphone. I wait anxiously for the bell to ring so I can dart up and get into lunch before the queue. Mr Thorpe is starting to make up a song about bad circuits, he is funny. I watch and wait for the clock to strike 12.45.

Jake Pemberton, 9L

12.31 p.m.

Art is a great subject and is my favourite the reason why I like art is because it is fun and you can draw and build things that you can't do in real life. Also you can give your brain a break if you work all day. If you are about five years old and do art it gives you in the future a lot of creativity which is good if you want to become an author when you are older. The most thing I like doing in art is drawing planes and making them in art.

Nabeel Jahan, Junior School pupil

12.33 p.m.

At lunch I eat my chicken nuggets. Then I go out to play. I have to take off my red apron.

Krish Bassi, 1B, Lovell House

12.34 p.m.

We are about to start the second half of a rugby match, which has so far been one sided. It is 15-0 to us. I score two tries and my team mate the other. We are playing against Mellers . The ball is kicked into the pitch. The opposition catch it and instantly get tackled. It is now a rook. They pass it across the pitch to the winger. He's running, the fall-back runs at him… The fall-back grabs on to his shirt but lets go! It's a try! A few tries later it is the 20-20 conversion to Mellers. It's Last kick of the game. He shoots, He scores!!! 20-22 to Mellers. I am very disappointed I we lost.

Francis Sidra, 7S

12.36 p.m.

It's really fun being at Nottingham High School because you can play outside for at least twenty minutes before going in! Lunch break is the best because it lasts for one hour.

If it is the turn of your class, you can either play on the football pitch or on the adventure playground (pirate ship). If you're lucky you might even get some equipment.

In morning break you're allowed to go to Senior School dining hall and eat there. If you're not as lucky you have to stay in for wet or snowing break.

And this is why I like this school.

Andrew Barish, year 3M, Junior School

12.37 p.m.

Its period five the last period before lunch and break. The task we thats set is to read through Macbeths first speech and add in emotions and actions that the reader should show when reading. We are working in groups of two with one person being the director and desiding what emotions and actions should be present while th other is the actor. In my group i am the actor and therefore have to listen to exactly what the director says even if i dont agree. After we have practised it we will perform it infrount of the class.

George Mumby, 9Y, age 13

12.38 p.m.

I put my coat on and go out to play for a long playtime. I like to play Spiderman and football. My friends are Shuban and Harry.

Namit Batra, 1B, Lovell House

12.39 p.m.

Everyone sits in biology anticipating the bell for lunch. Everyone slowly packs there bag putting their books back on the desk whenever the teacher looks. The bell rings and in a matter of seconds the classroom is empty. Everyone runs to the dining hall trying to sneak in early. Many are rejected but some are lucky. I am superior to people who buy lunch because I have a packed lunch meaning I can dine whenever I wish. I calmly walk into the dining hall seeing people pull out lunch passes from 2010.

James Beasley, 10H

12.40 p.m.

At lunch there is a big queue and it takes a long time for me to get my lunch. It is either a ninety per cent beef burger or a veggie burger, and for dessert it is crispy cake, fresh fruit salad or fresh fruit.

After lunch I go to my classroom to get ready for Games. When we are in the changing room we change into our black and white stripe shirts, black shorts, black shirt, long rugby socks and football boots. After getting changed, Year Three go outside for rugby.

Cole Tyler-Smith, 3W, Junior School

12.41 p.m.

The high school is very good at lunchtimes because I have a lot of things to do like, read a book, go to the library, the ICT sweets or do homework. The lunch meals are very nice the food is of high quality and I enjoy my meals a lot. Lunch at the high is a pleasant experience and that is why I look forward to every lunchtime.

George Fletcher, 8L

12.42 p.m.

I pack my books into my bag; the entire class is waiting for the bell to ring. Almost everyone looks at the door, then the clock, then the door again. The bell finally rings, and the whole class sprints out of the door and down the stairs, all wanting to get their pizza early. My friends and I make our way outside and over to the lunch queue, only to be sent out again by the teacher on duty, despite having got to lunch early. And instead of biting into our pizza we go back to the form room.

Dominic Duffy, 9Y, age 14

12.43 p.m.

It is the start of long break and I am first in the queue for the brasserie. I have just had quadruple maths and desperately need my panini. Soon I will be in the pod playing table football. After two months with a broken table, it has finally been fixed and now the number of students revising in the library during their study periods will halve. I should really be doing my maths homework but until somebody knocks me off the table I won't leave. I would still be there now if my teacher hadn't forced me to go off to lessons.

Bhargav Srinivasan, Year 13

12.44 p.m.

Only 60 seconds to go, 59, 58; the bell rings and the mad scramble starts. Two flights of stairs and one corridor and then I'm in. Fish Fridays, the best day of the week. I enter the dining hall and find a table. Only an hour and a bit to enjoy before period 6. Lunch can never be long enough.

Sam Steele, 10H

12.44 p.m.

Desperate for lunch, everyone is trying to hang on for another minute, eagerly anticipating the decision of the week: fish or pizza? Time seems to be slowing as we approach zero hour. Everyone is packing away, but then we are stopped by the infamous phrase: "stop taaaalking".

'Banter' throughout the lesson remains very high, but the notion of homework changes the atmosphere in the room. Everything goes quiet except from the rustling of bags as the students reluctantly lift their planners, heavy from a week of homework, out of their bursting bags.

Will it be more mass relations calculations?

Daniel Warrington, 10H

12.45 p.m.

Gerade hat es zur Mittagspause geklingelt. Wie eine Herde Elefanten stuerzen die Jungs die Treppe im "Weissen Haus" herunter in Richtung Kantine. Ich hingegen warte geduldig auf meinen Konversations-Kandidaten.

Ob er wohl kommt?

Soll ich mir einen Tee kochen?

Ich hab' die Nase voll und gehe ins Oberstufenzentrum!
Im Bistro – wo es all die leckeren Sachen gibt, die man nicht in der normalen Kantine erstehen kann – ist er nicht.

im "Pod" beim Computerspielen? Im Computerraum? Auch nicht.

Hoch zum naechsten Stock. Am Billiardtisch? Nein.

Aber da - ganz in der Ecke, fast versteckt hinter all den anderen Jungs, seelenruhig und gemuetlich, fast unschuldig ausschauend!

Grosse Augen: 'Oh Miss, I'm SO sorry.

COMPLETELY forgot!' Grrrrrr. Grrrrr.

Frau Bettina Krüger, *Assistentin,* German Department

12.45 p.m.

The bell goes to signal lunch at 12.45 am. We walk down to the schools front gates and wait for the buses to arrive. We hop on the bus at 12.50 and arrive at the grounds five minutes afterwards. We prepare for our one hour sports session (Rugby.) Starting off we run round the 1st team pitch as our warm up. We are split up into 2 teams t fighting tooth and nail to gain at least a try over one another. It usually ends up with the wingers out running everyone with a massive grin on their face (even when they are still doing the run.)Then we return back to school ready to eat a lovely meal.

Will Rock, 9H

12.45 p.m.

Lunchtime session: dyspraxic boy needs help organising his subject documents on laptop .

Carla O'Brien, Head of Learning Support

12.45 p.m.

The bell is ringing for the start of lunch break, after DT. All of the years eights are running to lunch from their lessons all over the school. It is the time of the week that everyone has been waiting for. Fish and chips! I charge across the school yard, to the door to the lunch queue, where there is already a large build-up of pupils. The queue is moving slowly today. The tedious moments pass at the rate of a snail. I can smell the fish and see the golden batter. Finally, I am there and the fish and chips are mine.

Cailen Ghadiali, 8T

12.45 p.m.

The bell rings, telling everybody its lunchtime. A sigh of relief hits the room as we quickly pack our bags and exit the classroom. I head towards the dining room with my friends. I leave my bag on the rack outside and hurry to the dining room. I remember its year 8's time slot for dinner, but when I arrive the queue is massive! Im starving and decide to go to the sandwich bar. There is still a fairly long queue here but I'll live. I finally pay for my sandwich and drink and find where my friends are sitting, I sit down and chomp in to my food.

Josh Almond, 8H

12.45 p.m.

Ring! The school bell echoes around the grounds, erupting from near silence. Were finishing putting the art equipment away and then hurriedly packing our bags and thinking about lunch.

Were running from the room and belting down the corridor.

"This is the first time I've been let out of art early," a voice next to me says. I turned round and I'm seeing Will.

Were jumping down the stairs, two at a time before dropping our bags off and then were rushing to the dinner queue.

'Pizza, yum, yum' I'm wondering aloud as I'm glancing at the laminated menu.

"What about fish?" says Will?

Harry Anderson, 8Y

12.45 p.m.

The bell rings, signalling the end of period 5, the English teacher reminds us of our homework before saying 'off you go.' There's a clatter of chairs and everyone rushes towards the door. It's a stampede, feet thumping down the school stairs to reach the dining room; our bags are deposited by the lockers, before the onrush of boys continue. It's not our sitting and the teacher on duty always sends us away, but it's always worth a try to see if we can get to a table and have lunch...

Ivan Wills, 9Y, age 14

12.45 p.m.

The bell goes, like a heard of gazelles we charge down the hall. We turn the corner, onto the ice rink that we call the playground. Together we charge at the doors, anticipation of a meal fixed firmly in our minds. The stampede slows only for the obstacle of a door and the hurdling of the barriers. Suddenly the lions come through the entrance blocking our route to food. This time we have failed, the race to the dinning is lost but we shall get lucky next time.

Harry Parker, 10T

12.45 p.m.

As the bell rings at the end of period five, we start to rush to lunch. It's fish and chips today, everybody's favourite. We're all tired, after a long week and a long Friday morning but nevertheless there is a surge of boys, all hungry for lunch, pushing and shoving as they try and win a place at the front of the never ending queue. As I near the front, I smell the strong cent of the beautiful meal that awaits me, my mouth is watering and my stomach feels like an earthquake. The fish is all gone, another gruelling five minutes to wait.

Charlie Hind, 8T, age 13

12.46 p.m.

The pure air gently caresses my raw cracked skin. The cheers and shouts of the people boom through mother natures crafted earth with exuberance. My foot lands and cold parted concrete. The concrete crumbles away, enough to percept the fresh, buff earth itself. Lunchtime is not only to eat your food, but also to cluster my thoughts. The constellations of my meditation-the bell. The only opportunity of the world to squander all inner peace that is as flat as an azure sea after a storm. I could hit the leather blanket of the football with my friends. The assiduousness was all too much. But the bell ends all peace.

Alex Podmore, 8T

12.46 p.m.

Thank Goodness! It's lunch break, the best time of the school day. If I quickly run upstairs from P3 to W17 I can meet my friends outside their last lesson and ask them to buy me a milky bar from Sainsbury's. Then I can take my JD bag from on top of my locker and sprint downstairs to get the best table in the dining hall, right in the corner so when my friends come back from we can 'crack' as many jokes as possible, and laugh out loud without annoying a single person. But there is a downside because every time my friend comes with his school lunch, it makes my packed-lunch look like prison food. But at least I can steal some of the ever flavoursome diced potatoes to warm up my cold tuna wrap. Now 45 minutes left of break...

Jaiden Samra, 11T, age 16

12.47 p.m.

Just out of maths, straight into the brasserie, just as every other Friday. Brief snatches of conversation with various people, all of it animated, none of it particularly important.

Now, sitting at a small table in the sixth form centre. There are eight people trying to find a place at a table suited for less than half of that number, but it's just the way of things, I suppose.

Time always shoots past when you have deadlines. Friday forum, or finishing that essay before the weekend? The days all seem that way now: a perpetual barrage of assorted unobtainable decisions.

Adam Hodgkinson, 6T1

12.47 p.m.

Es ist die lange Pause und ich muss sofort zu einer Big Band Probe gehen. Wir haben die Endrunde eines Wettbewerbs erreicht, also verbringe ich viel Zeit im Moment in der Musikschule. Um ehrlich zu sein, habe ich keine Lust zu dieser Probe zu gehen: Ich habe so viel Arbeit, und ich würde es vielleicht bevorzugen, Pizza im Oberstufezentrum zu essen! Jedoch entscheide ich mich, dass ich es bedauert hätte, wenn ich die Probe verpasst hätte – und ich habe Angst vor dem Dirigenten! Trotz meiner Gleichgültigkeit ist die Probe ungewöhnlich erfolgreich, aber am Ende bin ich total todmüde, und ich freue mich nicht auf meine nächste Doppelstunde Geschichte…

Christian Cummings, 6M2

12.47 p.m.

Today at lunch time, after our DT Lesson me and my friends are the first ones on the playground, and we start to play a football match. We decide teams ad start the match, so for about 5 minutes it is a 5-aside game until more people from our year come to play. Eventually it turns to a 20 to 30-aside match. At 1.10 p.m. my friends and me go to go eat our lunch, we spend about 20 minutes eating, and we have a laugh at the same time. After lunch we go back outside to finish our game.

Jassi Grewal, 9S, age 13

12.47 p.m.

I rush out of the art block, along with all of my classmates. As I walk across the playground, I look up at the huge main building. There are some boys playing football, using a pair of crumpled up blazers as goalposts. I walk into the quad, and I turn on my phone to look at the time- gosh, it's nearly 12.55; I'd better get my skates on. Walking into the Latin corridor, I am greeted by Mathew Sampson blocking my way and saying: "Where ya goin, Schlich!" Luckily, he gets out of the way and I can get my band music. I walk round the front of the school, and I think about the new piece that we will be doing in band.

William Schlich, 8Y

12.48 p.m.

Finally the bell goes for lunch, but as usual, the teacher tells us off and keeps us behind again! Once he lets us go, I run straight to the dinner queue and get in without too much trouble and have a really nice meatballs and pasta. I like to take my time eating and have a nice chat with my friends. Once I have finished it is gone 1 o'clock, but we still have another hour to have some fun and mess around. We do loads of things like talk to the passing girls (who are in sixth form) and listen to music really loud in our form rooms through our phones using speakers. Then as I am really having fun I realise that I have loads of homework to do from my German/ Spanish teacher who always sets us too much, because I didn't have time to do it last night because I had swimming. So I have to stop having fun and do stupid homework, again!

Joseph Wakefield, 8S, age 13

12.49 p.m.

I walk through the busy corridors, a hum of activity spread around the school, as one by one, students are let out from their lessons. Many run straight for the lunch queue eager to be first to get their hands on the delicious food. Others just sit in classes talking and playing on their phones or the occasional iPad. Most are outside in the fresh air: kicking the ball around, playing catch or simply sitting on the benches talking to their friends, teachers are strolling the yard, on the lookout for the occasional trouble makers. It's just a normal day.

Niall Vyas, 10S

12.50 p.m.

I can hear the stampeding feet behind me but I continue on, swiftly turning around the stairs. The footsteps are getting closer but I daren't turn around – every second is vital. I throw down my bag: any unnecessary weight must be lost. I thrust open the door at the end of the corridor and an icy cold blast of air smacked me in the face. I keep on running and a sharp left takes me through another set of doors. I weave in and out of the many obstacles – suddenly a crossroads. I have a choice now. Left or right? There is no time - I go left and at the end is my reward. A perfect slice of pizza with crispy golden chips on the side.

Sanat Kulkarni, Year 11

12.51 p.m.

I can feel the tension rising as the atmosphere builds and the different houses separate into groups. The captain's scream for control and the teams circle off into their houses circle. Respect, pressure and overall fright fill me and I can see into the opponent's eyes that they feel the pressure of a first house competition. I walk onto the pitch and shout encouragement this is the moment the captains see if their side was a worthwhile decision. The referee flips his coin and the kick is decided, silence, then the whistle.

Ralph Wills, 7H

12.52 p.m.

I am getting on the bus back to school in a good mood. I'm in a good mood because we won the house rugby. I look out the window at all the shops passing by me in a blink of an eye. I hear shouting and chatting in the background. I've just got back and I race to the line but I then notice that its only five past one so I decide to go and play dob with my friends. But I cant wait to get my fish and chips so I run back to the line.

James Stephens, 7s

12.53 p.m.

I am walking to the bakery to get a nugget and chips; walking into the bakery I grab a coke and order my nuggets and chips because I'm healthy. I am walking from the bakery to the art block to find out about the art trip to Edinburgh. When I get there I am confronted with the choice of more food that we are going to have in Edinburgh: a meal at Pizza Express. I find out about the trip; we are going to many modern art museums. I am going to enjoy it very much.

James Bell, 11T, age 15

12.54 p.m.

It is lunch time and I am bored due to a lack of interesting things to do at lunch. I would normally do football however the years football was kicked on the roof of the sports hall never to return, a bit like darth vader after he was killed. Because of this outrage I am forced to retreat to a form room where listen to music and then learn how to snap a pencil on my head. I am then encouraged to play fifa 13 on my ipod touch third generation, by Thomas Reilly (10s). I do this for the remaining time at lunch.

william gray, 10L

12.55 p.m.

I play Spiderman with my friends by running around the playground. I chase them around and pretend to spin a web over them so that I can catch them.

Raman Landa, 1B, Lovell House

12.55 p.m.

I walk into M5, hoisting my bag from my shoulder, and sling it under the desk I would sit at during my next lesson. Then, remembering my phone was still in my bag, I crouch under the desk and pick up my bag again, unzipping the front zip and pulling out my phone and placing it in my blazer pocket. I briskly walk out of M5 and next door to M4, where I see the lads sitting on the tables engaging in casual banter while Tom takes books out of his locker. I sit on one of the tables and join the conversation.

Sean Hill, 10L

12.56 p.m.

The blue sky hovers above me and the rays of sunlight uplift me as I walk to the music school. It reminds me about how fortunate I am at this moment of time. I then step into Room 13 to have a piano lesson. The principle of playing the piano is simple: pressing black and white keys to produce sounds. The difficult part is using the sounds to make a piece of music. And coordinating two hands at once are incredibly tricky. But I know that with practice I will find this much easier.

Timothy Lee, 10H

12.56 p.m.

I sit in the dining hall, with my chattering friends around me. Vinegar and fish fills the air reminding me of chip shops. Hearing the clatter of knives and forks on plates as people tuck into their lunch. My pals talk to me and I take my mind off the food; because of this, they leave before me.

Looking to the clock, it says 12.55, I have to bolt down my lunch otherwise I will be late for my lessons. Chewing the last mouthful, drop my tray off; when I swallow, I have my bag in my hand .GO!!!

Sean Kavanagh 7y

12.57 p.m.

The pressure is on. We were 15-0 down and now we are 20-20. This is the last kick of the game. It is a conversion. I have been elected to take it. I can feel my heart beating as fast as a cheetah chasing its prey. The referee has signalled this to be the last kick of the game. The whole of my team are relying on me. THUD. I kicked the ball. I can hear the screams in the background. Everybody is pouncing on me in joy. I have scored. We have won. One of the most dramatic matches in my life has just ended with me being victorious.

Sahrin Ahluwahlia, 7T, age 12

12.57 p.m.

I am surrounded by bits of paper in Studio One waiting for twenty boys to attend a meeting about the Art trip to Edinburgh next week except I only managed to tell the year elevens as I forgot to put notes into all form pigeon holes this morning. There are far too many bits of paper in my life and where are the students!?....I need to get and give information and they, most importantly, have to choose their pizza express food that I need to phone through yesterday. They eat a lot. I can see a repetitive long break ahead, four have just walked in. Sixteen to go!

Karen Skidmore, Head of Art

12.58 p.m.

Out in the Junior yard on duty once again. Sun shining and hardly a cloud in the sky, quite a change from the snowy weather we have seen recently. Most boys are still at lunch, but the younger boys begin to emerge, racing into the playground to enjoy their lunch break.

The Adventure Playground begins to fill with eager little boys playing on the Pirate Ship and swinging on the monkey bars.

More boys filter into sight and suddenly there are games being played everywhere; cricket, basketball, tennis. One small group of boys are having fun jumping over a skipping rope.

Mrs Lynne Sedgewick, Head of Maths, Junior School

12.58 p.m.

I run from the Junior School over to the Senior School sports hall, to get changed for Cross Country club and to practise for a race on Friday 8th. When I finish changing, Mr Allison drives us over to Wollaton Park, where we normally run. Then he tells us what we are focusing on.

Firstly, we run down to the lamp-post to jog between the first two lamp-posts then sprint to the third. After that we play a game which includes sprinting and jogging in a line.

For the final part of the session we jog lightly.

Ben Naish, 5A, Junior School

12.59 p.m.

Soon the bell is going to ring then I run around and put all the toys away. Then I line up in my class and we go back into school to do the register.

Shuban Yadavakrishnan, 1B, Lovell House

12.59 p.m.

I finish my lunch of sandwiches and a drink, clear it away, and then go out to play. It is mild weather outside. When I get outside, Hugo and Zachary are already there. They are playing a game of ropes which involves being tied up with skipping ropes. Later, Joe arrives and borrows a skipping rope to play a game of chariot races. This involves putting a rope around someone's chest and telling them where to go then yelling "CHARGE !". Soon after, Thomas comes along and once I spot him I have a game of Bashy with him.

Angus Timmons, Junior School pupil

1.00 p.m.

It is 1 o'clock and I am playing football in the yard with my friends. It is fairly warm but I cannot really tell because I am running around and I am hot.it is now 1.08pm and I am walking over to the dining hall door to queue up for lunch. Now I feel the cold, as I am not running around. I am very hungry and I wish that I had breakfast and the queue is huge. I just get my lunch and I sit down with my friends.

Tim Fitzsimmons, 9L

1.01 p.m.

I walk into the place where they are holding Schools Rugby trials. I feel nervous as I am warming up but then I start to feel more confident, I feel that I can beat men at will. Near the end the coach gives me a positive comment and my chest swells with pride. I only started rugby last year and important people are praising me already. I am so happy I could jump up and down on the spot for a very long time. I am also receiving praise from the other children that are there that makes my day.

Joseph Kenton, 8Y

1.01 p.m.

One to thirty minutes past 1 o'clock in my life stars with the ending of Games which in the first half of the spring term we carry with ruby till about 5 minutes passed one. We then get changed back into are school uniform and on go the bus back to school. When we reach school we rush to the canteen in hope to reach a substantially early place in the queue to lunch. When I have got are lunches I find the dilemma of who to sit with when have chosen I socialise till lunch ends.

Taylor Pearson, Senior School pupil

1.02 p.m.

My health is improving. As I sit on my sofa watching recordings of the golf, I wonder 'should I have gone in this morning?' A sick day at Nottingham High School is no easy decision. The next day's start with the relentless, non-believing attitudes of you peers hearing about your illness. Then lessons with 'have you copied up?' The guilt creeps in as I think about what lessons I am missing at this precise hour. The Quadratics test is a concern of mine, followed by the prospect of notes on Henry VI.

Tom Ravenscroft, 10T

1.03 p.m.

I am just about to go onto the bus after a close match in rugby.

I was in the whites in the B-team and we played Mellers and the score was 20-22. We only lost by two points! In the first half we were doing really well and winning 15-0. We scored three tries. However in the second half we only scored one more try and they scored four more tries. They were on the last conversion and if they got that conversion they would win and they did get the conversion. We were a good team but they were just a bit better. I wish we just scored one more try.

At the moment I am tired and hungry. I missed the first bus so now I have to wait even longer to be able to eat.

Louis Stravino, 7S

1.03 p.m.

I eat my delicious meal in the dining hall, I get ready for classes. But I still have a lot of free time left. So I go outside into the shining sun and blue skies. My friends and I take photos for the 500 year anniversary. After that I go on my phone to make a collage to send to the email for the 500 years photo. Still have quite a lot of time left. So I go to get a drink and a cookie. I also go to get a fizz fruit for my friend Tom Ward.

Henry Chiu, 8L

1.04 p.m.

I am queuing for lunch after a hard morning's work of English, French and Physics. I am being served my fish and chips very hungry and tired from a tough morning. 'Thanks chef' I say walking through the door to the tills. Having paid I walk into the bright open space which is the dining hall greeted by the loud and constant chatter from pupils hungry and excitable to enjoy their hour of freedom. I sit down and enjoy my food with the lads. Once my food is all gone I go outside for some nice fresh air.

Joe Williams, 11S

9. Lunchtime and Games

1.04 p.m.

Dripping with sweat and perspiration, I struggle to meet the physical and mental demands of our fitness training. We as a team are collectively very fit however; our coach wants to see we would react to challenges. We are hitting tackles bags hard and fast without much rest in between, and I am at the stage where I am looking is someone else to succumb so that I can do the same. We're going faster and quicker and I now see some people lagging behind. Stand up, run, tackle, and run back. I have now got into a zone that I almost cannot stop. I fall to the ground panting and fighting for breath. That is just an average day in Nottingham High School.

Kedem Morgan, 9H, age 14

1.05 p.m.

I am teaching GCSE Greek to Year 11. As usual, a couple of boys are late because they need to eat lunch first. As usual, it is necessary to go outside and tell boys in Year 8, who clearly do not like their form room being used for teaching, to be quiet a couple of times. We are working through prose literature, Herodotus' account of the Battle of Salamis. An interesting text, but lots of military specific vocabulary. The boys are working hard – it takes a lot of effort for them to study an extra GCSE in their spare time.

Mr Ben Harrison, Classics Teacher and Head of Year 13

1.06 p.m.

I am playing house rugby for Coopers A team. I am playing as winger and have hardly had a touch of the ball so far, but now I might have a chance, as the player with the ball is right next to me. We are losing 10-5 at the moment, but we will come back. It's a shame that there aren't many really good players in Coopers, and I am not looking forward to playing Whites next week. I am going to get really muddy, if I don't watch out, and I do not want to go in the showers.

Daniil Gerov, 7L, age 12

1.07 p.m.

I finish my intense rugby match on a cold winters day and I'm ready to go back to school, however I get changed as fast as I can to catch the first bus as I'm starving because I haven't eaten since breakfast. I look out of the window on my way back into the far distance. I'm thinking about how I could have made my performance more effective. We finally reach the school and I rush to the lunch queue. I can smell the steaming hot fish and chips in the dining hall.

Daniel Sterling, 7H, aged 11

1.08 p.m.

At break I play hockey as I'm part of the team. Playing defensive midfield I have to protect the defence while still dictating play with my natural creative flair. The opposition have the ball and we are penned in our D. Our team now win the ball and smack it out wide left. I make a central run and receive the ball, drag it right past one person and play a "beaut" of a through ball to the wider. He continues his run, as do I, and we play around their best defender, Josh Kerry-Smith, with a cheeky one-two. I receive it back on the top of their D with Josh breathing down my back and the goalkeeper charging at me. I lob it over the keeper but Josh predicts it, runs round him and was about to hit it out; but then he got cramp!!!

Dylan Mistry, age 17

1.09 p.m.

Time to get some lunch.

Susan Ford, cleaning manager

1.10 p.m.

A typical Friday lunchtime at Valley Road…..

The Year 7 pupils depart on the bus to enjoy the last sitting of school lunch PE staff can enjoy 40 minutes of peace prior to the Junior School pupils arriving at 13.50. Simon Payne, Stuart Whitehead and myself enjoy a sandwich, a cup of tea and an opportunity to chat about our week and indeed the weekend ahead. Soon enough Paul Allison and the Junior School staff arrive, followed immediately by a tsunami style wave of excited 7-11 year olds whose sea of smiles make for a very pleasant end to the week for all involved.

Mark Baker, school cricket coach

1.10 p.m.

Ten minutes past one o'clock, and the bell echoes down the down the corridor. Nerves building, anticipation waits, a voice calls; 'next!' I walk in to the newly developed Drama studio, a single light illuminates the vast space. The director says 'Read this please.' It is a passage from the infamous Canterbury Tales by Geoffrey Chaucer. My voice fills the room and unaware of its immense volume, I am transported back to London 1387, the time in which the play was written. Lines delivered; articulately spoken, the audition is over. I am brought back to modern day, February 1st 2013. 500 years from the day in which Nottingham High School was founded by Dame Agnes Mellers.

William.G.Robinson, 11Y

1.11 p.m.

I go and line up because the bell has rung. I am in Year 1. We line up between 1S and Year 2.

Ben French, 1B, Lovell House

1.12 p.m.

I'm running a fast as possible towards the double doors that lead to lunch the queue. On today's menu: an option of either pizza or fish and chips. In my opinion, there is no competition; the school's pizza is not nice, trust me. So as I am approaching the food my eyes widen. I'm starving. Eventually I get to the front and ask for a fish (without Lemon). Then, I transfer myself to the other 'food counter' and ask for a full plate of chips and beans, delicious. I quickly walk past the dessert counter, trying not to be tempted into getting one and then grab my cutlery. I also take a plastic cup and two packets of ketchup. Then I place my thumb on the scanner and after a few, long seconds later my details appear on the screen. Disaster! I haven't got enough money to pay. Oh.

Matthew Taberham, 9H, age 13

1.13 p.m.

Yum! I love chicken wings and herby diced potatoes. I often try to snatch at least three ketchups from the counter when I'm buying my food. I walk along the dining hall, holding my tray and looking for a table to sit at, preferably with some friends. I sit at a deserted table, seeing as I was one of the first people to come in for my sitting and get my lunch. Soon, other guys in my year come and sit at my table and keep me company. Stomach full, I leave the dining hall to get ready for lessons.

Ivan Ellis, 8T

1.13 p.m.

The bell rings and I stood still I am being told to put the toys away. The bell rings again and I am walking to line up the hill and lining up in 2W`s line. I am being collected by Mrs Williams and going to 2W`s classroom. I am sitting on the carpet and waiting to answer the register where I say good afternoon Mrs Williams. Jacob and Ashley are giving out the mental maths books and I am going to sit down in my afternoon place.

Rohan Banerjea, Year 2, Lovell House

1.14 p.m.

We are sitting tangled in a web of unidentifiable cables. Welcome to this week's session of Stage Staff - mission: to be able to identify these cables and to know their uses. With no prior knowledge, our aim is to come away a cables expert. After identifying and re-identifying them we move up to the Mixing Desk where we look for where to plug them in and discover what they do. Finally we learn how to set up the Amp with the Mixing Desk and end up with the voice of Aretha Franklin echoing around the Founder Hall, deserted apart from us.

Jacques Lachetta, 10H

1.15 p.m.

I am waiting in the lunch queue, I am starving we have 15 minutes until the doors open. The air is tense, we all know that when those doors open only one of us can get in their first. Until "Hey don't push in" I say but the rest just keep on pushing and pushing into the queue until we are 10 places back. We wait for a while until we say to ourselves if we can't beat 'em join 'em. So we walk to near the front and say "sorry just reading the menu" and then *DINGG* we are first in just by pushing slightly to the front!

Thomas Tristram, 7S

1.16 p.m.

When I get on the bus to go to games I am excited about another game of rugby. To be honest I did not like it when I first started, but each week it grows on me. Now I love it, even more since I got moved up into the A team. My favourite is when you get the ball and start running to score a try. However, it is not so good when someone comes in with a bone crunching tackle. Once, in a match, Josh did a smashing tackle and it really hurt. But not today, today they'll not catch me…

George Renton, Junior School pupil

1.17 p.m.

My mates and I have just accomplished the human pyramid with a great deal of success. All of us have worked up a great appetite and are eager to have lunch. However we realise that we still have 15 minutes to wait. There is only one thing that there is to do at this time, 'Fifa 13 on iPhone'!! I chose to go for a penalty shoot-out. I am Arsenal, and choose to play against the legendary Danish team, AC Horsens . First to step up for me is Olivier Giroud, I choose to shoot bottom corner, luckily I score. Now, H. Toft steps up for them, he slots the ball down the middle and I dive to the left, It is 1-1, my iPhone is out of battery so I will have to resume this game later.

Tom Reilly, 10S

1.18 p.m.

I am perusing the shelves of the City library searching through the few linguistics related books to aid in the onerous task of finding research for the Extended Project Qualification. I give up trying to find anything directly relevant and so grab a horde of books off the shelf and start scanning them through. My bag looks fit to burst with its bulky load and I am left trudging slowly back to school.

Hari Prabu, age 18

1.19 p.m.

We are doing the register. Mrs Baker says my name and I say 'Good afternoon'.

Alex Barish, 1B, Lovell House

1.20 p.m.

As I approach 1.20 on Friday afternoon, I feel a slight chill as I go outside to play football. At last our year has a football to play with, which is a shock as no one ever brings one in. I am really enjoying our game. Suddenly the ball is kicked onto the roof of the sports hall. Game over. I always knew that it would not last long as no game of football does when

I play. When the dismal game ends, I trudge inside to my classroom. In there I take out my IPod and start to talk to my friends.

Samuel Bowling, 8L

1.21 p.m.

J'aime arriver le lundi matin un peu plus tôt que les autres jours car j'utilise ce laps de temps afin d'imprimer les diverses activités en relation avec les thèmes. En règle générale, ce sont des activités que je trouve ou bien crée pendant le week-end .C'est un moment où j'apporte les dernières finitions aux travaux et où j'essaye d'imaginer comment je vais pouvoir exploiter ces documents au maximum, en faisant parler les élèves le plus possible et en essayant de les intéresser sur des sujets qui ne leur parlent pas forcément au premier abord. Une fois cette étape faite, c'est parti pour la semaine !

Laetitia Foureur, Assistante de français

1.22 p.m.

Languishing in E10 supervising work detention. Taste of fish in mouth, smell of vinegar on fingers are precursors of the weekend. Contemplating Saturday's agenda: refereeing U12 Rugby, watching two Six Nations matches, Party in the Quad. Might buy a new suit tonight. Tired. Sounds of whooping boys in corridor. Vibrating pipework in the corner. I was sitting in the same room thirty-six years ago in a sixth-form English lesson. Doesn't time fly when you're having fun?!

Andrew Winter, teacher

1.23 p.m.

I start my mental maths test with question one and it is really easy. I am doing questions 2, 3 and 4 and it`s getting harder and harder. I`m on question 5, 6 and 7 and they are getting very hard but I`m getting to 8, 9 and 10 are more difficult. Unfortunately 11 and 12 are extremely difficult.

Jacob Corne, Year 2, Lovell House

1.24 p.m.

I walk back across the car park and play cricket with Alexander for ten minutes. He starts batting so I only have one choice… to bowl. Alex says,"On 20 runs people always get me out and it is not going to happen this time". When I am on my fourth ball he has already hit three sixes, then he hits a two so he is on twenty. On my fifth ball he is out, and in the end he has twenty runs! There is a silence and then we both laugh. I say," I'm going to hit a six on my first go!" but instead of hitting a six, I am bowled out!

Akshat Singh, 3M, Junior School

1.25 p.m.

I'm outside in the school yard and I'm playing football with the Year 8's and some Year 10's (Mixed teams of Year 8's and Year 10's). My team are losing heavily but are dominating the match with commanding attacks but the other team are great on the counter attack. I barely have a touch of the ball before I get a chance to take a corner, I take a short corner but my teammate can't make the most of his chance. I have a chance at scoring a goal but the opponent's goalkeeper makes a good save and my team lose 6-2 in the end. Unlucky I think that we lost when really we should have won.

Liam McQuillan, 8H, age 12

1.26 p.m.

Rushing, rushing, rushing down the corridor to get set up for the competition. Will the boys come? Will they even remember? Get the computer set up! The wires, the plugs, the screen! Eat your lunch! Stuff it down! There's not long now before we must start. And then I see them start to arrive. A small huddle of lads. I sense the excitement. Who will win this Spelling Bee? And still they come…more and more Year 7s. Far more than I thought. And the first boy steps up nervously, tentatively to compete and his friends cheer and we smile.

Vicky Pidgeon, Head of French

1.27 p.m.

After lunch we did Handwriting and learned how to form my letters correctly, writing on the lines. Our handwriting books are red.

Chris Mok, 1B, Lovell House

1.28 p.m.

"The chips are dry ,there arn't enough beans and the fish is bredded. I'm going to start brining my own BBQ source".

Sam Lawrence, 11S

1.29 p.m.

Once lunch has finished everyone goes to their classrooms and gets their games kit and then registers. Everyone lines up in their year groups and then gets onto the buses. The buses take us to valley road where we get changed into our kits to play some rugby. We learn how to ruck, we have a demonstration where Dillon imagines he is being tackled, but he head-buts the rugby pad and we all laugh. Then Josh does it properly and we all copy. At the end of the lesson we play a rugby game, we then all get changed and go home.

Matthew Bousfield, Junior School pupil

1.30 p.m.

DT, 1.30 p.m. The deadline to finish my circuit board is becoming ever closer. Sweats drips from me. TICK TOCK TICK TOCK TICK TOCK TICK TOCK. I'm almost done but now I have only 10 minutes left. I solder the last components on and finish with 2 minutes to spare. Will it work? I attach the power to it and connect it to the computer. Disaster! The circuit doesn't work. I realise I forgot to turn the power on. Time for Attempt 2. It still doesn't work. It looks like I'll have to make a new circuit board.

Anouj Rajput, 11T

1.30 p.m.

Carry on with the references. Time soon passes and Dagmara arrives at 2.45p.m. to start cleaning the sixth form centre. Catch a few minutes asking Dagmara about her outfit for the party and who her guest is. She is bringing her mum, and says that she is very excited to be coming to such an event.

Susan Ford, cleaning manager

1.30 p.m.

As soon as the bell goes, all the Year groups from Year three to six grab their games bags for Rugby at Valley Road Sports Field. My trip there is on the top deck of the High School bus with my friend, Tom Barlow.

It is a cold, crisp, sunny day and I am shivering in my hooped rugby top and shorts. During the game, I am passed the ball. I feel excited and scared as I am running as fast as I can. My heart is pounding and at the end of my run, I am tackled, and am out of breath.

Nathan Harbinson, 5A, Junior School

1.31 p.m.

Frozen, I stand between the traffic cone and the green rubbish bin. It's the typical makeshift goal, and I am certainly a makeshift goalkeeper. Even on a good day, I don't consider myself the most agile, but with the chilling wind on my hands and face; this isn't the place to be. A shot dribbles towards me along the rough surface and I gingerly bend down to claim it. Disaster. The ball somehow evades my grasp and rolls kindly into the path of the striker to slot home, much to the amusement of my peers. 'I quit', I announce with a laugh. I've had enough embarrassment for one day.

Ollie Hayes, 11S

1.31 p.m.

I've finished my mental maths. I am swapping my book with Vuyo and Mrs Williams is giving me the answers to the questions on the board. I am marking the answers and I know I have one wrong and the question is what is the difference between 17 and 35. I have my book back and my score is 11 out of 12.

Zayan Baig, Year 2, Lovell House

1.31 p.m.

On Friday we leave our school at 1.30 get on the bus to go to Valley road to have our games lesson at 1.45 and get changed untill the time is 2.00 and go outside and play some warm up games like a jog around one or two laps a rugby pitch.

Then we play some tag rugby and do some pop passes with partners and then we play some quite long passes. After that we play a really fun game of tag rugby on the furthest rugby pitch away from the pavilion. Then we play tag witch is were have two courts which we play the game just like dob but with tags and when someone pulls your tag off they have to shout tag then it to go back to school.

Ethan Rathour, 3W, Junior School

1.32 p.m.

Penned up in a classroom, I laugh jovially with friends, watching school life unfold around me. Football outside, bell rings protruding from outside, as excited Year 7's prepare for the seeming highlight of their day, the school dinner. I see phones and iPod's buzzing around me, while a plethora of games and music are conveyed from them. There are pupils hastily putting together homework for the next lesson, as well as worried students doing last minute revision for the chemistry test. It is just a snippet of the world of Nottingham High School, a broad spectrum of learning, sport and entertainment.

Jack Sweeting, 10S

1.32 p.m.

On Friday I have Games, which is a triple lesson. I have a lot of fun at Games and we travel there on a double-decker bus. On the way there I sit on the bottom of the bus sadly, but when I come back to school I sit at the top of the bus!

When I arrive home, I prepare my bedroom because my nan and grandpa are coming from Birmingham. It takes one hour to reach Nottingham from Birmingham; I can't wait to see them. I am extremely excited to see them for a weekend!

Akash Singh, 3, Junior School

1.33 p.m.

I stalk the corridors alone, a drifting cell cloud. The walls peel past. I bank left, through the door and into the yard. With one eye on the tennis balls shooting across my path, I beeline for the Art Block, and make it inside unscathed. Upstairs, the 6th Form studio is locked, but the lock is very bad, so I open the door anyway. I layout paints and brushes and work on coursework : an image of a towering scaffold tyrant looming over a destroyed city.

Ben Brown, Sixth Form pupil

1.33.p.m.

Ravenous so get baguette from the sixth form brasserie.

Carla O'Brien, Head of Learning Support

1.34 p.m.

The hockey players in year's 5-6 come to the science lab with their equipment to get ready for this lesson. At 2.00pm everyone is ready and we all walk through the senior school playground to the sports hall where we catch up with Mrs Whittamore. We start with push passing to each other in pairs taking it slow but then we go into matches to show of our stuff.

This is extremely fun and I enjoy being at an amazing and enjoyable school for many years to come and for lifetime.

Hari Sagoo, 5A, Junior School

1.35 p.m

It is 1.35pm and I am departing for the playing fields at Valley Rd with my friends. We walk past the Senior School and past the stairs that lead up to the Founder Hall .We frog march past the war hero statue which stands there silently gazing at us and we go out of the front entrance, onto the sidewalk. 3 huge buses with our school name on have pulled up in front of the teachers. Year 5 go on the second bus. I am the first person to climb on the bus so I have a seat right at the front. When all of the boys have been seated and we have strapped ourselves in, the buses set off. The bus is filled with laugher and noise and we are ready to wrestle with mud!

Aadam israr, 5a, Junior School

1.35 p.m.

After we get changed for hockey in the science lab, we walk over to the sports hall where Mrs Whittamore is eagerly awaiting us. We start the hockey lessons by doing some warm ups with running. I am going to talk about the 15 mins of warming up. My most enjoyable warm up is where there are 6 cones. The first person has to run to the 1st cone. The second person has to run to the second cone and so on.

Nikhil Raj, 5A, Junior School

1.36 p.m.

We travel by bus to the Games field, but I cannot do rugby because I have an ulcer where my gum-guard is. It is torture to wear the gum-guard so I am excused from Games. The day is icy, so in way, I am glad to be excused.

My mum cannot pick me up because she is at her special Arabic lesson. I sit and read in the pavilion but the window is open and so I am rather cold.

William Tsang, 5A, Junior School

1.37 p.m.

I am in the DT block drilling my PCB for my GCSE project after finishing my lunch of fish and chips. After 10 minutes I have finished the drilling and after consulting Mr Thomas press forward with my project by starting the soldering. To my left sits Sanjay crouched over his project focusing intently on the task in hand. After a further 10 minutes I have finished my soldering for the day successfully finishing my resistor soldering, I stride out triumphantly into the playground to seek my reward of Sainsbury cookies, pleased with my lunchtimes work.

Isaac Carlisle, 11S

1.38 p.m.

On Friday 1st February 2013 all of the years go down to Valley road to play rugby. The year 4's learn how to ruck. I have really enjoyed the new year of rugby because we have started contact. We have a new teacher called Mr Dickson because Mr Allison is teaching the year 5's and 6's play hockey if they don't want to play rugby. At the end of the lesson we play a big match. We are split into 4 teams, I am the captain of my team, I have to arrange all the positions for people on my team.

Josh Shaw, 4C, Junior School

1.39 p.m.

I walk down the corridor towards my classroom, when I pass two boys. They ask me if I'm going to W22.

"Yeah, why?"

"Don't change anything, leave it as it is. It's hilarious!"

I note their comments and carry on. Entering the room, I discover that every single chair is facing the back wall! I chuckle to myself and decide to take a photo, as a possibility of submitting it for the 500 year celebrations. The camera on my phone clicks as a photo is taken. I laugh again, moving slowly over to my locker to take out my books.

Jack Hadfield, 11Y

1.40 p.m.

We depart to Valley Road for our games session. When we arrive we eagerly talk about what might happen on the games field today. It is muddy in places when we walk across the pitches and we are split into our usual groups. I am in the B group with all my other friends and then we start with our actual lesson. Mr Shaw is our teacher and he teaches us to perform a ruck in this session.

To do a ruck we have to use tackling pads to prevent hurting ourselves. When a player in my team is tackled to the ground he lies sideways and holds the ball in such a way that we can get hold of the ball. However, as this happens the opposition try to snatch the ball for themselves. In the ruck the tackler's team-mates cannot touch the ball directly but we are allowed to pick up the ball if we are on our feet.

Soon the games session is over and it is time to go back to school. We are tired but have had lots of fun.

Abhishek Thakar, 4, Junior School

1.40 p.m.

I do not know what to do. I had sat down a few minutes earlier and started my lunch. By this time I am sitting in the same place with my friends finishing off my lunch and chatting. We then decide to go and play hide and seek outside. But unfortunately it is my turn to be on this time.

I count to fifty and wait for my friends to run away and hide. I start with the west block as that is where they would normally hide and then I make my way across to the east block where I find them. They have all decided to hide together. It is simple, try and dob as many people as possible. In the end I think I tagged 3 of them and then we manage to find where the others' new hiding place was.

Owain Dunn, 8L

1.41 p.m.

We do Games every Monday and Friday. On the school bus to Valley Road, I am Joshua Lloyd's partner. We talk to each other a bit, then we notice that we are already at Valley Road.

Next we go to the changing room and change quickly into our rugby kit. After that, we walk to the games field to start rugby. For the warm up we run two laps of the rugby pitch, then we all put on our tag belts, ready for two tag rugby matches. The first match we draw 1-1, the next match our team win 3-2.

Finally we have a warm shower, dress nicely and go home. We have an exciting and tiring Friday.

Milad Fadakar-Bany, 3W, Junior School

1.42 p.m.

I'm out in the yard on lunch duty – it's a mixed blessing. It's so cold again today, but there's space and time to stop and think. I'm thinking about how to capture the day with an image and suddenly remember I should try to do so in words too – it's not my medium. What a simple and timeless scene it is; a group of boys rushing round in pursuit of the ball, playing by rules that they seem to intrinsically understand and respect. They've got themselves organised, don't need any encouragement or intervention and are happy to put in real effort. Now how can we capture that and bring it inside?

Mrs Gill Riley

1.43 p.m.

In Handwriting we write letters neatly. We write with a sharp pencil. I like Handwriting.

Kapil Krishanand, 1B, Lovell House

1.44 p.m.

I've finished marking my mental maths I've got 8 out of 12. Rayan is collecting the books in to give to Mrs Williams and I am being given my Handwriting book. I am watching Mrs Williams form the letters on the board which are oe, oa, ow and she is asking anyone to give some words with those letters in them. I am now writing the words that are on the board they are toad, store and foal I think my writing is looking neat and tidy.

Krrish Mehrotra, Year 2, Lovell House

1.45 p.m.

We all arrive on the bus back from the playing fields, aching from our big house Rugby match. We rush to the dining hall, flinging our bags onto the bag racks. It's Friday, fish and chips day. We all push and shove to get into the queue, our mouths' watering at the thought of hot food. I eventually get to the front of the meandering line of hungry pupils and teachers. Luckily, I get the final fish of the batch. I find a seat next to my friends and dig into my lunch. I chat and have a bit of post-match banter with the other players before finishing off my food and walking to my locker to get my books for the next lesson. Let's see... French, Maths, Latin. All as boring as each other...

Tom Whittingham, 7S

1.46 p.m.

Lunch has just ended. I have finished doing some last minute biology refreshing before my test on the on the heart and tubes, e.g. arteries and veins.

During lunch I spend most of my time fine-tuning our groups robot for the VEX robotics tournament on Tuesday.

As I walk to the science block a swift breeze sweeps my revision notes right from my hands. After retrieving them I continue on my way to lessons. As I come into biology the second bell rings. I have just made it. I take my seat on the second row as the tests are being handed out. Time to se what I have learned.

Alex Carroll, 9L

1.47 p.m.

I wipe the sweat from my brow and mutter under my breath. The ball fizzes past me and I watch as Ben intercepts the wayward pass and lays the ball off to me. This high octane environment is the weekly 2nd team hockey training session, and I, for one moment at least, am in control of the ball. I attempt to slip Neel through on goal and as the ball bobbles and skids across the sports hall floor it looks to be perfect, but just before Neel collects it the pass is cut off by the scrambling defender. I wipe my brow again. The sports hall is always warm at lunchtime.

Charlie Flear, 11L

1.48 p.m.

A double lesson on the inter-war German economy is over, a sandwich and drink hastily consumed, and a dozen Year Seven exercise books are gladly dropped onto the 'marked' pile. Soon the two o'clock bell will sound, summoning me back to the classroom and the complexities of Tudor England with Year Eight. For now, I allow myself fifteen minutes of blissful relaxation, in which my thoughts drift to the river and the sight of hungry trout, sipping in Large Dark Olives, at the start of what will hopefully be another productive season with the fly rod.

Dr Clark Colman, teacher of History

1.49 p.m.

I have decided to write about our Games session at Valley Road.

As soon as you get off the bus, you know you're in for a good time. The 100m sprint courses are spotless and all of the equipment is neatly packed to the side.

When you get onto the games field, you get a rush of excitement as you start the fun activities that make up your games session. Firstly, we normally start with a heart-working warm-up. Secondly we begin our activity then bring that into the game.

Personally, games are overall exceedingly enjoyable.

Frazer Lim, 5A, Junior School

1.50 p.m.

It is time for the boys to get ready for PE. They go into the cloakroom a few at a time to collect their PE bags. Now the fun begins! All of the boys start to undress and get their PE kits out of their bags. They are getting changed into black tracksuit bottoms and black and white striped rugby shirts, with trainers. Some of the boys are finding it tricky to independently get changed, but they are having fun 'dressing' the chair with the clothes they take off. This helps to avoid clothes getting lost and keeps them in one place! Finally all boys are ready, and they line up for their PE lesson. Their PE teacher comes to collect them (Mr Farman) and off they go. Half an hour's peace ahead, while I write this week's class blog with a coffee!

Julie Higgins, Reception teacher, Lovell House

1.51 p.m.

We are sat in the warm changing rooms, sheltered from the arctic winds outside. My teammates and I, that is. Nottingham High School Hockey 2nd

XI is our official title. Friday training sessions pit the team against each other in an epic battle for personal pride. We've just finished; now, drenched in sweat as though we've just been on every ride in a water park, we sit slumped. The energy-draining heat in here leaves you reflecting on the performance and – I don't mean to boast – I usually enjoy the four or five goals I score. It keeps me going!

Ben Maher, Year 11

1.52 p.m.

On Friday we go to the Games field. When we arrive, we go into the changing rooms and we get changed and talk for a bit, while we are waiting for our teacher to arrive. Then some names are called. My name is called out but only the better rugby players' names are called out. I am very pleased. We go out to get the equipment then we make our way across the field. Afterwards we do a warm up and we have to jog around two rugby pitches. It is extremely windy, but I still come fourth in the warm up.

Zak Ilyas, 3, Junior School

1.53 p.m.

Football continues against the year 9s. Check the watch, ten minutes until I have to go to lessons. Double English.

The crucible- what a bore! Walk in to W21 and pack my bag for lessons. Only two hours until the weekend. I can't wait. Enter the classroom and sit down.

Turn around and talk to 'the clever ones' whilst the English teacher walks in. We start the crucible and I look at the clock.

It feels like an hour has passed but it has only been five minutes. It feels like the weekend is never going to come.

Lewis Dickinson, 11Y

1.54 p.m.

I go to my music lesson in the music room and sing monster songs and play maracas with Mrs Kavalec. I learn some new songs today with my friends. Then I go to Games with Mr Farman.

Nikhil Sanghera, 1B, Lovell House

1.55 p.m.

On a Friday afternoon, the whole Junior School goes down to Valley Road Games fields. We travel there by double decker buses after lunchtime. The weather is sunny but cold. We get changed and afterwards we split into our groups. For the first exercise we run around the field. Then we practise our rucks. One person holds a tackling pad and the other person tackles them. They fall on the ground and hold up the ball so that their team can grab the ball. Then we have a mini game of rugby.

Zachary Rudd, 4c, Junior School

1.55 p.m.

It is a cold, bright afternoon at Valley Road and Junior School Games has begun. I am taking the Year 4 Rugby group and we are just beginning to develop our skills in rucking. The weather is incredibly windy today and this is making the boys excitable... it also means that stray passes could lead to the ball being blown away! Still, the boys are enjoying themselves as they practise charging into tackling pads, cleaning out arriving players, and being able to run into each other at speed without breaking any school rules.

Richard Shaw, teacher, Junior School

1.56 p.m.

I am doing my handwriting and writing oe, oa, ow on one line at a time. I am now copying the words from the board which are toad, foal and store my writing is looking good and I am keeping in the lines. I am now collecting in the books with Toyan. I am now going to lining up for chess and am standing in the middle of the line

Rayan Mammood, Year 2, Lovell House

1.57 p.m.

I walk from the dining hall, collect my bag and walk to E4. I wait outside the classroom for my Latin teacher. I go inside and prepare for the lesson. I am told we are going to take part in a reading challenge and to get into our groups. My group and I rehearse and practice, then listen to the three other group's performances. We then do our performance and then review other groups. We wait for our Latin teacher to tell us the results. He tells us our results and I am fortunate to go through to the final.

Simon Onions, 7H, age 12

10. Mainly Rugby

1.58 p.m.

Firstly we jog on to the pitch at Valley Road playing fields in our rugby kit. It is extremely cold with a howling wind. We split up into our groups, the 'B' game and the 'A' game. I am in the 'A' game with Josh and Matthew.

We do warm- up exercises, then we practise our rucks and we do well. After that we play a game which is mixed up of A players and B players. I am hooker.

The game goes very fast and suddenly Mr Shaw blows the whistle loudly. The final score is 1-1.
We are all muddy and tired. We have hot showers and get back into our uniforms.

Harry Easton, 4, Junior School

1.59 p.m.

Dyslexic year 10 boy needs to learn history topics and we try using his phone to record the information. Eureka it works!

Carla O'Brien, Head of Learning Support

2.00 p.m.

It's 2 o'clock. The bells echo round the school to let us know that lunch is over and that it is time for our next lesson. My friend is informing me that the next lesson will not be just any normal period six but that a special guest is coming into school. We are being instructed by our form teacher,

Dr Burton, to make our way as quickly as we can to the large lecture theatre. Thoughts start to race through my mind. I have no idea of who this visitor could be or even if there is a visitor and not just a teacher who wants to tell us off. So with only two minutes to go I switch off my phone and head to my class where I am going to be registered. So, we arrive at the large lecture theatre, gasping for breath from the stairs I have just run up. I catch my breath, sit down with my class and wait for the arrival of our special guest, completely oblivious to who is going to walk through the door.

Samir Sanghera, 8L

2.00 p.m.

At the moment we're doing rugby. We have been tackling, passing, scrums and my favourite smashing through people's defence. This time the A and B groups are mixed together to make it a fair match. At first I didn't know how to play rugby but now I know the rules and can get involved more. We are with a teacher called Alex who is replacing Mr Simpson. I enjoy this session because we haven't played many matches and we have more scrums than usual.

I think Rugby's the best!

Euan Lim, Junior School pupil

2.00 p.m.

I come down the stairs from 2W classroom to chess in the after school room. I walk in and see Mr Williams and he tells me to find a partner to play. I ask Naveen if he will be my partner. I go over to the table with Naveen where there is a chess board. I sit down with Naveen. Naveen makes a move, I make my move with a pawn. Naveen makes a move with his Knight and takes my pawn.

Vuyo Mukange, Year 2, Lovell House

2.01 p.m.

I hear the bell ring and think that it is the 3rd sitting bell. I look at the bell and see that it is the end of lunch. It isn't possible. I have only just sat down. I put my tray away and head for the door. I get my bag and go to maths. I realise that I have physics next so I go to get my P.E bag. I walk through the door and see that only half of the class is there. I get my books and pencil case out and sit down. I look at the board. OH NO! We are handing in homework. I get my exercise book and start to skip through pages. I get to the last page and realise I haven't done it. The teacher walks up to me and asks me for the homework. I look down and flip through my book. All of a sudden I see a page stuck together. I open it and realisr that I have done the homework. I let out a sigh of relief. I proudly hand it to the teacher and write down the title. I then pray that I have done the physics homework.

Abarnan Koneswaran, 8S, age 13

2.01 p.m.

I leave the classroom as the five minute bell rings, I have already packed my bags, and I head down the stairs talking to some friends as I make my way towards the last few lessons of the day. It's unfortunate, however, that the first of these is double maths. That's 4500 seconds of pure boredom, and it ticks away incredibly slowly. I leave the classroom, however, with only 40 minutes left until home time. As I wander into the next class aimlessly the penny drops, we have homework due in this lesson, but I can't remember whether I have done it.

Jack Wildgust, 11S

2.01 p.m.

Fantastic! Another afternoon of exhilarating rugby. Fresh air, sunlight, freedom!

The 'B' group (the group I am in) are split into perfectly fair teams. I am ready to embrace the pain as my friends are now, temporarily, my enemies!

Yousef runs at me with great pace, ready to score a try, but there is only one thing blocking his way... ME! He runs straight towards me as I know my team are counting on me to push him back. We collide with ferocious impact. I know I am not strong enough to take him down on my own, but with adrenaline and pressure I push him back onto his own ground. At the very end of the tiring match we draw three all!

Ben Webster, 5A, Junior School

2.02. p.m.

The end of the day's growing near, but what is that I have next, double Maths? Great. An hour and a half of solving pointless equations and theories I will have no use for in future life. But what can you do; it must be done. I take my seat, get my books out and the lesson begins. Fortunately, we get on with our teacher and have a laugh and a joke before we really got on with the hard graft. Today's lesson? Trigonometry, my favourite. The phrase "time flies when you're having fun" came to mind; however in this instance it wasn't the case.

Kam Khalil, Year 11

2.02 p.m.

Today is the School's 500th Birthday. After assembly and when all the writing subjects are completed we go to valley road [the games field]. When year 5 have got changed group 1 stage down the stairs and I think it is group 2, so I follow. When group 1 start doing their activity David walks over he has followed me, then David sees group 2 strolling along so we sprint over there but then they are just walking to the pitch straight next to Mr Bakers group 1 that makes angry later. After games I am really muddy and tired. I reluctantly go to the changing room.

Henry Robson, 5S, Junior School

2.02 p.m.

My 20 minutes of my day are about hockey. Hockey this week is with Mrs Whittamore and we learn the skill of dribbling. We play a match with teams of 6. In my team there are Thom, Alex, Harry B, Kasim, David and myself. We play two matches, win one and lose the other one. The first match is not easy, however the second match that we play goes well. After that we change back into our uniforms.

Everyone is excited because it is the 500th anniversary and we all know that this day will go down in history.

Matthew Justice, 6S, Junior School

2.03 p.m.

Reaching W2 after a short walk from my set of lockers, I take my seat between Bhaskar and Simon. I immediately unpack my utensils before Mr Grant strides boldly into the room; consequently, we all rise from our chairs. Mr Grant politely asks us to sit, and he then commences the register. After the register, we recap what we covered last lesson before reading about a "haruspex" (or soothsayer) who read the future by examining the entrails of dead animals. After a gruesome few minutes learning about these gruesome people, we study the ancient Roman gods and goddesses.

Nyle Cockell, 9Y

2.03 p.m.

I receive the prize for the most house points for Tonkin's in the previous three weeks. This is in form period. I give in more than ten stars and also get a merits certificate equalling 10 house points. I work very hard on maths, English, RE, MFL, ICT, games, music, swimming, history, PE, PSHE, science, maths ICT, art, chess and geography. The prize for each house is received by a student in form 3W. This is very special for Miss Walster and I am very pleased. Nottingham high school is five hundred years old and I am very proud to be a pupil here.

Charlie Varcoe, 3W, Junior School

2.03 p.m.

I line up patiently outside the library doors. The voice of Mrs.Wheeler, our English teacher, calls us in. Enthusiastically, we all enter....

A vast array of colourful books, immediately strike me, exciting my senses. Enticed, I wonder what to read... After many book proposals, my eyes move towards the shelf labelled 'F'. I settle for an Ian Fleming novel, a Bond book: 'The Man with the Golden Gun'. Picking up the volume, I stride over to my customary seat, on the last table...my little nook; my treasured time.

A few notices later, opening the book, I begin to read...And Action!

Ziyaad Surtee, 7Y

2.04 p.m.

I finish my break in which I have pizza. I arrive to my art lesson on time and quickly settle down to continue my art project on 'Animal Studies.' I do this on my table with Jyzu; a fellow peer. Our table is, however, quite clogged up with miss' books and so we feel it appropriate to move them. I search into my pockets to find my headphones but remember my phone doesn't have much music on. I am saddened by this but continue to work and instead talk to Jyzu. I enjoy the art lesson.

Jed Mellors, 10H

2.04 p.m.

On Friday I do Games at 2:00-2:30pm. In Games we are doing Tag Rugby and Oscar scores 1 all. Then he tries to score again but Mr Coldwell blows the whistle. We come to him because the game has finished. Mr Smith says his game was awful. After that he says, "Next time I want everyone to listen, now everyone to the changing rooms! I want everyone ready in 10 minutes."

When I get on the bus, I have to sit at the top next to my friend Luca because the bottom is full.

The tree branches crash on the windows as the bus goes on the road.

Mojetoluwa Shonde, Junior School pupil

2.05 p.m.

"Aah Jack mon, where have you been ? try and get here on time ! " I get out my booklet and we start to discuss if judges are neutral and independent from the executive. I am looking forward to the end of the lesson so I can leave promptly and dash home. I then have to quickly get changed and return to school to get the school bus to my friend's house. I always look forward to my two free periods on a Friday afternoon.

Jack Green, 6Me 1

2.05 p.m.

after lunch I walk to Music and we do different types of composition like homophony.

Lucas Wilcock, 10S

2.05 p.m.

As I run out on to the games field on a cold crisp afternoon, I am wondering if 500 years ago, Nottingham High School even played rugby or any kind of sporting activity. I wonder what type of activities the boys enjoyed as a form of exercise? If only I could travel back in time to see what they did - that would be amazing! I could tell them about the truly wonderful opportunities we have now at this school. I think they would be astounded to know it has survived through five centuries and is now the Sunday Times best prep school in the country.

Alex De Silva, 5S, Junior School

2.05 p.m.

I'm walking into maths, expecting another boring lesson where I'll probably get told off for talking too much, as ever. I sit down in my usual place and reluctantly get my books out. I ask Harry whether or not he has done the homework. Since he has we compare answers, just to make sure that we've got them all right. Mr Barr-Smith says we won't need our books today, and tells us to get into pairs. I instantly look at Harry who is sitting next to me, surprised and also relieved that we won't have to do any maths today.

Edward Hirst, 11H

2.06 p.m.

Year 8 are murmuring, chattering quickly and quietly under their breath as they enter the Large Lecture Theatre, where "Chariots of Fire" is pulsing grandly through the speakers. As the clip finishes, a woman limps in. It is the Para–Olympian swimmer, Elizabeth Taylor! I am on the edge of my seat, craning my head forward to hear every word as she speaks about how she overcame her disabilities as a child; for instance she used her brother's skateboard to move around the house! We are extremely privileged to see her medals – two bronze and a silver from the 2000 Olympics.

Michael Fletcher, 8Y

2.07 p.m.

This week we are focussing on contact rugby in the 'A' game.

As I am really strong and people fear me, this is my favourite part of it. It all starts off with the warm up, which involves jogging around the entire rugby field. Then Mr Baker, our coach, tells us to sit down and he explains what to do. Our first task is to get used to the bags and my group are taking turns on them while the others in my group are driving the bag forwards.

Alex Bellamy, 5S, Junior School

2.08 p.m.

Just settling back into lessons after lunch for the final lessons of the school week: history followed by maths! In history, we have recently finished studying World War I and are now looking at German politics after the war. It is interesting to see the recovery of a troubled nation in a short amount of time. In today's lesson we are looking at the effect WWI had on Germany, leaving the Kaiser's regime in disarray. The new political system, known as the Weimar Constitution, brought democracy, stability and freedom of speech to Germany.

Matthew Law, 10S, age 15

2.09 p.m.

It is a surprisingly sunny day on this cold January afternoon. Unfortunately, it is like Maths and me; the two just don't mix.

I am quite relaxed at the start of the lesson as it is almost the weekend. The teacher arrives unusually silent and it turns out he is not pleased with my homework and begins to have a rant at me; he says I'll be lucky to pass GCSE. This takes me aback as I do not expect him to come out with such a statement. The silence in the room feels like laughter ….. well, I still can't believe I got zero out of ten on the homework.

Anees Hussain, Year 11

2.10 p.m.

Year Four play rugby at the games field. My favourite part is when we perform a ruck. Matthew Eastland runs into the training pad. After that Joseph and I perform a ruck and shortly afterwards Adam Woodings and Jai Varma join in. We train like this for ten minutes so we have five minutes at the end for a game. I have a very, very strong team. For most of the match we are in scrums. I am Tight Head Prop, our Hooker is Tom C-DF and our Loose Head is Oliver Hulme.

Alex Cochrane, 4C, Junior School

2.11 p.m.

My friends and I are waiting outside the Large Lecture Theatre, intrigued about what is going to happen. After a while we have been let in and now everyone has sat down someone is walking to the front. It is Elizabeth Wright, a Para Olympic swimmer who competed in the 1996 and 2000 Paralympics. I was impressed that she had achieved more than people with 4 limbs, and with a life with a disability she can still do ordinary things. We are lucky enough to see some of her medals and one of her races in which she one Silver. It is a great inspiration for me and a once in a lifetime opportunity.

Harvinder Mehat, 8Y

2.12 p.m.

At around ten past two I am ready and changed for a great lesson of games.

First of all, year five A game walk over to pitches seven and eight where we start our warm up. In our warm up we practice passing in contact, this is when you get tackled you have to pass it behind to the next person so he can run until he gets tackled where he would pass the ball. Soon that exercise ends and we go straight onto the game earlier than usual. As soon as we start, it isn't going well the other team score very early in, sadly they score a lot more and we never make a comeback.

Tom Barlow, Junior School pupil

2.13 p.m.

Dr Swain begins to move swiftly over to the video player in the history lesson. I am waiting eagerly for the title of the video to be announced. He utters the most inspiring phrase ever omitted by any human. The Somme as told by Richard Holmes. My eyes are growing with great excitement, but a dark thought spreads like a plague through my mind, this will be the last Richard Holmes video we will ever watch. The master of beige on beige, tweed on tweed, will return to our screens for one last valiant performance.

James Stevenson, 10H

2.13 p.m

During games we work on rucking over and defending the ball. We all really enjoy it thoroughly, after that we play a rugby match.

To begin with we don't know how to ruck over so we set up a ruck situation, by putting people with protection bags at one end of the room, one person runs up with the ball and presents the ball two more people link up and push the bag person backwards the last person "scrumhalf" picks up the ball and passes it to the next group.

Robert James Dowsett, Junior School Pupil

2.14 p.m.

Today is the School's 500th Birthday. After assembly and when all the writing subjects are completed we go to valley road [the games field]. When year 5 have got changed group 1 stage down the stairs and I think it is group 2, so I follow. When group 1 start doing their activity David walks over he has followed me, then David sees group 2 strolling along so we sprint over there but then they are just walking to the pitch straight next to Mr Bakers group 1 that makes angry later. After games I am really muddy and tired. I reluctantly go to the changing room.

Henry Robson, 5s, Junior School

2.15 p.m.

The current lesson is Latin in which we are reading about the Roman religion and empire in our books. However halfway through the lesson one of my class members at the back of the classroom, Saaras, stands up to retrieve a shoe. It turns out the shoe belongs to someone at the front of the classroom, Matthew Moir, therefore shoe was returned. How the shoe ended up at the back of the classroom will forever remain unknown... After this slightly unusual interruption we continue reading the passage which is now focusing on sacrifices.

Henry Murray, 9Y, age 13

2.16 p.m.

On the 1st of February 2013, our school (Nottingham High School) celebrates it's 500th anniversary. Each pupil of our school are asked to write a short piece of writing, which expresses our most enjoyable, exciting moment of the day. Well, this is my favourite part of the day: hockey training. If there is one thing in the world that I enjoy, it's hockey! The moment I walk in, I feel the blood pumping in my body, getting exciting and preparing for the **big** game ahead of me. With our excellent teacher (Mr Cowley), nothing can ruin our game...

Rishi Ambalkar, 6L, Junior School

2.17 p.m.

I am playing chess with Marcus and I am moving my Knight and I am taking his pawn. Marcus moves his Queen away. I am taking my turn and I`m taking his Queen with my Bishop. I have just lost my game oh no!

Toyan Garland, Year 2, Lovell House

2.18 p.m.

When I go to Games as usual, I run over to the 'B' game to start our warm up. The warm up is to pass the ball to each other but there is a defender so it is very hard for us three to pass the ball to each other without getting caught.

After about 10 minutes, Mr Shaw, our Games teacher, says that seeing as we are doing so well he will give us an extra five minutes to do exactly the same thing but when you pass the ball you have to move and when you get the ball as well.

Yuvraj Singh, Junior School

2.19 p.m.

Today at valley road, our school does House Cross country. I am scared, happy, excited and hoping I am going to win or at least come within the top five. When we arrive at the games field we all go to get changed into our games kit and wait for the year threes to do their race. Then it is our turn to do our race. Year four line up at the start line. Mr Allison says ready, set, go and we all shoot off like missiles. I take the lead and I absolutely storm down the left hand side of the flags and before I know it I am at the scrum machine. I know it will be a really close race as my friends Thomas, Alex and Dillon are really fast. Amazingly I win for Tonkin's and I get a medal. Daddy is really proud of me because he was in Tonkin's when he was at the school. I come 1st, Thomas Cassidy de Falco comes 2nd and Alex comes 3rd. I tell all of my family as well as my dad and they are proud of me as well.

Harry Hammond, 4S, Junior School

2.20 p.m.

We are told that a visitor is coming into school. We find out that this person is a Para Olympian who swam for the Australian team in the 1996 and 2000 Olympic games.

Elizabeth Wright shows us the medals; they looked amazing. I have the pleasure of asking questions about how she began swimming and about her disability. This is an amazing insight to a Olympian lifestyle

Tom Ward, 8L

2.21 p.m.

My favourite part on Friday is when we are at the Games Field playing Rugby. All of Group 1 take part in a tackling event. We start a Rugby game so we can all get warm and our team score a try. The try is set up by the scrum. Meanwhile, the other team has a breakaway from another scrum and Harry Tyler-Smith gets the ball and runs forwards quickly. I am the last line of defence so I move forwards and flatten Harry but his knee collides with my funny bone. However, I do not find the pain funny although everyone else laughs.

Oliver Hulme, 4C, Junior School

2.22 p.m.

I put the bag of chess pieces and board away into the box. Mr Williams tells me about the chess tournament the Grand Prix. I now go up the stairs to 2W where Mrs Williams is. I am asked to get my book bag and Miss Clarke gives me my reading book and maths homework and I put them in my bag. I am told to go down and get my coat and swimming bag on and find a partner.

Harvey Jenkins, Year 2, Lovell House

2.23 p.m.

On Friday, I am included in a fixture for a rugby match against Birkdale. This is in the 'B' team match.

Our coach is Mr Payne, who is refereeing the match. I am with Mr Payne and the rest of the class, exercising till the pupils from our opponents arrive. I am extremely excited as I am warming up. Finally, our opponents arrive at our games field, (valley road), and are all prepared for the fixture. Birkdale start off with the ball and that is when the intriguing fixture begins.

Hassan Zeb, Junior School pupil

2.24 p.m.

The Under 11's rugby match against Birkdale is at Valley Road, following the 500th year celebrations.

The cold air rushes around our goose bumpy legs and our hands are too scared to reappear from the pockets of our shorts. The seemingly large pitch (for the First 15) stretches out before us. Our fly half has the ball cocooned in his hands and the whistle blows...

The ball spirals in the air, into their outside centre's hands. Legs pumping, running into our line, the fierce tackle is made. 32-0 defeat.

Archie Symes, 6G, Junior School

2.25 p.m.

I am sitting in Biology just a single period today not the usual double. Its 10 minutes from the end until our class makes our way to geography whether that's a good thing I don't know. Mr Cook is talking about the lamb's heart we dissected last week. All the chambers of the heart are being labelled, on the white sheet of paper.

5 minutes left just counting down the minutes before you hear the distinctive sound of the bell just outside the classroom door. Finally 14.40 everyone starts to pack away while Sir just rounds the lesson off. Now nothing will stop us getting out the classroom down the corridor and into the outside breeze.

Alex Dowie, 9L

2.26 p.m.

As I walk onto the pitch at Valley Road, I feel really nervous, playing in my first match for Nottingham High Junior School. The game starts and I feel scared but I settle into it as time goes on. Our first try is scored by Adi and the conversion is scored by Toby. Birkdale score twice but miss their conversions.

At half- time I am subbed off and Aryan takes my place as right winger. After that I run up and down the side line to keep up with the game and to keep warm. The game finishes and the score is 12 points to Nottingham and 20 to Birkdale. As I walk back to the pavilion, I feel that I have done well in my first rugby match of the season.

Jonathan Steele, 6S, Junior School

2.27 p.m.

I make my rugby debut for NHJS B-Team on Friday 1st February against Birkdale an experienced team from Sheffield. The match is pretty eventful; I reckon we have possession of the ball 50% of the time.

The game starts off well. We give some well-trained tackles; within the first 10 minutes we score a try and convert successfully. Score: 7-0 to NHJS. Another few well-played minutes pass, Birkdale score a try but the conversion is missed.

Then we let our performance slip. To our disappointment they score a 2nd try but the conversion is missed. Score: 7-10 to Birkdale.

Matthew Raw, Junior School Pupil

2.27 p.m.

On the first of February 1 2013 an excellent rugby match takes place at the Nottingham high schools rugby pitch at Valley Road at 2:30 Pm our opponents are Birkdale School. The match starts and we are the first to score a try, the person who scores the try is Toby Bashforth and is set up bye myself. However we think we have this game in the bag so we aren't playing as well as we would if we were behind rather than in front, we all play our best and that's all that matters. This is a brilliant match for Nottingham High Junior School.

Hugo Fielding, 6G, Junior School

2.28 p.m.

7S have nearly finished French with Mr Brown. It is ten minutes until we go to Maths. We are filling in some missing words on a sheet in our exercise books, which are to be sung in a French song. It is sung quite quickly, so it is hard to hear what the woman and man are singing. Some words stand out in the song such as 'la musique'. We are trying to write down all the missing words (there are nineteen of them), before the lesson ends. So far, I have done about five because I cannot really catch what the woman is singing.

Brandon Harbinson, 7S

2.29 p.m.

On Friday we have reasoning, double science then double English. Science is good because we are doing microbes at the moment and it is an interesting subject. On Mondays and Fridays we go to games, in the winter we play rugby, in the summer we play cricket and in autumn we play football. At the moment we are playing rugby. On Friday the 1st of February we play against Birkdale. The match goes well in the first half but then they start scoring more tries so eventually we lose. The score is 20-12 to Birkdale. Overall it is a great match and we do well.

Joshua Bolton, 6G, Junior School

2.30 p.m.

I am lining up with my coat on and swimming bag on my back with my partner Krrish. Mrs Williams is telling the boys to be quiet when we are walking past Reception and Year 1. I am walking through the school and outside to the car park and I am now waiting for it to be safe to cross the road.

Isak Ibrahim, Year 2, Lovell House

2.31 p.m.

The rugby match starts and I have never felt that much tension in a long time. All the parents are cheering on their sons and the coaches are shouting at their players, giving them orders.

As soon as the whistle blows, everyone starts shouting, as if the pitch is a battlefield. The contact has come to life, with players running and calling for the ball.

When the first try is scored, the crowd are chanting as loud as they can. The match turns from a fun game into a fast- paced and rough battle. All the parents are thrilled by the action in the game.

When the game is finally over, the noise has dropped into complete silence. The opposition has won however that game was unforgettable for both teams.

Zain Ahmed, 6S, Junior School

2.32 p.m.

Today is not quite my normal Friday as I sit at home recovering from a small operation. It is 14.30 and I am currently sitting at home managing the cover and detention system for the coming week so that I can send emails to Clare at school so she can make print outs. Whilst doing this I have to listen to my four year old boy, Oren play 'Angry Birds – Rio' on the iPad. I am feeling frustrated at not being able to move but understand that I have to stay still to recover!

Paul Spedding, Senior Teacher, age 37

2.33 p.m.

I quickly glance at my watch, whilst stifling a snigger: some of my classmates are getting told off for something they didn't do. Everyone else is working quickly and effectively at the thought of finishing some of their homework. Additionally, our Latin teacher has promised us the weekly treat of biscuits; however, that dream doesn't seem too likely anymore due to our previous disruption. I stare longingly through the window, at the thought of a break, and then at my teacher, who has seen me looking at the biscuits. Finally the teacher agrees to our demands-a bad mistake...

Rahul Menon, 9Y, age 13

2.34 p.m.

On the 1st of February 2013, we are scheduled to play a rugby match against Birkdale School. However, I didn't know anything about this fixture. As far as I was concerned, it was just a normal day at Valley Road. When Mr Paine, my rugby teacher, tells me that I am in the team, I am ecstatic! It is my first rugby fixture ever!

After we change, Mr Paine leads us to the pitch. On the pitch, both teams start practising equally furiously. I don't practice very much because I have been told that I will be coming on at half-time. Once the teams are warmed up, Mr Paine blows the whistle, indicating start of the game. The game gets off to a slow start, but after about 10 minutes, the match becomes really exciting. At about 12 minutes, Birkdale have a chance for a try, a player is bursting down the wing with an almost clear path.....but after a ferocious tackle from Zain, the player's fate is sealed.... the first try won't go to Birkdale!

Next, after a couple of scrums and a few skirmishes, a crucial point in the match arrives. Jonathan, our speedy winger is charging down the wing with a *literally* clear path, when, suddenly, a horrible tackle to the neck stops him in his tracks.

The remaining game is quite hard-fought and the final score 20-12....... to Birkdale doesn't do justice to the effort put in by our team. We have tried really hard and have given our best and, therefore, can hold our heads high.

Achintya Dixit, 6S, Junior School

2.35 p.m.

7th and 8th period on a Friday is when I have a R.S lesson. There's nothing better than a debate to end the day. Even when we are meant to being something different, it always pops up. Everyone has their say and me, being an atheist; it's quite hard to question my views than someone who believes in Christianity or Islam. Though it can become quite heated, at the end of the lesson there's all smiles showing the respect between the class and that's it just an opportunity to share your views and have a laugh at people responses.

Russell O'Brien, 10T

2.36 p.m.

We have a tough rugby match against Birkdale. The whistle blows to start the match. I am playing full back and it is our first time playing together all year.

They are a very strong team which I know as soon as they break through our line of defence, rucking over as fast as a bullet, striking their tackles with killer force. Then the worst thing happens.

The Birkdale player steps on me and my fellow team- mate to score the try. We hope the conversion will not go through but it is straight through. Then the whistle blows for half- time.

We are down.

I am thankful to be at this school at the 500 anniversary.

Finn O'Regan, 6S, Junior School

2.37 p.m.

Nottingham High Junior School year 6 A-team face Burkdale in a rough rugby game.

We win the toss successfully and Ben Peirce nervously does a huge drop kick to then let Nott's High to move up in a magnificent line to win the ball, however Burkdale one the ball and move quickly. Swiftly they pass the ball down the line to their fast winger to score a well-earned try.

Their fly-half then comes to step up to the challenge of the conversion and he successfully kicks the griped ball through the giant looking posts give his team two more points.

Max Coppel, 6S, Junior School

2.38 p.m.

We are at games, it is Birkdale vs. NHJS in rugby at Valley Road. The B team are captained by Toby Bashford.. We are playing in the second half when I have been substituted; I have an assist to one of my classmates Hassan Zeb. I am running and have been tackled by one of there players and I hold the ball out for Hassan Zeb, he grabs the ball and scores the try I feel that I have achieved a part in one of our tries.

Final score Birkdale 20-12 NHJS.

Edward Roberts, Junior School pupil

2.39 p.m.

Today we go to the Games field to play tag rugby. We change and run out to the field. We warm up by jogging twice around the rugby pitch then we put on our tag belts and rugby tags. We play against the Reds first and we win 2-0. Alex scores both tries.

After we have played the Reds, we play the Yellows. We start in a V shape and I pass the ball to Alex. He runs around the corner but is tagged so he then passes the ball to Oliver. Oliver passes the ball back to Alex, who scores a try. The Yellows get the ball then and Isaac scores a try by running the whole length of the pitch without stopping or passing. No-one is able to stop or tag him. We lose the game 2-4.

Then we change back into our uniforms and return to the school on our school buses.

Vijay Sundaram, 3W, Junior School

2.40 p.m.

I leave the large lecture theatre, and collect my bag for the last two periods of the day. We have just had an inspirational speech from Elizabeth Wright, an Australian Paralympic swimmer who won a silver and two bronze medals. Small groups of people make their way off down the different corridors, as the crowd disperses for different lessons. We have geography, when we will start a new unit about the energy we use, and where we get it from. We learn about the different types of renewable and non-renewable resources, and find out where we get each from.

Euan Kirrage, 8L

2.41 p.m.

On Friday 1st February 2013, I play tag rugby between 2.30 and 3.00 at Valley Road Sports Field. First I get changed and then I stand in a line at the door. After that I go out onto the sports field and put my tag belt on. Soon I am playing tag rugby. Ben's on the run. Does he score a try? YES! He scores a try and 1-0 to us. Rio (who is on the other team) is coming and he scores a try. Bad luck. 1 all. Next Issac's on the run. Does he score? YES!! Another great score from our team. Meanwhile I am tagging. At the end of the match we win so we go back to the sports pavilion and get changed. Soon I am back on the bus and going back to school to get my things and go home. I really want to play again soon!

Tom Gibbons, Junior School pupil

2.42 p.m.

Today it is a tiring day so far; I have just finished my library lesson. I am walking to drama tired. Just before, we have done 2 periods of house rugby; I was in coopers B team it was great fun. After climbing 5 flights of stairs I am wandering what we were going to do. Our drama teacher is running late because she has to run to the staffroom to get something. After 5 minutes our drama teacher returns so we enter the classroom/small hall. I thinkit is going to be a boring lesson but I am WRONG!!!!

anonymous pupil, 7Y

2.43 p.m.

I am walking up the hill to go swimming and to the traffic lights. I am now crossing the road and watching the green man as I am walking I am going into the High School through the gates and up the stairs and now I am walking down the stairs to the changing rooms.

Jack Stockley, Year 2, Lovell House

2.44 p.m.

We are in the middle of a double lesson in ICT 1 with 7L. Scratch is being used to create an Aquarium Game and other Games. I never thought teaching would involve creating and playing computer games in a lesson. Sofyan has just announced `I have eaten 18 fish`! Joe is just helping Archie with his shooting game. Harry has now finished his game on shooting slendermen! Oh to be teaching Mathematics.

Mary Mills (recently retired Maths teacher)

2.45 p.m.

Everyone in the Junior School goes to the games field which is opposite the City Hospital. Year 3 play a game of tag rugby and we have to wear black tag belts. We play a lot of little games and my team wins more times than we lose. It is very cold while we are playing, but we keep warm by running around a lot to tag people.

After rugby we go inside to have a nice warm shower which makes us feel much better. We get changed and catch the bus back to school.

Reuben Crawford, 3M, Junior School

2.47 p.m.

At the start of the afternoon we travel on the bus to the games field. When we arrive we get changed before playing a brilliant game of rugby. I score six tries and my team win which makes me feel brilliant. My friends and I celebrate by saying well done and clapping each other on the back, one of my friends starts running around in excitement. After the game, we go on a steady jog around one of the pitches to cool ourselves down. I really like my game of rugby, because I am very competitive and I like sports.

Isaac Morledge, Junior School Pupil

2.50 p.m.

It's 2.50p.m: the second period of English. The lesson is fuelled by heated debates and points between teacher and student. At three o'clock it is homework time. 'A day in the life of' is the title. Photo madness begins at the mention of the phrase '500th anniversary'. A seemingly endless frenzy of clicking begins. With the odd click, the lesson restarts. A classmate at the front fiddles with something he found as he sits down. The teacher tells him to put it away. A joke reveals itself and a circus of laughter rises around the classroom. It dies down and the lesson continues, refuelled by the jokes and banter made seconds before...

Alex Kumra, 11H

2.51 p.m.

I and my class, 8S, are held outside of the classroom because we produce much noise. Our Physics teacher once again lets us in and we sit in our seats in silence, for we do not wish to be in trouble. Our class is learning about sound. Most of our class are not listening, until our teacher mentions the word balloon. We are given the opportunity to pop a balloon. As my friend holds the balloon I lunge my Lamy fountain pen at the balloon and it pops. We then have to throw the remains of the balloon in the bin.

Muhtasim Thakur, 8S, age 13

2.54 p.m.

I am in the changing room and I'm hanging my bag and coat up on the pegs and they are quite high up so I have to stretch. I am now getting my clothes off and putting my swimming trunks on and I am going to give my towel to Miss Clarke. I am sitting down and then I go into the shower.

Marcus Smart, 2W, Lovell House

2.57 p.m.

Catch up with emails; go to reprographics to get photocopies; phone call from parent; phone call from Paediatrician about a boy being referred; write summaries of testing done in the week and have a longed for cup of tea!

Carla O'Brien, Head of Learning Support

2.59 p.m.

On the 1st of Febuary at games the top year 4 rugby group are doing rooks and malls and at first we step over the person on the floor and push the other person behind away and when Alex is on the floor Jai accidentally stands on Alex's neck by accident. Also in that lesson we have a match and I am a winger and don't get the ball very much but even though I don't get the ball much it is still fun! The best bit about rugby is that that we all have fun and everyone enjoys it which is great. So that is my 15 minutes of the day.

Joseph Podesta, 4C, Junior School

3.00 p.m.

Time for another cuppa before getting ready for the evening cleaners who will arrive at 4.00 p.m.

Susan Ford, cleaning manager

3.01 p.m.

I am sitting in Geography and we are watching a video about illegal immigrants from Mexico. Though I am mainly focusing on the video, the teacher is writing facts on the board to do with the video, so I read them. I don't think many people are going to read the board but it is fairly interesting and helpful with the homework. I am mainly thinking about how boring it must be for the immigrants sitting on a train as they don't have anything to do. The video is fairly interesting; though for some reason it is by an Arabic company. We watch a fair few videos by them in geography I then realise.

Fred Hudson, 9L

3.02 p.m.

I sit, eagerly waiting to begin the lamb's heart dissection we were promised a week ago. The teacher comes past and lifts an irregularly shaped floppy object from a bowl of tinted liquid. He carefully lays it on the dissecting board in front of me and the person next to me, who prods it with a pencil. Over the next few minutes we slowly dismantle it. I suddenly realise I'd forgotten to record our findings and frantically scribble down a few details into a blank table. Two Atria, Two Ventricles and a weaving web of vessels and valves.

William Baldwin, 9S, age 14

3.03 p.m.

I am in German, we are learning about where we live and how to describe our houses and our street. I like German; however I am going to have drop it in order to French and Latin. In German I sit next to Ritho or Lewis. After German I go to my maths set, I am usually very confused by the things that we do in maths. After a tiring day I go home to and practise my guitar, playing sweet melodic blues and rock, usually the Black Keys or Led Zeppelin.

Joseph McNamara, 8T

3.04 p.m.

At this time my form are in Geography where we are learning about our new topic after our Brazil project on energy. Our teacher is giving us a power point presentation to explain the pros and cons of different energy resources and the effects they give on the environment. It is very much an informative lesson as we also watch a video concerning fracking, how will help us in the future but cause earthquakes at the same time. As much as I find it interesting; I still can't wait to go home from school after yet another tiring week of lessons.

William Myers, 8L

3.05 p.m.

I'm sitting in physics right now and doing an experiment to try and calculate the acceleration due to gravity using a metal ball and some string. Although it is not the most sophisticated equipment, our teacher claims that pupils usually get reasonably accurate results. Having said this, our set seem to be struggling a little, despite the fact Galileo was able to do this fairly accurately about 400 years ago. At least its more interesting than studying electricity.

Arjun Nehra, Senior School pupil

3.06 p.m.

I am doing pushing and gliding in my swimming lesson with Mrs Whittamore. I dive into the swimming pool and swim to the other side. It feels great and I really like diving because it is my favourite thing and I am really good at it.

Ashley Holmes, 2W, Lovell House

3.07 p.m.

Year 9 boys are dissecting hearts. It's the end of the week but all seem eager to get stuck in. I make my way round the lab with a trolley, the organs sloshing around in a pool of red. One boy imitates a flight attendant: "would you like anything from the trolley today sir?" Faces light up as hearts appear on dissecting boards in front of them. One lad looks a little pale; I must check on him later. The trolley catches on something and red liquid splashes my face. Did the boys see? Of course they did.

Dr Andrew Bingham, teacher of Biology

3.08 p.m.

When we are at the games field we get changed and line up beside the door. Mr Smith tells us to go to the games field. Before we play tag rugby, we do some training. We have to go in and out of the cones and put the ball down on every cone we stop on. The tag rugby game that follows is exhausting. The final whistle blows, thank goodness, it is time to go home.

I rush into the bus and the bottom row is full up, so I go to the top row. I sit at the front and Zak is with me. As the bus drives off, Zak and I find a mirror in front of us. We see the driver through it.

Rishav Ahluwalia, Junior School pupil

3.10 p.m.

Friday afternoon and sitting in English, bored out of my mind as my English teacher's voice drones on, trying to get my class to work like a stuck record, repeating the same mantra over and over again. The clock ticks closer and closer to 4 o'clock, and the weekend gets even closer every second. He explains to us that the particular writing task pains him more than it does us, but I don't even think that is possible at the moment. I realise that I've forgotten the homework I promised to hand in. Hopefully he doesn't remember.

Ben Davies, 11T, age 16

3.11 p.m.

Ich habe eine Freistunde am Freitag in der siebten Stunde aber das ist zu spät in der Woche, um wertvolle Arbeit zu machen. Deshalb sitze ich jetzt hier in der Bibliothek. Vielleicht werde ich Musik hören oder ein interessantes Buch finden. Mein Freund, der Daniel heißt, kommt an und wir quatschen über sinnlose Dinge und was jeder von uns am Wochenende machen wird. Wir warten auf unsere letzte Stunde, in der nicht so viel Arbeit gemacht werden wird, weil jeder Schüler und sogar der Lehrer sehr müde sind. Ich freue mich auf den Schulschluss, wenn ich zu Hause gehen kann.

Oliver Woodhouse, Year 12

3.12 p.m.

I am in the swimming pool and it is very cold. It feels like you are in the ocean and that there is a shark following you! I am practising swimming on my back and my front by swimming lengths from the deep end to the shallow end and back. I prefer swimming on my front because when I swim on my back it hurts.

Finlay Cullen-Draper, 2W, Lovell House

3.13 p.m.

Dammit, Faraaz is drawing rude pictures on my folder again. I've got to stay vigilant, Michael is looking for an opening too. You would think they would pay attention in Chemistry, oh well. Nihal opens the door, the bell rings, end of lesson YEEAAH TO CHICKEN! We walk out of the Science block and there are the rude little kids trying to spray us with a water bottle, we need to bully these kids more, enforce the pecking order some more. Back through the pod to the Sixth Form Centre to debate with Jack about how the Tory's are evil.

Omer Elhassan, age 18

3.15 p.m.

I walk through the school with a great thought on my mind I have English- next period (English is my favorite lesson). I slowly trudge along observing the interesting posters on the walls. A poster that particularly catches my eye is one of the recycling posters; I like the poster because of the vibrant colors and surprisingly large font. The poster says: "Recycling is good!"I find this particularly effective because it is near one of the many recycling bins dotted around the school.

When I finally step through the doors of W21- my English room - I see my teacher handing out books. I prefer reading to writing so this is a good start! As I usually would I sit down on the second row with my friends and await further instructions. The book we are reading is one about Frankenstein. Frankenstein is about a scientist who creates a monster, who he later rejects and calls a 'hideous' creature...

Ali Samatar, 7T

3.16 p.m.

On Friday 1st of February, and we have games, in our games session, we have tag rugby and we play matches foe the entire time. My team unfortunately don't get a very good score because we lose one and draw one. I still enjoy it very much and it is worth having a try because the teachers encourage everyone.

Mr Caldwell and Mr Smith encourage everyone to play. When we are on the bus returning back to school, I have a chat with my friend Rishav about how good the games session was.

Mohammed Zeb, 3w, Junior School

3.18 p.m.

On Friday in maths, I now sit in a different position in the classroom after everybody got moved and we had a new seating plan. In today's lesson we are doing 'converting fractions to decimals'. I particularly like this topic. We also now have another new teacher, our third teacher this year. He is a very enjoyable and kind teacher though. I am working on page 195 exercise 2E. I complete questions 1 to 10 whilst the boy I sit with takes much longer because he thinks that he knows the solution. It turns out I have the exact same answer but I have done six times the amount he has done in twenty minutes . He is a very friendly boy and works hard. I struggle to concentrate but now I am sitting closer to the front I find it much easier to concentrate. I also talk to the teacher quite a lot, but not about maths.

Harry Smith, 8S, age 12

3.20 p.m.

My friends and I walk down the corridor, we open the doors and the sunlight hits us. We begin to make the long journey from the art block up to the mathematics classrooms on the top floor. We enter the main building and approach the long set of stairs that will lead us to our classrooms and the search for further knowledge. As we get to the second floor my friends disperse to their individual lessons. I will have to make the last part of the journey myself. I reach the classroom and sit down; I greet the boy on the desk next to mine and open my bag. That is when it strikes me. My mathematics books are on my desk at home. I will have to tell sir. I approach his desk, my heart thumping; I wipe the sweat of my brow as I take the final steps forward. 'I'm sorry sir, but I have forgotten my books' I say in a meek voice, I look at him watching for any sign of emotion, he nods and tells me to get some spare paper. He understands the mistake; it is going to be OK.

Tait Grundy, 10L

3.21 p.m.

Finally I go to maths to learn about translating graphs. It is hard but I eventually understand with some help and advice.

Lucas Wilcock, 10S

3.22 p.m.

I walk from the large lecture theatre all the way to W7 to my Geography class. We have just seen the paraolympian Mrs Elizabeth Wright. She showed us her bronze and silver medals from the Sydney and Atlanta Olympics. She told us about her life and had a question and answer session.

We arrive at Geography and get back parts of our Brazil project which I enjoyed doing. Mrs Lemon tells us that we're starting a new project on electricity. We're going to be finding out about what America does and about fracking-this is where gasses are drawn from the ground. We watch a power point and a video on it, so now it's off on our way to Spanish to have a test.

George Alexander, 8L, age 12

3.23 p.m.

It's the last period of the day- Physics. One more round, then it's home time. Those words haven't got any less sweet since primary school. I don't mind Physics, but after double Maths I just don't have the energy anymore. We all wait outside for as long as possible (no need to make this longer than necessary). Eventually, it's noticed we're all outside. We troop in and sit down. I pull out my Physics folder, red of course, by the ancient traditions of Nottingham High School. The teacher starts his lesson, while we all get on with our conversations.

Robert Jackson, 11S

3.24 p.m.

I am having a shower after swimming, they are very cold when you first get in and then if you wait a while they get warmer. Mrs Williams gives me my towel from the rail and I get dry and then I go into the changing room to get dressed. I have to get dressed quickly and then I put on my coat and my bag. I sit and wait for everyone else while we all count down from fifteen.

Naveen Bala, 2W, Lovell House

3.26 p.m.

In games we are playing tag rugby. There are four teams red, blue, yellow and green. The reds play the blues and yellows play the greens. All the teams go seven meters back, and they pass to each to each of the players. Then the other team pull a tag off. The green team score 2 trys as well as the red team. The blue team scores only one. But the yellow team score the highest 3 trys. The teams swap over, and they play. All the players are very happy. Then after the game, we go on the bus back to school.

Niranjan Muthuswamy, 3W, Junior School

11. Ending the Day

3.30 p.m.

I am going towards my history lesson just after watching some illegal immigrants cross the border of the USA in geography. I get there early even though it is the last lesson of today. It is quite crowded because we are waiting for the teacher and some people think we can go in. the teacher arrives and asks politely for people to get out of his way , as usual, so he can open the door. We all rush in, unpack and sit down (with a few slow people left behind outside the room). We are asked to open our books near the back and find the dates of different battles against the Japanese. Two people, who are sitting next to me, get a really good start, finding the dates with ease. I am sitting there wondering how they do it.

Will Moorby, 9L

3.31 p.m.

I have just finished afternoon play and I am coming in to do handwriting. Then I am eating fruit with all my friends and Mrs O is reading us a book.

Luca Vergari, 2M, Lovell House

3.33 p.m.

I am currently practising 'The Pink Panther' so It can be recorded by our teacher. Many of us are playing as loudly as we can to show off or knocking on doors, and looking through, pulling funny faces, and when we come to the door, running off, trying to distract us, however I am ready and waiting to be recorded. The wait is nerve racking. Painful. But I know not to be distracted. Keep practising until it is my turn to record, else, and I'll give in. Now I've performed, I feel much better. It went well; and I'm glad!

Oliver Simpson, 7Y, age 12

3.40 p.m.

At 3.40 I am in E1 doing Spanish in the lab with Mr Picardo and Miss Williams. I start the Spanish vocab test. The test is on the 1st half of section 5. There are ten questions, five Spanish to English and five English to Spanish. Certain people in the class collect in the test for Mr Picardo to mark. Our next instruction is to go on vocab express and learn some more vocab on section 5 till the bell rings at 4.00.

James Bennett,
8L

3.42 p.m.

I am getting ready for home time with my book bag. I will have a piece of fruit on the way out. In my book bag is my reading book and homework.

Noah Bhatia, 2M, Lovell House

3.43 p.m.

On the 1st of February 2013 Nottingham High School has a big celebration because the school has been teaching for exactly 500 years. These are indeed 500 years of excellence. In the morning we play before lessons. Our first lesson is English and in that lesson we do a test which is for a spelling test of different kinds of words. The second and third lesson is Maths and in these lessons we do very challenging mathematical investigations. Last of all we have ICT and in that lesson we practise logo programming which is very difficult but we all do it well.

This day is supposed to special, happy and memorable and indeed it was!

Neel Badhe, 4S, Junior School

3.44 p.m.

The boys have their hats and coats on and are sitting at their tables and ready to go home. They have their black Lovell House book bags which contain their reading diary and homework, plus library book. From where I sit I can see parents outside by the painted fence waiting to collect their children. Two boys are not being collected as they go to After School Club. I wait with them until 4.00 and then I take them to the hall to await registration for the club. When I go back to the classroom I tidy my desk and get ready to go home.

Julie Bignall, Teaching Assistant, Lovell House

3.45 p.m.

RING! There goes the bell as I scamper down to the cloakroom to collect my things. I quickly slip on my hat and gloves and then hurry to the Hall, as I do not want to be late. I tell the teacher that I have arrived at the queue for the bus. Once everyone has been ticked off the list, the line starts moving and we exit the school via the boys' entrance. Once we have moved to the statue of Albert Ball, the pilot, then the teacher stops to make sure that no-one has been left behind at the Senior School. Once we have reached Balmoral Road, the teacher stops all cars in the road so that we can cross into the bus lane. When we have all arrived at the bus lane, we walk down the queue of buses, to board the one that takes us closest to our homes.

Mark Sperry, 6S, Junior School

3.46 p.m.

It's half time, and we're 1-0 down to the side that has beaten every team they've played in the tournament so far. Beaten is an under-statement, they have destroyed their opposition by margins as large as 10-0! We are already out, playing for pride, having let ourselves down so far in the tournament, but a win will gain 3rd place. We are not going to be push-overs.

The whistle blows, here we go. 15 minutes to turn the game around, to guarantee 3rd place. We send constant waves of pressure towards them, we want this more than they do. Finally, a short corner. The ball is crossed into me, I pass it to our striker, who swivels and scores! We've done it, an equaliser! But the whistle is blown, celebrations are cut short. Their umpire rules it out, we don't know why. But we don't stop trying, a final push, and our striker is knocked down, rugby tackled! Penalty flick surely! But no, the same umpire says no. We lose 1-0, but we go out fighting.

Harry Croasdale, 9H, age 13

3.47 p.m.

Just 13 more minutes till the end of the week and the day. During such a fun music lesson we are practicing for the grand performance of The Pink Panther. We are very nervous when Mr Reid comes to film our performance. We do very well. He says that he wants us to recreate the Pink Panther theme song. The task is disrupted by a strange blackout which also makes the light switch on and off. We all run away run away, scared. We find out that boys were trying to play a trick.

Rishabh Mehrotra , 7Y

3.48 p.m.

We have to win this match, we have not won a match, and everyone is frustrated. We are 1-0 down, and the other team are leading in the tournament. They have obliterated some of the teams; we know that we can't go through to the next round. Only two teams will go through. We are raring to go, willing to not go back without a win. The whistle is blown we trudge back onto the pitch, only 15 minutes left we have to score at least one goal. We get two short corners within a couple of minutes. The ball is passed in, it is travelling two slow, and I won't have enough time to make a decent shot. I shoot, powering it towards the goal, it hits the foot of one of their team. Shot corner again this time it is our captain shooting, he passes it; it goes to our centre midfielder. He shoots, he scores! The whistle has gone, it is disallowed. We lose the match. Disappointment spreads throughout our team!

Benji Chivers, 9H

3.49 p.m.

I am cycling home with my Daddy and my little brother. My brother is on my Daddy's bike. I ride my own bike. We are going to Close Cottage.

Orlando Baker, 2M, Lovell House

3.49 p.m.

I go to my Arabic class. My Mum takes me to the lesson which is from 4.00 until 6.00.

Azaan Mahmood, 2M, Lovell House

3.50 p.m.

I listen to the lesson on the Spanish Transition to Democracy. The teacher puts in a Powerpoint and shows us a video, in Spanish, of the day that Spain switched from being a dictatorship under Franco to a free, democratic state. The atmosphere is friendly because of the upcoming trip to Cádiz, and the fact that it is almost the weekend. The bell goes for the end of the lesson, and the class quickly file out of the classroom. The school day is over and now is not the time for reflection. The weekend is here.

Thomas Pownall, 6M2

12. Free at Last! Free at Last!

3.51 p.m

It is History now, the last lesson of Friday. The last lesson of the week. The weekend is just round the corner and I can't wait. The only bad part is the last 10 minutes of the last lesson on Friday seems much longer, it feels like an hour has already been, but actually only one minute has been. All that is being said by my history teacher, just pops in my ear and jumps straight back out. My mind is so elapsed on the clock as it counts down to four o'clock. It is 3.59 and the last dyeing embers of Friday go by, I quickly anticipate when the bell will ring to signify the end of school and chuck all my books in my bag and rush out the room. There is only one message in my mind which is just running to the bus stop to seal the front seat at the top of the bus so it will be a relaxing ride back to home, where my freedom for the weekend awaits me.

Aaron Stanyard, 9L

3.52 p.m.

Il pleuvait des cordes sur la mer orageuse. Je n'avais jamais rien vu de tel – le bateau en bois sur lequel mes pieds glissaient tanguait toutes les quelques secondes. J'avais les jetons – comment suis-je arrivé ici ? Ça ne tenait pas debout... Lorsqu'un autre bateau essayait de voguer vers nous, je jetai un coup d'œil autour de moi. Et en voyant la tête à mort sur notre drapeau, j'ai dû tomber dans les pommes.

Quand je me suis réveillé, j'avais été ligoté. En face de moi était le capitaine, qui portait un grand chapeau de pirate noir. Il sourit, en me montrant ses dents pourries. « Bonjour, mon petit chou, » il mangea ses mots, puisqu'il était clairement ivre. « Je tire mon chapeau à toi – alors, tu as voyagé avec nous clandestinement ? » Tous les corsaires rirent de manière menaçante.

« Tu parles Français comme une vache espagnole, » dis-je héroïquement.

« Aahhh, tu penses que tu aies le melon ? Mon petit chou, qu'est-ce que tu penses de notre vaisseau pirate ? »

« C'est pas le Pérou, » je dis.

« Quoi ?! » En un clin d'œil, il semblait un peu blessé. « Tu ne l'aimes pas ? » Puis, il sourit encore, et ça me rendit nerveux. « Je t'aime bien, passager clandestin. J'ai pris une décision. Je n'aime pas tourner autour du pot— au lieu de vous forcer à subir le supplice de la planche, mon petit chou, tu seras mon capitaine en second, et nous parcourions le monde ensemble ! Tu as ton cul bordé des nouilles, non ? Nous allons avoir une baleine d'un temps ! » Il m'étreignit. Je restai bouche bée. Si j'avais pu m'évanouir dans les airs, j'eusse été profondément soulagé.

Et à ce moment-là, je me réveillai. Tout le monde me fixait du regard dans ma classe de français.

Raghav Sudarshan, Year 11

3.53 p.m.

As the match draws to a close, we have almost lost, losing 3-1 to Worksop College in the County Cup despite playing some of our best hockey. I am shattered on the wing, having a constant tussle with their German winger Anton, as we duel to see who can get past the other and attack the space behind. Suddenly we break, and the emaciated faces of my team mates surge forward to try and get back in the game. I follow. As we enter the circle, luckily the ball finds its way to me and with a hopeful slap, I place the ball in the corner of the goal. It is 3-2; only seconds remain…

Tim Venkatesan, 6F1

3.54 p.m.

Time to draw to a close whatever I have achieved in my free period and go to the bus lane for my weekly bus duty.

Grahame Whitehead, teacher of German, age 53

3.55 p.m.

Merely five minutes of Physics to endure but as I haven't completed copious labour all lesson, I pack away now, I'm set to dash from P4 to make the glorious 4:01 tram. 4:00, the bell alarms, I drive my way out the door and gallop along the passageway trusting that any professor I pass will have disremembered by Monday so I chance to overlook the 'no running indoors' rule. Out the exit, up the footsteps, up more steps and then the slalom in-between junior school families afore the ultimate sprint and plunge through the closing doors.

James Mellor, 11L

3.56 p.m.

It's only 4 minutes till the end of school. The French teacher slows down time, every second feels like a minute and every minute feels like an hour. In French we are learning about French nouns, the most boring thing ever. Finally the bell rings. I pack away as quickly as I can then I frantically run out the door. The corridor is jam-packed with people trying to rush home. I fight through the crowd. I arrive at the year 7 corridor, pack my bag and head of to the scout hut in the freezing weather.

Wojciech Cajdler, 7L, age 12

3.57 p.m.

Can't resist discussing photocopying job with Resources Assistant.

Grahame Whitehead, teacher of German, age 53

3.58 p.m.

I look at my watch as the final sixty seconds of the school week begins. After a busy five days of homework, lessons and extra-curricular, this is it. The final sprint before the weekend. I am sitting in maths while my peers and teacher feel the same as me. Fifty-seven... fifty-eight... fifty-nine... and the bell goes. The whole class springs to life and gets ready to leave school for the weekend. In a short space of time, the caretakers will lock the school until we return on Monday for another week of school.

Ben Wellings, 7H, age 12

3.59 p.m.

As the class chatters away, I focus on my translation exercise, trying to seclude myself from the noise. 'Son las diez menos cinco,' what could that possibly mean, I... suddenly I am rescued from the imprisonment of the ICT room, the bell rings.

School is over! I desperately cram my Spanish books into my bag, and struggle the straps round my shoulders. Anxiety pumps through and then... we are allowed to leave! I dash through the door, sprint across the cramped corridor, grab my sports kit and head out of the door. IT'S FRIDAY!! Joy races around my body as I realise, the weekend has begun. Freedom, freedom at last!

Fin Strathern, 8L

4.00 p.m.

The bell rings and immediately sheer joy is evident on all the faces of every member of Mrs Howat's maths set, including Mrs Howat herself. The weekend is finally here, after a long week of homework and tests, excitement levels are high as for the next 48 hours or so, we have been released from the perilous grasp of school life. As I am packing up my 'GCSE Mathematics 1' Textbook (by 'B.V Hony'), all I can think about was the prospect of little homework, Birmingham City v Nottingham Forest and the Superbowl all contained in what would be an exciting, tense and sporadic weekend.

Alex Olds, 10S

4.00 p.m.

The bell rings at 4.00 p.m.and I go out the door as it rings in a rush for the bus. I walk quickly through the forest and hope either the bus is late or the wind is behind me. I get my head down and fast walk as quickly as my legs will take me. I emerge from the trees and see the green and white 58 (Nottingham City Transport) pulling up. I squeeze through the shutting door at 4.06; my swimming kit nearly got trapped. I go upstairs as always, the regulars are all there. I sit near the back, but in front of the camera. I plug in my Beats headphones and listen to my music (mainly made up of 'Drum and Bass' and 'Rap'). The bus approaches Sainsbury's in Arnold, my stop. I get up, brace for the mini round about then walk downstairs. I get off, say thanks and make my way past Sainsbury's and up the hill of Church street and all the way home. I open the gate, switch off my music and knock on the door. My weekend has begun.

Daniel Parker, 9H, age 14

4.00 p.m.

As I walk out the school at 4.00 p.m. I meet my sister at the school gates. Together we walk down Arboretum Street in the park, across the tramline, up the hill and take a right in to the park estate, where we live. Especially today (Friday), it is hard to walk home as my school bag is very heavy and I have my games kit from the house rugby competitions. It takes 20 minutes to walk this route every day and it is very tiring but I have to do it.

Will Hammond, 7H, age 11

4.00 p.m.

D-d-d-d! There's no better sound than the school bell at end the day; it is sweet music to my ears. Making my way towards the lockers I find a tsunami of Year 7 heading in the same direction. I face another fight with my games kit to get it out of the locker; this is a match I'm determined not to lose! Why is everything such a challenge at this time of the day? With a yank I win. Leaning on the school wall to help support the weight of my heavy bag, I wait for Dad.

Aown Janjua , 7Y

4.00 p.m.

Bell goes. Late, but can't find the energy for a serious dash. Collect coat and scarf from car, but the need is hardly urgent – what a contrast to the snow two weeks back when my NGHS opposite number was wondering whether to risk a long journey northwards.

Grahame Whitehead, teacher of German, age 53

4.00 p.m.

The bell rings. The end of the day has finally come! I feel a feeling of joy. School is over, two whole days of no school. I am looking forward to the exciting rugby match that's taking place early tomorrow morning. I packing my bag and head for the bus lane. I step outside, feeling the cold brush past my cheeks; the wind erupts in my face. I can't wait to get on the lovely warm, comfy bus that will take me home. I am with my friends with not a single care in the world.

Matty Pickering, 8Y

4.00 p.m.

I hear the bell sound throughout my classroom and immediately pack my items away, following the large group filing out of the door, each individual glad of the oncoming weekend. I proceed towards the statue as I am due to meet up with a group of people within my year that walk into town: passing the buses, walking just outside the arboretum and up the large hill reaching the local shop, just outside the park. Londis. After I purchase a small amount of food, I return to my home.

Kieran Fowler, 10T

4.00 p.m.

The final bell rings for the end of school, a sigh of relief encapsulates the room. The clanking of chairs. The bustling of feet. The chaos in the corridor. Schools finished for the day, bring on the weekend! Yet in the back of my mind looms the unwelcome thought of the homework I have to complete. However the anticipation of two days rest overwhelms this. No teachers to listen to, no lessons to attend and nothing to worry about. After a short walk I clamber upon my bus for the one hour journey home. Yet another week over.

Ben Allen, 11H

4.01 p.m.

I walk out of school and into the light, contemplating what I will do when I get home. Then I realise it's the weekend. Freedom from the menace of school and the tyranny of homework for yet another week. I can relax, sleep late and not think about school until Sunday. I walk down to the bus thinking about what the rugby score's will be and whether England will beat the Scots. Whether the U15's will be victorious against Northampton Grammar School. The thought of work are far from my mind as I settle in to the the relaxed time of the weekend.

James Lord, 10S

4.02 p.m.

I finish my last lesson of the day and briskly walk to the school music block to have a final practice for my band's gig later in the week. As I approach the building I notice again that one of the S's in 'Music School' on the wall is upside down and I notice that the foundation stone was laid on my birthday as I do every time I pass it. Grabbing my guitar I hurry upstairs to meet the rest of the band who are already set up and waiting for me. I greet them, quickly get out my instrument, check the tuning and without another word begin playing our opening song.

Tris Ellis, 11L

4.03 p.m.

I think to myself, 'it's the end of the day.' I walk to the music block as it is my favourite part of the school. I am waiting here for someone who I am walking home with. I take out my headphones and plug them into my phone. I unlock my phone and go to the music app. I put on my favourite music and I sit and wait until half past four.

Oliver Bosman, 9S, age 13

4.04 p.m.

I quickly get my maths books packed away from yet another gruelling maths lesson. Quadratics. Urgh. As I clumsily pack the books away, I keep thinking meet Richard outside the junior school, do not forget. I then leave the room and get my overnight stuff. Richard told me his parents are nice, I will have to see when I spend the night at his house. After I have collected my stuff, I meet Richard, he says "Are you ready?" I naturally answer yes. We get the tram to the bus stop and get on the bus. My journey into the unknown begins.

Ross Jackson, 10L

4.05 p.m.

I am being sent out of my maths lesson in W3. I head for my locker and brace myself for push through the surge of boys collecting their bags. I pull out my key and grab my bag. I sprint outside to wait for the bus. The bus arrives and I jostle my way on. We judder and move. I look out of the window and talk to my friends. We keep on driving and I can see all kinds of people out of the windows; in cars and on the pavement.

Bilial Qureshi, 7Y

4.05 p.m.

Heute bin ich ziemich müde, jedoch muss ich nach der Schule bleiben, um Altgriechisch zu lernen. Es gibt nur zwei Schüler und der Lehrer bringt uns die griechische Sprache und auch die Literatur bei. Ich finde, dass es nicht nur interessant sondern auch spannend ist. Zusätzlich lernen wir immer neue Sachen über die Kultur der Alten Griechen und neulich haben wir ein Verständnis von ihrer Lebensweise entwickelt. In dieser Stunde werden wir einige Kapitel von Xenophon übersetzen, die ziemlich einfach sein werden, denke ich. Ich bin auch froh, dass die Klasse sehr klein ist und deshalb können wir viel lernen.

Andy Wright, Year 12

4.05 p.m.

It is 4.05 p.m. I am staying over at my friend Jack's house. As he does scouts on a Friday I am going as well. When I get there we start playing football, there is no real goal so no one is keeping score. The scout leaders tell us to go to the backroom of the scout hut. The leaders are talking to the regulars about a Duke of Edinburgh trip. I have not had any scout training in the past but I give it my best shot I. We play a game called jump the rope to, I lose.

Max Briggs-Goode, 8Y

4.06 p.m.

I arrive at the scouts hut: a bungalow at a height from the main school area, surrounded by multi-coloured cars. There seem to be only two fellow scouts, none who are in my year. So I wait for a minute or two and soon my friends arrive and we find an orange sponge ball that has many torn bits. We play football; at one point the ball is in one of my friend's possession and he kicks it with much force causing it to narrowly miss my head. I pick up the pliable toy ball and I kick it aggressively.

Rishabh Motiwale, 9Y

4.07 p.m.

As I walk out the school doors I can feel the calming breeze gently caress my face. I can hear the low rumbling from the boilers and the sound of children calling to their parents. I can smell the reek of exhaust plumes from the cars constantly passing by. I can taste that same smoke but also my lunch stuck in the crevices of my teeth. I can see the cars, the streets and the people, one of which is my brother who barely acknowledges me partly due to the headphones in his ears. It is time to go home.

Thomas Wakefield, 7L, age 11

4.08 p.m.

I wait for my brother with my friend at the top of the junior school steps. He takes while but we can eventually make a move towards the tram. As we walk towards the tram we see and hear the junior school children running and shouting. As usual it is quite cloudy and looks like it is going to rain, so we quicken our walk a little. When we get to the tram stop we see the Hucknall tram is four minutes away so we decide to take cover under the shelter just in case it rains. As we look around we see a few people coming to catch the same tram and some other people catching the tram on the other side. The tram on the other side comes just as our tram comes so we all hop on. My friend and I talk as my brother finds a seat. We have a fun time until my friend gets off at Moor Bridge and my brother and I wait for two more stops till Hucknall. We get off at Hucknall and start our walk home, which takes about 12 minutes whilst my brother and I have a fun talk.

Tim Stuttle, 9H, age 13

4.09 p.m.

I have just finished putting all my books into my locker. I am ready to walk home with my two friends, however I look around the corridor and they are no-where to be seen. So, I look around for them but can't find them, I then ask someone else where they are in frustration and they say they have left a few minutes previously. As soon as the other boy tells me this, I sprint out of the school into the yard to see my two friends; we then all walk to the bus stop and go home.

Joshan Gangotra, 9Y

4.10 p.m.

I walk wearily up to the classroom after a windy Games session of Tag Rugby with Year 3 pupils. As I reach my desk I am struck by the fact it is still light outside. I check my e-mails on my laptop and gaze out of the window on to the Junior School yard, where only hours before there was a cacophony of noise and activity from the boys playing ball and other games at lunchtime. The school is eerily quiet now, with boys, parents and staff all leaving early to beat the rush hour traffic and I can hear only the whirring of the heater in my room.

Tim Caldwell, Teacher, Head of Humanities, Nottingham High Junior School, age 33

4.11 p.m.

At this time I am at school for 15 minutes after school until it is 4.15 when my dad picks me up from school. But I'm looking forward to having a warm cup of hot chocolate with succulent marsh-mellows to warm my cold winter day up. And then I get to play on my Xbox which is my fun time of the night for 1-2 hours!

Brandan Samra, 8T

4.12 p.m.

I have just walked past the board with the names of the 40 Headmasters of Nottingham High School on. As I sit here in my office reflecting on their contribution to the long History of the School, I am humbled to be listed on that board. The successes, the buildings, the people they have employed, the support of so many benefactors have all gone to create this brilliant school as have no doubt along the way some failures, some tears and some difficult situations to face. I am so fortunate to lead this superb school 500 years on.

Kevin Fear, Headmaster of the High School

4.13 p.m.

The engine of the bus starts. I come back from the sixth form centre. I am not empty handed. I have a pack of doritos, chilli heat wave. I'm SO hungry. I sit on a damp seat at the middle of the bus. As I open the sealed packet. Out comes a sensational spice of chilli. I love it. I continue to savour each crisp. But, before I know it, I am holding the last dorito of the packet. I drown my sorrow by listening to my iPod for the rest of the journey. Almost there.

Aqdas Burney, 8T

4.14 p.m.

I'm waiting outside school for my parents to come and pick me up. I watch as the amount of people hovering around outside the gate decreases, until I am the only one left, still waiting for my ride home. It is eerily quiet, apart from the cries of children from the nursery across the road. Every time a car approaches, I glance over to see if it is my car, but I am disappointed each time. I check my watch; it's now 4.30. I've been here for 15 whole minutes. My mum's car finally pulls up and I jump in.

Jack Hadfield, 11Y

4.15 p.m.

The last two delayed buses set off. All over for another week.

Grahame Whitehead, teacher of German, age 53

4.15 p.m.

When I first wake up I look forward to another day at Nottingham High Junior School. So I quickly get up, go to the bathroom and brush my teeth. Then I get dressed, have my breakfast and start my journey to school. When we get there I play for a little bit with my friends and then when the bell rings, go down to the Junior Hall for our assembly. After the assembly our first lesson is Reasoning. Later, we have double Science. They are both fun and enjoyable but sometimes the work can get a little tricky. Following that we of course have English. Afterwards we have triple Games and in that we play triple rugby. That is the end of a day in the life of a Nottingham High Junior School pupil.

Mathew John, 6L, Junior School

4.16 p.m.

I am on the tram with my nanna. I am just finishing my sweet which is a chocolate éclair.

Harrison Skinner, 2M, Lovell House

4.17 p.m.

I find some of the discussions we have in the staffroom amusing. Teachers can get animated over all sorts of mundane things. Today is no exception. Half a dozen male staff are agonising over what to wear at tomorrow's staff 'Party in the Quad'. The instruction 'dress casual' elicits lots of opinions; for some it is a suit, for others their best jeans that haven't yet developed holes. Fortunately, the Seventh Cavalry arrives in the shape of the Headmaster who says smart casual is intended to mean no ties or jeans, basically nothing formal.

Dr John Swain, teacher of History

4.18 p.m.

I am in the staff room, having a conversation with Messrs Winter, Ruff, Williams and Dr Swain about what to wear to the Staff 500th Anniversary Party in the Quad tomorrow night. It appears that our interpretations of the 'Smart Casual' dress code differ wildly along the smart to casual spectrum. Fortunately, the timely intervention of the Headmaster brings some much needed clarification – suits and ties not required! This is quite possibly the most detailed conversation ever to have been held among male members of teaching staff about what to wear to a staff social in the school's long history.

Mr Ben Harrison, Classics Teacher and Head of Year 13

4.19 p.m.

I'm in the library waiting for my mum. I decide to read for a bit thinking that my mum will arrive soon so I can just enjoy my weekend. It is 4.20

and still no luck. I decide to go to the brassiere for a quick snack. When I get there do you know what find? No more snacks. Seriously!!! I am still really thirsty so I decide to just get some water. It isn't as refreshing as an oasis or something but still refreshing. My mum's here. Weekend here I come.

Maqhawe Ndebele, 7Y

13. Home or Homework

4.20 p.m.

I go to Birmingham in a car with my uncle Dasi, my aunty and my baby cousin. My baby cousin is very cute and funny. We stop at a shop to buy a clock for my new bedroom and some sweets for my family. The clock is a Cars clock in a square shape. When we arrive, we watch some episodes of Peppa Pig with my baby cousin.

Amarjit Singh, 3W, Junior School

4.21 p.m.

On the first of February 2013 the Nottingham Boys' High School celebrates its five hundredth anniversary, however, I cannot attend as I have a horrible cough and a nasty cold. This is particularly unfortunate as it is my only day off school so far this school year!

I spend the day reading my book, 'the Pearls of Lutra' (a fictional book from the "Redwall" series by Brian Jacques) and sitting in bed.

To conclude, this is probably the worst day of my school career to miss and I also miss an English grammar and punctuation test that I now have to retake.

Dan Kittmer, 6G, Junior School

4.22 p.m.

Sadly, on Friday 1st February I cannot come to school due to a nasty virus that I have had for the entire week. This will mean I will miss the Assessment Week and the practice SATS exams! The virus has caused a nasty fever, cough and a bit of vomiting. In the morning I wake up with a fever of 39.7 degrees Celsius, however I do recover with a good dose of

Nurofen. For the rest of the day I feel exhausted and have to stay in bed. I pass most of the time reading the hilarious book, 'Just William'. Overall, my day isn't brilliant but I'm glad that I am feeling better now.

Dhruv Gupta, 4, Junior School

4.23 p.m.

I am in the car with my mum and friend; we are going to a skate park called 'Flo'. I'm really looking forward to it because I love skateboarding!

Just about to go in to the park with my helmet and pads for protection! We are going to be skating here for another two and a half hours so it's going to be fun and hopefully we will learn lots of tricks.

Matthew Sampson, 8L

4.24 p.m.

I'm getting changed into my blue football kit and once I am changed I go to my lesson.

First I practice my skills and then I play a game of football.

Mohintan Athavan, 2M, Lovell House

4.28 p.m.

Once I get home from school, I run to my room and begin my weekly routine of polishing my guitar. I look down to see my face reflecting in the now shining headstock of my guitar, I begin to reflect about the advancements of technology and the way people live that have changed over 500 years, and the way things have changed for the whole world (such as the invention of the guitar), and I begin to feel lucky I am to be born at this particular time in the school's history.

Daniel Scriver, Year 10, age 15

4.33 p.m.

I arrive home from school, hungry and tired after a long day. I am told by my mother that my Uncle and his son are coming to Nottingham for a football match. My cousin is coming down on the team coach and my Uncle is driving down from Sandbach. My cousin will be playing for Stoke City u8's in a friendly against Nottingham Forest. None of us has ever been to Nottingham Forest Academy before and when we arrive in the dark, it is beginning to rain and my Uncle Andrew is nowhere to be found. To make it even worse my Mother nearly slaps the bald head of a stranger, thinking it is her brother. Eventually though, my Uncle arrives five minutes after kick-off but without his son noticing his lateness. For ninety minutes straight the children play several different matches of intense footy. The two teams are very equally matched and I am extremely impressed by how good my cousin is. Overall, I have a good night watching my cousin playing football and he is very excited too.

Connor McCourt Hanrahan, Senior School pupil

4.36 p.m.

I'm running for the train, it's going to leave in five minutes and I've only just got off at the tram stop in Station Street, my platform is on the other side of the station! I run to the ticket machine, damn! There's a queue of four people. After waiting for two minutes (three minutes left) the queue finally moves away from the machines and leave me open to punch in my train ticket details, hurriedly drag the ticket from the machine and belt down the train station corridor to my platform. I check my watch and think about how long it took those amateurs to get their tickets-took me half a minute to get mine and took most of them at least two(lucky there were three machines.) speaking of time I realize there's only a minute left to catch my train. I find my train and leap through the train door and still maintaining my running speed, I thud down into the nearest seat. My next thought: Spanish test on Monday, I had better revise.

Toby Pendleton, 10s

4.37 p.m.

Just about to go in to the park with my helmet and pads for protection! We are going to be skating here for another two and a half hours so it's going to be fun and hopefully we will learn lots of tricks.

Matt Sampson, 8L, age 13

4.38 p.m.

I am on the bus after yet another school day. I am just passing the QMC on my way to my house near Beeston. It is still half an hour until my expected arrival time. I am with another pupil from my year, and he has recently got a new tablet computer. Emulating old games on it, we play Super Smash Bros from the N64. He is playing as Kirby, and I am playing as Pikachu. I am able to use a Wii remote, which is easier to control than the touch screen, and as such, I knock him off the arena many times. There is no score, but I know I won. He gets off, leaving me to sit and wait quietly to arrive home and begin my homework.

Rowan Lee, 11L

4.39 p.m.

I wait at the front of the bus and look at my watch, the weight of my homework hurting my shoulder. The bus stops and I walk off it and down the road to my front door. I ring the bell and wait until it opens and I finally escape the cold rain and into the warm, comfortable heat. I run upstairs, flick my shoes off and jump onto my bed, my gaze settling yet again on my bag with the weekend's homework bulging out of it. I give a sigh, pick up my bag and sit down on the chair opposite my desk.

Bilal Shiekh, 10H, age 15

4.40 p.m.

At 4.40, I am still on the bus home, but nearly at my stop, a restaurant called the Rushley. Soon we are at my stop but my mother isn't there. After a five minute wait she arrives my brother and I jump into the car to go home. When we get home we have spaghetti Bolognese on the table waiting on the table. When I have finished I get changed then start some of the many home works I have to complete over the weekend.

Connor Shaw, 8L, age 12

4.42 p.m.

I get off the school bus in my hometown of Ruddington. I walk, as I usually do towards the Car Park of the Bricklayers Arms. I often wait for my mum who turns up late on certain occasions. But, on this wintery night, she is waiting for me in her car. I jog towards the car, whilst saying goodbye to my friend who lives near the Bricklayer's Arms. As I get in the car, my mum turns on the radio. The song on is my favourite, Gangnam Style.

Sam McKenzie-Small, 8H

4.43 p.m.

I walk sleepily into the house and I am welcomed with my 4-year old brother bounding towards me, before slamming into me. He drags me excitedly to his cars and makes me play with him. I play with him for a little while until I get bored and focus on trying to annoy him. He runs to my mother, wailing and screaming as I try to catch him. He reports back to my mother and I am told off badly and sent back to my room. My mother calls me back for food and I am met with the warm, succulent smell of steak and chips, slam into my face. She asks me about school and I recount my school day. I ask my sister to get me something to drink who reluctantly gets up to get it, complaining how I don't do anything for her. I argue with her and my mother gives a massive lecture on how I shouldn't say the word "stupid" because I'm being a bad influence on my brother.

Rowan Thomas, 8S, age 13

4.46 p.m.

Having just arrived home, I have a quick snack and make some final edits to my R.E. homework. I attempt to print the homework out. The printer just freezes instead, probably because we have a new wireless router installed, which is connected to a total of zero gadgets, which are all still connected to the old one. So while my Dad tries to fix that, I start with my Maths homework, until eventually my Dad gives up and asks me to play

Table Tennis with him, during which I 'accidently' hit the ball off the table and into his tea. Well almost…

Jithin Kurian, 7Y, age 11

4.47 p.m.

There is a knock on the door of WH2. I shout 'come in' and Mr Harrison opens the door and tells me that he is leaving to go home. We have a brief chat about the 100 words that each of us are going to write for the School's 500th anniversary and we both agree that we will write something about our experience of Greek teaching at NHS. He leaves and I get back to translating Xenophon's 'Anabasis' with my two Greek students. It is the first time I have taught this text since I was taught it myself – it was the first Greek text I read in the original when I was at school. We translate a couple more sentences and then it is time for one of my students to catch the tram. I have enjoyed finishing the week each week this term translating some Xenophon.

Mr RCS Grant, Head of Classics, aged 39

4.53 p.m.

After travelling for just under an hour, my vast yellow school bus arrives at my local leisure centre. The bus brakes suddenly as I walk down to the lower saloon and I happily hop off the bus. I walk approximately 20 meters down the pavement and there I arrive at the great leisure centre. I enter the leisure centre and strol over to the reception desk and I ask 'one for the gym please.' As I hand over my card. I walk down the long corridor, ready to start my training in the hot, wet, steamy gym.

Luke Easton, 8H

4.58 p.m.

I am playing with my brother whilst my mum is making dinner. I play cars with my younger brother Aarya.

Arnav Sovani, 2M, Lovell House

5.00 p.m.

I look up from my book and see my village loom up illuminated by the street lights. I close my book earmarking it and eagerly await my arrival home. When I get home I look up at the clock above the oven. I Put my bags down and take off my coat and put it on the rack. I feel a moment off euphoria it is the weekend And I tear off upstairs to play on my computer.

Devang Nigam, 8H

5.01 p.m.

I get home from school. School was such a tiring and hard working day. The last lesson was Biology. We hat to dissect a lamb's heart. I changed my clothes and. After I get changed and I do my homework. I need to do three homework's. They are Biology, Spanish and German. I am doing my German homework. It is quite difficult because you have to write about what you wear at a party, what you wear in the summer/winter and what would you rather wear. I like German. It is fun and the teacher is really nice and helpful.

Ismail Zia, 9S

5.02p.m.

The bus judders to a halt just before the A52 slip road. I hop off the bus and turn around to watch it disappear round the bend. It's already dark and I am not able to see much further than the bridge. I wait until I can take my chance of crossing the slip road. Traffic is a continuous flow and when I finally cross, I trek over the bridge and pause to view the headlights whizzing beneath me. I continue walking past the kennels and past the cricket club until I can see my house.

Adith Thomas, 8T

5.03 p.m.

Siempre conduzco a casa del colegio, pero los viernes lo hago con una sonrisa en la boca. Ni siquiera los innumerables semáforos o las grandes colas de tráfico que serpentean de camino a casa los viernes me pueden negar la satisfacción de una feliz sonrisa. Feliz porque vuelvo a casa a pasar el fin de semana con mi familia, pero también feliz por lo mucho que hemos aprendido y avanzado esta semana.

Ed se sienta a mi lado, relajándose, jugando con mi móvil – ya somos dos los que volvemos a casa los viernes, pronto seremos tres. Él, cansado, también sonríe.

José Picardo, Head of Modern Languages

5.05 p.m.

I am playing dressing up with my brother Sasmeet. I dress up as Obi Wan and my brother dresses up as Darth Vader from Star Wars.

Saahat Satyam 2M, Lovell House

5.09 p.m.

I can't do my homework,
I have asthma and endless wheezing.
I have headache after headache,
And never-ending sneezing.

I can't do my homework.
My skin is oh so itchy,
Oh so blotchy, oh so hivey.
Malaria, heat rash, toothache
And that dreadful poison ivy.

But yes, I'm still alive,
And for that, I take a bow.
Can I do my homework?
No. I don't see how.

Anvarjon Seviour, 10S

5.13 p.m.

I am having my dinner and I am having chicken nuggets. They are my favourite!

Thomas Bavin, 2M, Lovell House

5.19 p.m.

I am playing with my brother and my mum is making our food for our evening meal.

Jagpal Singh, 2M, Lovell House

5.29 p.m.

I come home from Mosque and there is a load of work just waiting to be done. All I do is sigh. The worst piece of homework is English, because the teacher always gives you homework that has to be two sides long. All I do is watch the Simpsons and then I can start to focus on my homework. I start doing my French which is really easy because all you have to do is a couple of exercises. I start my English and I just leave it all till Sunday afternoon.

Bilal Sadaq, 8T

5.33 p.m.

I am having my bath and my dad comes home from work.

Rayan Kapur, 2M, Lovell House

5.36 p.m.

I trudge up the hill, trying to keep up with two tremendously energetic dogs. They are really flying, moving at a remarkable pace, I push myself to keep up with them. They eventually begin to tire and start to slow down. I reach the top of the hill - a marvellous sight to behold. The supernatural red sky contrasts beautifully with the bustling city in the far distance. I sit down in the long, dense grass, staring intently at a mass of birds, frantically flying around the gorgeous red sky. I fall into a deep state of relaxation. Perfect. I lean back, whistle my dogs over. They both curl up into a ball and fall asleep. I find myself a small patch of soft grass and close my eyes. I couldn't have been more content. What a wonderful world.

Edward James, 9T

5.39 p.m.

I am watching my sister's swimming lesson and I'm playing on Mario Kart on my Nintendo DSIXL.

Ujesh Sakariya, 2M, Lovell House

5.52 p.m.

It's dark outside now, but there's still a pile of work to finish before I can switch the light off and go home. I can hear the soft buzz of the vacuum cleaner outside the office door; soon she'll be in to empty my waste paper bin. I wonder whether anyone else is still in the building? My mobile rings – it's my husband wondering when I'll be home. I tell him it may be a while yet. Poor man – but he's used to it by now. At least, today it's Friday........

Judy Brown, Marketing and Admissions

5.54 p.m.

I am eating my sausages with chips and I'm getting very full.

Robert Goodwin, 2M, Lovell House

5.55 p.m.

As I gaze up and stare in awe at the School building, my mind drifts back through the years to ponder over what the first lesson will have been like half a millennium ago. A few children with some desks in their local church learn about their world whilst a gentle snow flurry comes down outside. Nevertheless, the school looks grand; as it's size and majestic architecture dwarf the people who inhabit it. Each brick, each tile and each window are testament to a different age and the people of it.

Saaras Mehan, 9T

6.01 p.m.

I am at home and am doing my homework. I have got to do lots of homework to do and one of them is revising for my physics which is quiet easy. My physics revision is on energy and is about all the different types of energy. Another homework I have to do is revise for my Biology test and that is about microscopes and animal and plant cells. The final home work I have to do is finish my English homework which is this and I have a couple more words left. After that I read my book.

Karam Sangha, 7H, age 11

6.03 p.m.

At around 6.00pm, with my headphones on, I am walking outside the school grounds towards Sainsbury. I grab the milk and scan for anything else. Nope. Eventually, I am on the bus back home.

Kevin Lau, 602

6.06 p.m.

I cycle through the gates, cross Forest Road and weave through the new green bollards at the entrance to The Forest; rumble over the cobbles then swoop down the hill, floating smoothly over the new tarmac, following my bright beam of light towards the bustle and drone of Mansfield Road. For a few seconds, it's dark and silent around me and I know that I've left school and work behind, and that the weekend has begun. I feel the wind pick up and I drop my head to the handlebars and click into top gear.

Andrew Martin, Head of Psychology

6.09 p.m.

The warm scent of centre parks that comes over me like a cloud of smoke is immense. Just by merely slowly winding down my window I feel the aromas I feel every year. It almost feels as if I am home. We pull in the sign towering over me with its sparkling lights afoot. Finally we have arrived the excitement hits me like a boxer with a k.o punch. Time for a weekend of relaxing, I think to myself. I am woken from this endless fantasy when the lady asks. What is your surname please? I think finally here we go...

Alex Pereira, 8Y

6.11 p.m.

I am just having my dinner, steak and chips. When I have finished I go and pack my rugby kit ready for the game against Northampton. I remember playing them in year 7 and getting beaten. I hope the result will be different tomorrow as it is the exact 500th birthday of the school. Because I have no homework to do I go upstairs and turn on my computer. I am a big fan of Ali-A on youtube and I see if I have any videos to catch up on. There are no new ones today though.

Eddie Meakin, 8H

6.14 p.m.

On Friday I go to a karate lesson in the dojo. First I put my gi on in the changing rooms then my purple belt. I come out the change rooms and wait for the class to start. When the class starts we line up in belt order. When sensei Aiden tells us to, we bow first, then we split the class into brown belts and above with sensei James and purple stripe and below with sensei Aiden. We practise our katas and mine was hian godahn [a kata is a sequence of moves]. In hian godahn I start off with utchuki yakazuki then we all started partner work. I am against a brown belt and I know who is going to win so I try my hardest but still lose.

Alex Winter, 3, Junior School

6.17 p.m.

This is it. I am in the championship. I run towards the goal hoping to strike and secure the title. I try with every bit of my strength to score but I narrowly miss the target. They power the ball wide, almost gaining an advantage. My players are quick and soon after I am charging forwards to the goal, but their defender takes me down. I step up to take the penalty. Sweat is pouring over my face and I shoot the ball, my heart beating as I do and I miss. I can't believe it... My phone has lost battery.

Anish Bagalkote, 8Y

6.22 p.m.

Phew, another week finished!!! Pick up KFC on the way home to have for my tea. I get changed for Kids Club after tea. We do some colouring and play ZONK and I win 5 sweets. When I get home from Kids Club I watch the end of A Question of Sport with Phil Tufnell and Matt Dawson. After I get changed into pyjamas I go into Mummy and Daddy's bedroom and watch the recording of Arsenal vs Liverpool from Wednesday night which ended 2-2. After this, I go to bed. It has been a very, very busy day.

Ptolemy Bowen, 3W, Junior School

6.33 p.m.

I am having my sensational dinner, pizza and chips with a bit of salad, and a lovely fruit cocktail with ice cream for dessert. After that I have to finish off my homework in detail my and after that I have a warm shower and do my fine hair with a comb and hair dryer. Then I dry my hair and go to sleep at 9.00 p.m. so I can be able to wake up at 6.45 a.m.

Brandan Samra, 8T

6.42 p.m.

I'm sitting at my desk, trying to catch up on all those tasks that can't be done easily during a busy teaching day. Marking Year 7 projects; replying to a parent concerned about their son's progress; checking off-site visit applications; and logging into iSams to enter distinctions and, rarely for me, a couple of detentions. The Year 11 class was 'pesky' during period 8 and I'm drained! The school empties quickly on Fridays and a reassuring calmness returns. I check the emergency telephone; pick up the contact folders for the two trips on Sunday; and look forward to getting home.

Mr Richard Willan, Head of Geography

7.07 p.m.

I am working on my French homework; I am on the last sentence... and I am finished. My French homework is finally finished which took 30 minutes. After an extremely tiring day at school and one hours of homework, I trudge down the stairs as slow as a snail to receive my tea. I am as happy as a cat eating a mouse! If there was school tomorrow, I would have broken down into pieces. My mum has made a curry! As I have my first bite, I turn the television on. The cricket is on.

Deep Desai, 8T

7.16 p.m.

As I walk into the restaurant I chat with my brother and tell him how I helped Maples win in the house rugby against Coopers. Whites are next. We approach the table after a 20 minute wait and discuss the events of the day. Dad is interested in the I.C.T project which is based on programming. I have downloaded the software onto my computer at home so I can work on project in-between lessons. I am designing a Pac Man game at school and I have recently finished it at home.

Matthew Davey, 7H

7.27 p.m.

I lie on the sofa and watch the Simpsons inside my room not worrying about my homework. My mom calls me for some food. I walk like a zombie to the kitchen to see what there is. It is pizza, my favourite. I can't believe that I have pizza, as my mom would never let me have this kind of food before. I take about three slices of pizza before I sprint to my room and stuff my face with pepperoni.

I finish eating and go downstairs to go onto the PS3 and play some FIFA 13. I read a book that makes you want to read more and more but I have to stop because I have to go church and play the drums for my church. I come back from church and sleep walk back to my bed and sleep for ever and ever but I will have to wake up and play Rugby.

Joshua Sinkaiye, 8S, age 12

7.35 p.m.

Still at school with the florist sorting flowers for the staff and former staff 500th anniversary party tomorrow night. Almost everything from today's checklist ticked; tomorrow's plan written. Early start - 9am IKEA for table decorations; 10am giant five zero zero balloons arriving; 11am front of house set up team should arrive; 12 noon hope kitchen prep starts; 12.30 – 3pm printing and guillotining tasks - menu cards, guest lists, golden tickets .... Can't wait to see the School Dining Hall and Player Hall transformed into event venues. Anxious and excited; hope all goes well and everyone enjoys themselves.

Katrine Scott-Mitchell, Development Director

7.47 p.m.

After my homework: I submerge, I can't breathe. Its dark and I can't think, my head is spinning. My head bursts through the surface and I remember I am in water. I swim slowly to the side anticipating the next lethal wave, as it hits I lift my body as best I can so my head is above water. Suddenly a shadow arises from the depths and clamps onto my leg. I realise it is only my sister and she's been pulled under. I concentrate on now and remember I'm in a pool and I'm not going to die!

Josh Ghattaora, 8H

8.00 p.m. – 9.00 p.m.

Although they were given, more or less, a fairly free choice of their time of day, of the 1,500 or so people who were asked to contribute to this current project, not a single individual seems to have done anything during this hour.

Perhaps they are all recovering from the first thirty minute episode of the television soap, "Coronation Street", which started at 7.30 p.m., and then eagerly watching the second at 8.30 p.m.

John Knifton, organiser and author of this work

9.00 p.m.

Me despierto hacia las siete y media, me ducho a las oche menos veinte. Sorry, got Spanish on the brain. I try and do an hour of Spanish every evening, although I'm very pernickety when it comes to work so I usually end up angrily punching letters into my poor laptop, trying forever to better my quizlet scores. At work, I'm based in the MFL office. Sometimes we call it the landfill site, sometimes it's the boiler room, but personally I like 'club saddo'. I sit nearest the printer, which means I can perform a 180-degree spin to retrieve documents.

Chris Brown, Teacher of French and German, age 25

9.25 p.m.

I am having so much trouble to stay awake. Homework is decaying me bit by bit. English is slowly making me fall asleep – essay after essay. Also the numbers are just jumbling up in my head. On the other hand chemistry revision is keeping me awake by the symbols and the symbolic drawings. However, I'm looking forward to having a lie in (till about 2 p.m.) and the dreams that I will experience when I'm sleeping. Also playing on my PS3 (games console) all day long. I have finally finished all of my pieces of work; I can finally go to sleep.

Raaid Humdani, 7T, age 12

9.41 p.m.

At home my wife cannot persuade me that Silent Witness is worth watching on the television. Instead I read the recently published 2012 edition of the School Yearbook. Although drawn towards the report of my own History Department's trip to Berlin, I also reflect on Mr Ruff's review of the Yearbooks of 1977 and 2002; some names from the past certainly spring out. And then to the back pages with the photograph of the leavers from 2012; where will they be in twenty-five years?

Peter Dowsett, teacher, age 41

And, now the very last word……

11.57 p.m.

On sitting in a dark, gloomy and slightly therapeutic room, in my house, I have time to think to myself on why I left it so late, to do this simple task of writing one hundred words on the five hundredth anniversary of my school. The vivid light of the lamp pierces through dark abyss and I can hear the soft, slow and comforting breath of my dog as he sleeps on the floor beside me; providing a relaxing environment to which I type these very words that you are reading. Moreover, as the analogue clock on my computer slowly ticks towards a new day, I think to myself: what a five hundred years it has been.

Dayal Sekhon,　10Y

Printed in Great Britain
by Amazon.co.uk, Ltd.,
Marston Gate.